# Immigrant and Minority Entrepreneurship

# Immigrant and Minority Entrepreneurship

The Continuous Rebirth of American Communities

Edited by John Sibley Butler and George Kozmetsky

Westport, Connecticut
London

338.6422
I33

**Library of Congress Cataloging-in-Publication Data**

Immigrant and minority entrepreneurship : the continuous rebirth of American
communities / edited by John Sibley Butler and George Kozmetsky.
  p. cm.
  Includes bibliographical references and index.
  ISBN 0-275-96511-2 (alk. paper)—ISBN 0-275-96512-0 (pbk. : alk. paper)
  1. Minority business enterprises—United States.  2. Entrepreneurship—
United States.  3. Immigrants—United States—Economic conditions.
4. Minorities—United States—Economic conditions.  5. Community
development, Urban—United States.  I. Butler, John S.  II. Kozmetsky, George.
HD2358.5.U6I46 2004
338.6′422′0973—dc22      2003057980

British Library Cataloguing in Publication Data is available.

Library of Congress Catalog Card Number: 2003057980
ISBN: 0-275-96511-2
      0-275-96512-0 (pbk.)

First published in 2004

Praeger Publishers, 88 Post Road West, Westport, CT 06881
An imprint of Greenwood Publishing Group, Inc.
www.praeger.com

Printed in the United States of America

The paper used in this book complies with the
Permanent Paper Standard issued by the National
Information Standards Organization (Z39.48-1984).

10 9 8 7 6 5 4 3 2 1

**Copyright Acknowledgment**

Every reasonable effort has been made to trace the owners of copyright materials
in this book, but in some instances this has proven impossible. The author and
publisher will be glad to receive information leading to more complete acknowl-
edgments in subsequent printings of the book, and in the meantime extend their
apologies for any omissions.

# Contents

# Introduction

*John Sibley Butler and George Kozmetsky*

This book is grounded in scholarship that looks at the contribution of newcomers to the economies of natio- states. Indeed, it has been argued that the impetus for the overall study of what we now call entrepreneurship lay in the attempt by scholars to understand how immigrants, or new members of societies, develop a sense of economic stability through the entrepreneurial process. In Georg Simmel's groundbreaking work that appeared in the late 1800s, he called newcomers "strangers."[1] They were distinct ethnic groups who were not part of the established host society and thus came to play the merchant role. Max Weber, in his classic turn-of-the-century work, *The Protestant Ethic and the Spirit of Capitalism*, paid attention to this population. His argument was that because of exclusion by nation-states, certain ethnic groups were forced into economic activity.[2]

Present day research on immigrant entrepreneurship is a natural extension of these classic works. Although the concept of immigrant entrepreneurship has replaced that of stranger, the general theoretical question remains: How do newcomers create business activity for economic stability? Throughout American history, newcomers have been immigrants from foreign lands, the children of former slaves who were transported to America, and the first generation of large numbers of female entrepreneurs.

We should note that this tradition of work is very different from research on immigration that takes as its starting point the idea that immigrants are a burden to nation states. This research, which has produced a wealth of important information, is based on assumptions about how immigrants arrive on American shores and compete for jobs, space in educational institutions, and other community services.[3] There are policy recommendations that range from limiting immigration because of strains on community financing to closing the doors of immigration.

This volume takes a different approach by concentrating on how immigrants and other newcomers revitalize America and create economic stability within communities. As early as 1953, a President's Commission on Immigration and Naturalization noted the following: "The richest regions are those with the highest proportion of immigrants. Their industry, their skills and their enterprises were major factors in the economic development that made these regions prosperous."[4] In *Immigrants and the American City,* Thomas Muller examines how immigrants enrich what he calls Gateway Cities. These cities, such as Miami, New York, and San Francisco, owe their population growth, especially since the 1970s, exclusively to immigration. For generations, however, immigrants have flocked to these cities, revitalizing them and adding to their continued economic stability.[5] Consider the following quotation, which comes from the literature on the experiences of Cuban refugees in Miami. As they started to arrive, city officials predicted the further economic decline of a declining city.

> All statistical projections were dismal. Experts foresaw a prolonged siege of medical crisis, economic stresses, and ethnic friction; a teeming burden of "social disorders," needs for housing, welfare, and simple hygiene, an impossible load for the already afflicted social services of the city. Here in one economically stagnant urban area, over a period of just two years, thronged some 200,000 . . . immigrants. . . . It was an influx about one-fifth the size of the entire Dade County population in 1960, an inundation more rapid and overwhelming than any previous migration to one American city. . . . Nearly 60 percent of the exiles had been common laborers even in Cuba, and all had lost most of what they had accumulated at home. Poring through the press coverage of the day, it is difficult to find any observers who saw this human flood as anything but a tribulation for southern Florida or a problem to be solved by saviors at HEW and the Immigration and Naturalization Services, or the U.S. Marines.[6]

Instead of being an absolute burden on the city, the new arrivals contributed to the revitalization of not only south Florida and Miami but also the southern Latin corridor. With entrepreneurship and institutional building clearly at the center of community, the Cuban community was instrumental in turning Dade County into one of the fastest-growing entrepreneurial counties in the country during the 1970s.[7]

The importance of business activity for community stability is reflected in perhaps the oldest research in this tradition, which takes black Americans as data. Indeed, the very first research agenda on black Americans placed entrepreneurship at its very center. In 1898, W. E. B. DuBois published *The Negro in Business.* This documentation of the building of community, business, fraternal, and religious organizations by newcomers to the American marketplace is path breaking, and predates the systematic booming of the nonblack ethnic literature by over 70 years.[8] In 1913 Henry Minton published *Early History of Negroes in Philadelphia,* a work dedicated to the building of the business community of that city prior to the Civil War.[9] A host of other books, including Abram L. Harris's *The Negro as Capitalist* (1913) and Joseph A. Pierce's *Negro Business and Business Education* (1947) continued the documentation of, and problems associated with, business development among black Americans.[10]

The research on black Americans, as well as on immigrant nonblack groups, gives consideration to the involvement of women in the entrepreneurial process. More recently, that involvement has become more systematic, especially as applied to white females as a group, who were seen in early literature as having a special place in the home and did not have a strong history of any kind in marketplace participation. At this point in history, women's entrepreneurship is generating more research, as we understand the relationship between gender dynamics from all racial and ethnic groups and the process of entrepreneurship.

This present volume presents research on immigrant entrepreneurship. It presents data on how immigrants contribute to and build American communities. It also contains work that points to the issues of nonimmigrant groups such as black Americans and females of all groups.

The first chapter, "African American Entrepreneurship: The View from the 1910 Census," takes us back to a time when communities of black Americans were newcomers and placed entrepreneurship and self-employment at the very center of community. One of Margaret Levenstein's most striking findings is that black Americans during this time period were more likely than white Americans to be employers, and almost as likely as whites to be self-employed. This work, although not driven by immigration, informs us of the importance of entrepreneurship for black Americans as they went from slavery to freedom.

In contrast to the findings of Levenstein, Hayward Derrick Horton's chapter "Black Entrepreneurs, 1970–1990: A Demographic Perspective," notes that during this time period blacks were significantly less likely to be self-employed than all ethnic whites. His analysis also informs us that by 1990, black females were just as likely to be self-employed as black men. The most recent data suggest that black Americans are returning to the strategy of past generations. In the October 7, 2002 issue of *Business Week*, a headline read: "The Return of the Black Entrepreneur: A century ago, African Americans were the country's most ardent small-business owners. A new study suggests history is repeating itself."[11] The data source was the most recent release on entrepreneurship by the Ewing Marion Kauffman Foundation of Kansas City, Missouri.

Min Zhou introduces the theme of immigration in "The Role of the Enclave Economy in Immigrant Adaptation and Community Building: The Case of New York's Chinatown." Using the experience of Chinese immigrants as data, she shows how ethnic entrepreneurship creates job opportunities and builds community for members of the Chinese community. She also concentrates on the influence of social capital on entrepreneurial activities at the community level.

Stephen J. Appold and John D. Kasarda, in "Building Community through Entrepreneurship: Lessons from the United States and Vietnam," look at how business ownership is a hallmark of personal success, and how it helps to level the economic playing field for groups that have experienced discrimination or whose paths are blocked by the normal avenues of career development. Their analysis reveals how we are just starting to really understand the relationship between entrepreneurship, crime in communities, and residential stability.

Samia El-Badry, in "Fitting In: The Arab American Entrepreneur," presents a detailed comparison of community success around the country for the Arab American population. Her work is in the genesis of understanding immigrants from the Arab world and their relationship to America.

In "The Minority Community as a Natural Business Incubator," Patricia Gene Greene and John Sibley Butler explore the methods by which a Pakistani community capitalizes and maintains business enterprises. The greatest contribution of the chapter is that it gives a strong consideration to the literature on business incubators and shows how a community-based incubator provides some of the same kind of services. This paper is fueled by Ivan Light et al.'s "Korean Rotating Credit Associations in Los Angeles."

Patricia Gene Greene and Candida Greer Brush, in "Women Entrepreneurs: An Explanatory Framework of Capital Types," provide an overall view of women's enterprises in America. Greene and Brush note that the numbers of women entrepreneurs have increased significantly and that the enterprises that they build tend to be small companies. She explores strategies for growth and the relationship between growth and community.

This general theme is continued in Margaret A. Johnson's "New Approaches to Understanding the Gendered Economy: Self-Employed Women, Microcredit, and the Nonprofit Sector." Her chapter is concerned with providing a theoretical framework to help us understand the impact of microenterprise nonprofit organizations that support the rapid growth of women's self-employment.

Finally, Ivan Light, Im Jung Kwuon, and Zhong Deng, in "Korean Rotating Credit Associations in Los Angeles," give insight into how rotating credit associations support the entrepreneurship of selected immigrant minorities in North America and Europe. One key finding of this research study is that about one third of the Korean entrepreneurs examined in this study made significant use of the Korean rotating credit association in capitalizing their enterprises.

It is our hope that this work contributes to the overall understanding of the relationship between entrepreneurship, immigration, community, and society. We understand that entrepreneurs, both immigrant and minority, have always been part of the process of the continued rebirth of American society, and it is our wish that this volume contributes to the importance of placing the practice and study of entrepreneurship at the center of community for its growth, development, and economic well-being.

The authors would like to express a special thanks to Coral Franke and Margaret Cotrofeld for their dedication in helpng bringing this manuscript to press.

## NOTES

1. For a discussion of this literature see John Sibley Butler and Patricia G. Greene, Ethnic Entrepreneurship: The Continuous Rebirth of American Enterprise, in Donald L. Sexton and Raymond W. Smilor, eds. (1997), *The State of the Art of Entrepreneurship* (Denver: Upstart Publishing Company), pp. 267–290. Simmel's original work is reprinted in K. Wolf (1950), *The Sociology of Georg Simmel* (Glenco, IL: Free Press).

2. Max Weber. (1930). *The Protestant Ethic and the Spirit of Capitalism* (New York: Charles Scribner's Sons).

3. See, for example, Frank D. Bean.

4. Report of the President's Commission on Immigration and Naturalization (Washington: Government Printing Office, January 1, 1953). Quoted in Thomas Muller (1993), *Immigrants and the American City* (New York: New York University Press), p. 111.

5. Muller, p. 111.

6. George Gilder. (1984). *The Spirit of Enterprise* (New York: Simon and Schuster), p. 95.

7. For a discussion, see Gilder, pp. 93–111; Alejandro Portes and Robert L. Bach (1985), *Latin Journey* (Berkeley: The University of California Press).

8. W. E. B. DuBois. (1898). *Economic Co-Operation among Negro Americans* (Atlanta: Atlanta University Press).

9. Henry M. Minton, M.D. (1913). *Early History of Negroes in Business in Philadelphia.* Read before the American Historical Society, 1913.

10. Abram L. Harris. (1913). *The Negro as Capitalist: A Study of Banking and Business among American Negroes* (The American Academy of Political and Social Sciences); Joseph A. Pierce. (1947). *Negro Business and Business Education* (New York: Harper Brothers).

11. *Business Week online,* The Return of the Black Entrepreneur, October 7, 2002. www.businessweek.com/smallbiz/content/oct2002/sb20021074298.htm.

# African American Entrepreneurship: The View from the 1910 Census

*Margaret Levenstein*

Despite limited study in recent years, entrepreneurship plays a crucial role in economic growth, both in society at large and within specific communities.[1] In a capitalist market economy, firms initiate and coordinate a wide range of ongoing economic activity and have increasingly been the site of innovation. The formation and nurturing of firms, of organizations that can create and sustain economic activity, is the most basic of entrepreneurial activities. Understanding who forms businesses and why they succeed or fail should be of great importance to economists. Understanding how those processes have changed over time should again be an important area of study for economic historians.

Successful entrepreneurs often rely on networks for the provision of information and resources that give them a competitive advantage—privileged access to information about product markets, sources of labor or capital, production technology, and management organization. Sometimes these networks are based on family and extended kinship. Other networks are based on common racial, ethnic, or religious identification. Historians and sociologists have focused on these "noneconomic" networks to explain ethnic and racial differences in patterns of entrepreneurship (Butler, 1991; Light, 1972). Less formal, and less visible when not associated with a distinct "minority" group, are networks based on common membership in professional, craft, educational, social, or cultural institutions. More generally, overlapping business and personal associations can be thought of as highways for the flow of resources and information. Firms, industries, communities, and nations succeed when they are at a major intersection, where mutually sustaining networks intersect. Whereas sociologists and historians have focused on personal, familial, and cultural networks, economists have implicitly. assumed the existence of private firms whose business is the creation of such networks, and the sale of the information obtained. Banks that build networks of borrowers and lenders, employment agencies with networks of employers and workers, and direct marketing companies with networks of consumers for sale to potential suppliers are examples of firms whose business is the construction of such networks.

An examination of African American entrepreneurship implicitly or explicitly must ask three questions: First, to what extent have the informal networks on which white Americans relied in forming businesses been replaced by more formal businesses who sell information and resources to customers; second, do African Americans have access to those resources and information at the same prices and quantities as do white Americans; and third, to what extent are there informal networks within the African American community on which entrepreneurs and potential entrepreneurs can rely?

Understanding the dynamics of African American entrepreneurship is of particular importance today. There has been increasing attention given to policies that emphasize African American entrepreneurship. But these policies have been informed by little historical study. A historical perspective may shed light on today's lack of African American entrepreneurship and suggest the kinds of networks and institutions that would be able to support successful entrepreneurship.

This chapter takes a small step toward filling in this missing historical picture. It presents a snapshot of the African American business population in 1910, based on two public use samples from the 1910 Census of Population. This was the first census to include a question on employment status (employer, own account, or employee) and is thus the first nationwide survey to include information about both business ownership and race. This study focuses on a period before the great migration of African Americans northward, which may have disrupted existing networks among African American businesses. It was after, however, the first "Buy Black" political movement and the formation of the National Negro Business League, so we know that there existed a vocal, if not large African American business community. Although support from large white businesses gives historical visibility to these political movements, there has been no systematic attempt to measure their impact on the number, size, or distribution of African American businesses. Booker T. Washington (1969) estimated that there were 9,838 African American businesses requiring capital in 1900 (p. 12). If that number is accurate, the findings here suggest a considerable increase in the number of African American businesses in the decade following the upsurge in the "Buy Black" movement. The most comparable figure that one can draw from the census data is the predicted number of African Americans employers outside of agriculture. In 1910 there were almost 19,000 such businesses, almost double Washington's estimate of a decade earlier.

One of the most striking findings of this study is that, in 1910, African Americans were more likely than white Americans to be employers, and almost as likely as whites to be self-employed (Table 1-1). This contrasts with the mid-1990s when African Americans were only a third as likely as whites to work in their own businesses. This raises questions about claims, such as those of Light (1922), that African American culture is unsupportive of entrepreneurial activity, or that "cultural differences may explain black white differentials in self-employment" (Meyer, 1990, p. 26). If cultural differences are to explain late twentieth-century differentials in self-employment, they must be a twentieth-century development.

## AFRICAN AMERICAN ENTREPRENEURS IN 1910: WHERE WERE THEY?

As suggested in the introduction, the overall rates of entrepreneurship (defined here as the proportion of the labor force that was either an employer or working on one's own account) were roughly equal for African Americans and whites in 1910 (26 percent of African Americans compared with 29 percent of whites; Table 1-1). This contrasts sharply with the situation in the mid-1990s, in which white entrepreneurship was significantly higher than that of African Americans. Again in con-

**TABLE 1-1  Distribution of Employment Status by Race (in percentages)**

| Race | Employer | Own Account | Worker | Total |
|------|----------|-------------|--------|-------|
| White | 12.52 | 16.30 | 71.18 | 82.21 |
| African American | 13.91 | 12.88 | 73.20 | 17.25 |
| Asian | 7.96 | 9.33 | 82.71 | 0.54 |
| Total | 12.73 | 15.68 | 71.59 | 100.00 |

trast to mid-1990s findings, entrepreneurship was significantly more common among both whites and African Americans in 1910 than among Asians (those of Japanese, Chinese, or Hawaiian descent; Table 1-1). This latter change probably reflects differences in both the characteristics of cohorts of Asian immigrants and the opportunities which they faced in the United States.

In aggregate, 15.68 percent of the labor force was self-employed, 12.73 percent an employer. The distribution of entrepreneurs in agriculture differs from that in nonagricultural sectors (Table 1-2). As the paths to and meaning of entrepreneurship are different in the two sectors, they will be analyzed separately. However, because the vast majority of African American entrepreneurs were in agriculture and a sizable proportion of white entrepreneurs, it would be misleading to ignore the sector altogether, as is frequently done in modern literature.

Although overall rates of entrepreneurship of whites and African Americans were comparable in 1910, there are three important differences in the pattern of entrepreneurship among African Americans and whites. These differences may help us to understand the decline in African American entrepreneurship over the twentieth century. First, the sectoral distribution of African American entrepreneurs was different from that of whites; African Americans were much more heavily concentrated in agriculture (Table 1-3 and Table 1-4). Second, there were differences in the patterns of entrepreneurship among men and women (Table 1-5). In general, men were more likely to be entrepreneurs than women. But African American women were more "entrepreneurial" than white women and also made up a larger proportion of the African American labor force. Finally, the distribution between employers and the self-employed ("own account") was different for whites and African Americans. Overall, African Americans and whites were split about evenly between "employer" and "own account" (Table 1-1). But this apparent similarity disappears when the data are disaggregated by sector and gender (Table 1-3, Table 1-4, and Table 1-5). A large proportion of African American men in agriculture were employers, and a large proportion of African American women in services were self-employed. In both cases, the proportions were higher than among their white coun-

**TABLE 1-2   Distribution of Employment Status In and Out of Agriculture**

| Employment Status | Percent of Nonagricultural Workforce | Percent of Agricultural Workforce |
|---|---|---|
| Employer | 5.15 | 27.17 |
| Own Account | 11.53 | 23.67 |
| Worker | 83.32 | 49.16 |

**TABLE 1-3  Distribution of Male Employment Status by Sector and Race**

| Sector | Employer | | Own Account | | Worker | |
|---|---|---|---|---|---|---|
| | African American | White | African American | White | African American | White |
| Agriculture | 34.43 | 29.33 | 15.42 | 30.14 | 50.15 | 40.53 |
| Mining | 0.30 | 1.51 | 0.30 | 2.79 | 99.40 | 95.70 |
| Construction | 3.00 | 10.41 | 9.73 | 10.92 | 87.27 | 78.66 |
| Nondurable Manufacturing | 0.56 | 4.99 | 2.24 | 2.69 | 97.20 | 92.31 |
| Durable Manufacturing | 0.35 | 2.95 | 0.42 | 1.57 | 99.23 | 95.48 |
| Transportation, Communication, and Utilities | 1.02 | 1.80 | 0.77 | 1.11 | 98.21 | 97.09 |
| Wholesale— Durables | 3.75 | 10.56 | 20.95 | 21.31 | 75.30 | 68.12 |
| Wholesale— Nondurables | 0.00 | 10.63 | 7.70 | 15.07 | 92.30 | 74.30 |
| Retail | 3.15 | 16.96 | 12.25 | 23.66 | 84.59 | 59.38 |
| Finance, Real Estate, and Insurance | 0.00 | 5.64 | 3.30 | 23.15 | 96.70 | 71.20 |
| Business Services | 8.64 | 8.99 | 27.16 | 32.65 | 64.21 | 58.37 |
| Personal Services | 2.12 | 15.73 | 8.49 | 21.52 | 89.39 | 62.75 |
| Recreation | 0.66 | 7.07 | 15.99 | 18.27 | 83.34 | 74.66 |
| Professional Services | 0.00 | 3.43 | 10.42 | 38.43 | 89.58 | 58.14 |

terparts. Outside of agriculture, African American employers were relatively rare. I discuss each of these three issues in turn. Finally, I conclude with a discussion of the particular nonagricultural industries in which African American entrepreneurs do appear in significant numbers.

The sectoral distribution of African American and white businesses was very different. Seventy-three percent of all African American entrepreneurs were in agriculture.[2] White entrepreneurs were also concentrated in agriculture—because the average number of workers on any farm is relatively low—but, with fewer than 60 percent of white entrepreneurs located in agriculture, were less so than African Americans. When one examines the concentration by gender, the lack of diversification of African American entrepreneurs becomes even more noticeable. Fully 92 percent of all African American male entrepreneurs and over 97 percent of African American male *employers* were in agriculture

**TABLE 1-4   Distribution of Female Employment Status by Sector and Race**

| Sector | Employer | | Own Account | | Worker | |
|---|---|---|---|---|---|---|
| | African American | White | African American | White | African American | White |
| Agriculture | 5.46 | 20.00 | 3.17 | 11.28 | 91.35 | 68.72 |
| Mining | 0.00 | 0.00 | 0.00 | 2.78 | 100.00 | 97.22 |
| Construction | 0.00 | 7.35 | 0.00 | 4.41 | 100.00 | 88.24 |
| Nondurable Manufacturing | 0.75 | 0.46 | 0.75 | 1.23 | 98.50 | 98.31 |
| Durable Manufacturing | 0.00 | 0.32 | 0.00 | 1.59 | — | 98.09 |
| Transportation, Communication, and Utilities | 0.00 | 0.46 | 6.47 | 0.15 | 93.53 | 99.39 |
| Wholesale— Durables | — | 0.00 | — | 5.00 | 100.00 | 95.00 |
| Wholesale— Nondurables | 0.00 | 0.58 | 6.33 | 1.73 | 93.67 | 97.69 |
| Retail | 10.00 | 3.98 | 18.75 | 11.16 | 71.25 | 84.86 |
| Finance, Real Estate, and Insurance | 0.00 | 0.91 | 4.54 | 4.88 | 95.46 | 94.21 |
| Business Services | 0.00 | 2.63 | 30.07 | 45.26 | 69.93 | 52.11 |
| Personal Services | 0.24 | 2.45 | 30.38 | 23.24 | 69.38 | 74.31 |
| Recreation | 0.00 | 0.80 | 0.00 | 11.20 | 100.00 | 88.00 |
| Professional Services | 0.00 | 0.21 | 9.68 | 13.17 | 90.32 | 86.62 |

(Table 1-6). The comparable figures for white men were 64 percent of all entrepreneurs and 68 percent of all employers (Table 1-6). Almost 93 percent of African American female employers were in agriculture, but only 61 percent of white women (Table 1-7). The only sizable group of African American entrepreneurs who were *not* concentrated in agricul-

**TABLE 1-5   Distribution of Employment Status by Race and Gender**

| Employment Status | White Men | White Women | African American Men | African American Women |
|---|---|---|---|---|
| Employer | 14.53 | 3.77 | 21.11 | 2.97 |
| Own Account | 17.14 | 12.65 | 11.14 | 15.54 |
| Worker | 68.33 | 83.58 | 67.75 | 81.50 |

**TABLE 1-6   Sectoral Distribution of Male Entrepreneurs**

| Sector | Employer | | Own Account | |
|---|---|---|---|---|
| | African American | White | African American | White |
| Agriculture | 97.35 | 68.43 | 82.58 | 59.60 |
| Mining | 0.03 | 0.41 | 0.06 | 0.64 |
| Construction | 0.60 | 5.38 | 3.69 | 4.79 |
| Nondurable Manufacturing | 0.08 | 3.01 | 0.60 | 1.38 |
| Durable Manufacturing | 0.15 | 2.75 | 0.35 | 1.23 |
| Transportation, Communication, and Utilities | 0.44 | 1.33 | 0.63 | 0.69 |
| Wholesale—Durables | 0.03 | 0.40 | 0.32 | 0.69 |
| Wholesale—Nondurables | 0.00 | 1.30 | 0.23 | 1.56 |
| Retail | 0.61 | 11.86 | 4.51 | 14.03 |
| Finance, Real Estate, and Insurance | 0.00 | 0.74 | 0.17 | 2.58 |
| Business Services | 0.18 | 0.76 | 1.10 | 2.33 |
| Personal Services | 0.51 | 2.66 | 3.86 | 3.08 |
| Recreation | 0.01 | 0.25 | 0.41 | 0.55 |
| Professional Services | 0.00 | 0.72 | 1.50 | 6.85 |

ture were self-employed women. (Only a small proportion of self-employed white women were in agriculture as well. Running a farm on one's own does not seem to have been a popular option for women.) Among both African American and white women, about 10 percent of the self-employed were in agriculture. Because self-employed women make up a significant portion of the African American workforce, they introduced a degree of diversification out of agriculture for African American entrepreneurs in general. The quantitative importance of agricultural businesses to the African American business community is one of the most striking, even if predictable, findings of this study. This sector has been almost completely ignored by the historical literature, which has focused on sectors such as personal service, retail, banking, and insurance. Promoters of African American business at the time recognized the importance of agriculture. For example, at the 1911 national convention of the National Negro Business League, the "important subjects" addressed included "Raising and Shipping Fruits and Poultry," the "Pickle King," "My success as a Horticulturist," as well as several discussing wholesaling of agricultural products (Work, 1912, p. 22). The concentration of African American entrepreneurs in agriculture suggests that the relative lack of entrepreneurial behavior on the part of African Americans today may have little to do with cultural attitudes

**TABLE 1-7   Sectoral Distribution of Female Entrepreneurs**

| Sector | Employer | | Own Account | |
|---|---|---|---|---|
| | African American | White | African American | White |
| Agriculture | 92.74 | 60.65 | 10.22 | 10.19 |
| Mining | 0.00 | 0.00 | 0.00 | 0.03 |
| Construction | 0.00 | 0.58 | 0.00 | 0.10 |
| Non-Durable Manufacturing | 0.33 | 2.33 | 0.06 | 1.87 |
| Durable Manufacturing | 0.00 | 0.35 | 0.00 | 0.52 |
| Transportation, Communication, and Utilities | 0.00 | 0.35 | 0.06 | 0.03 |
| Wholesale—Durables | 0.00 | 0.00 | 0.00 | 0.07 |
| Wholesale—Non-durables | 0.00 | 0.12 | 0.02 | 0.10 |
| Retail | 3.32 | 13.74 | 1.19 | 11.47 |
| Finance, Real Estate, and Insurance | 0.00 | 0.35 | 0.06 | 0.55 |
| Business Services | 0.00 | 0.58 | 0.16 | 2.98 |
| Personal Services | 3.61 | 20.02 | 86.99 | 56.64 |
| Recreation | 0.00 | 0.12 | 0.00 | 0.49 |
| Professional Services | 0.00 | 0.81 | 1.23 | 14.94 |

toward risk-taking or the desire for the independence, authority, and responsibility associated with owning one's own business. Rather it may reflect the extreme concentration of African Americans' entrepreneurial resources, and the networks of African American entrepreneurs, in a sector that was undergoing long-term decline. This also suggests that further research on the effect of agricultural policies on African American entrepreneurship may shed light on the decline of African American entrepreneurship.

One might claim that the presence of a large number of African American employers and self-employed in agriculture reflects the heavy concentration of African American labor, generally, in agriculture, and not entrepreneurial behavior *per se*. It is certainly true that African Americans generally were concentrated in agriculture (about 56 percent of the total African American workforce). But African American men in agriculture were actually more likely than whites to be *employers*, not simply self-employed. This is true even if one compares African American and white men within the South, where the lack of mechanization increased labor requirements relative to the North.[3] Though the concentration in agriculture may reflect existing skills and human capital specific to agriculture, it may also reflect barriers to entrepreneurial activity outside of agriculture. And the experience of being an employer or self-employed in agriculture, while certainly different from owning a factory or a store, is still one in which the individual has the responsibility and assumes risk for a wide range of decisions: what and how much to produce; what inputs, including labor, to buy; where to sell. As in other sectors, entrepreneurs in agriculture are interacting with the market, locating markets, locating inputs. This distinguishes them from employees who, having located an employer, relate to that employer, that firm or farm, but do not, as producers, continue to have a direct interaction with the market.

There are very large differences in the pattern of entrepreneurship between African American men and women (Table 1-5). To some extent they reflect the same patterns of gendered participation in labor markets as do whites. Both African American and white women are less entrepreneurial and less specialized in agriculture than their respective male counterparts (compare Tables 1-3, 1-4, 1-6, and 1-7). They are also both much more likely to be self-employed than employers (Table 1-5). There are actually more African American male employers than self-employed, and the two groups are divided about evenly for white men. Unlike the concentration of male entrepreneurs in agriculture, the largest groups of female entrepreneurs, both white and African American, are in personal service (Table 1-7).

There are several important differences between the entrepreneurial behaviors of African American and white women, however. First, women made up a much larger proportion of the African American labor force than of the white labor force (40 percent and 19 percent respectively). Thus patterns of entrepreneurship among African American women have a larger impact on African American entrepreneurship as a whole. Second, the overall rate of entrepreneurship of African American women was somewhat higher than for white women (Table 1-5). As with males, this slightly higher average rate masks a difference in the distribution between employers and self-employed. White women were more likely than African American women to be employers, and less likely to be self-employed. Finally, while neither white nor African American female entrepreneurs were heavily concentrated in agriculture, African women were much more concentrated into a few sectors than was the case for white female entrepreneurs (Table 1-7). Seventy-four percent of female African American entrepreneurs and 87 percent of female African American self-employed were in the personal service sector. This was the largest sector for white female entrepreneurs as well, but the concentration was significantly less (48 percent of entrepreneurs and 57 percent of self-employed). For both African American and white female entrepreneurs the next largest sector was agriculture. And again, African American entrepreneurs were more concentrated than white women. Twenty-three percent of African

American female entrepreneurs were in agriculture, and only 22 percent of white women. (Ninety-three percent of African American female *employers* were in agriculture, and only 61 percent of white, but the number of employers for both African American and white women was quite small.) So 97 percent of all African American female entrepreneurs were in either personal service or agriculture, compared to only 70 percent of white women. The concentration of African American female entrepreneurs in these two sectors again reflects their overall labor force behavior, and may reflect their exclusion from other sectors. But, as was the case for African American men in agriculture, the concentration of entrepreneurs is greater than the (very high) concentration of the labor force as a whole. (About 78 percent of all African American female employees were in either agriculture or personal service.) African American women's entrepreneurship cannot be dismissed as simply America's twentieth-century peasantry. Perhaps because of exclusion from opportunities to engage in wage labor, African American women set up businesses in sectors where they had skills and could find customers. But their concentration into two sectors, both of which experienced decline over the course of the century, did not bode well for the long-term success of these efforts.

The last important difference in African American and white entrepreneurship is in the division, discussed briefly earlier, between employers and self-employed. African American men were more likely to be employers than to be self-employed (Table 1-8). This pattern was at variance with that observed for any other group, and is explained by the large proportion of African American employers in agriculture (Table 1-3). Over 34 percent of African American men in agriculture were employers (Table 1-3). This led to a difference in the pattern of entrepreneurship between African American men and women, who were more than five times more likely to be self-employed than to be an employer (Table 1-5).

Outside of agriculture, the difference in the rates of entrepreneurship between African American and white men was quite large. African American men were about a third as likely as white men to be employers or self-employed (6 percent of African American men, 17.4 percent

**TABLE 1-8  Distribution of Employment Status of Men**

| Race | Employer | | Own Account | | Worker | |
|------|----------|--|-------------|--|--------|--|
| | Outside Agriculture | Agriculture | Outside Agriculture | Agriculture | Outside Agriculture | Agriculture |
| White | 6.94 | 29.33 | 10.48 | 30.14 | 82.58 | 40.53 |
| Negro | 1.16 | 34.41 | 4.23 | 15.34 | 94.61 | 50.24 |
| Mulatto | 2.13 | 34.53 | 6.78 | 15.80 | 91.09 | 49.68 |

of white men). There were small but significant numbers of African American male entrepreneurs in construction, retail, and personal service. In each case there are about three to four times as many self-employed as employers, but with significant numbers of each (Table 1-6). Extrapolating from the samples suggests that there were almost 5,000 African American male *employers* in construction, 2,500 running eating and drinking establishments, 2,000 running barber shops, 1,500 repair businesses, and a thousand grocery stores. There were smaller numbers with trucking businesses, taxicab businesses, shoe repair shops, and dry good stores. There were somewhat larger numbers of individuals, in these and similar industries, working on their own account. In addition, there was a significant number (about 4,000) of self-employed African American male professionals with no employees. (There was not a single African American professional in the sample with an employee.) Most of these were mulattos. Every African American lawyer in the sample was mulatto; over 60 percent of the medical professionals were mulatto. Mulatto men made up only 16 percent of the African American male workforce.

As suggested earlier, African American female entrepreneurs outside agriculture were heavily concentrated in personal services. Three industries had more than 1,000 female employers: lodging places, private household services, and eating and drinking establishments. Among African American female self-employed, over 50 percent worked in personal household services. These were not simply misclassified maids; the census distinguished them from a much larger (three times as many) group of African American women workers in private household services. The next largest group of African American female self-employed was dressmakers, of which there were about 35,000. There were over 10,000 African American women running boardinghouses ("lodging places, except hotel and motel"), 1,750 with their own beauty shops, and nearly that many with their own restaurants and clothing stores. There were also over 1,000 African American women who were self-employed health practitioners (presumably midwives) and a similar number providing educational services.

The number of African American entrepreneurs outside of agriculture was dwarfed by those within it. But even excluding agriculture African Americans were more likely to be entrepreneurs in 1910 than in 1990 (6 percent of African American men in 1910 compared to 4.4 percent in 1990; Fairlie & Meyer, 1994, p. 1). This reflects a decline in self-employment throughout the American economy over the course of the twentieth century. The rate of decline in self-employment, outside agriculture, seems to have been the same for white and African American men—about 25 percent over the 80-year period. Thus there has been no convergence in the aggregate pattern of entrepreneurship outside agriculture over the century. This also suggests that virtually none of the entrepreneurial skills reflected and developed by the large numbers of African American employers in agriculture were transferred into entrepreneurial activities outside agriculture as agriculture declined.

## ANALYZING THE DETERMINANTS OF AFRICAN AMERICAN ENTREPRENEURSHIP

With a somewhat clearer picture of the extent and location of African American entrepreneurs in 1910, we would like to be able to address the fundamental social and economic questions raised in the introduction. How was African American entrepreneurship affected by differential access to resources from the formal, commercial sector? Were African American entrepreneurs discriminated against in credit markets? Did differential treatment in labor markets affect African American entrepreneurship? Did African Americans turn to entrepreneurship when wage labor was unavailable, or did they, presumably like white Americans, use wage labor to accumulate wealth and experience as a path to entry into entrepreneurship? Did African American customers "Buy Black?" Did African Americans prefer to work for other African Americans? Although the 1910 census provides virtually no financial information about individuals with businesses, or the businesses themselves, it does allow a limited exploration of these questions.

Table 1-9 and Table 1-10 summarize the results of a series of logistic regressions estimating the likelihood that an individual will be either an employer or self-employed as a function of things that we can measure using the 1910 Census. These include two very crude proxies for the accumulation of human capital—AGE and LITERACY—and one very crude proxy for personal wealth—home ownership (HOME). Because the observed pattern of entrepreneurship is so different between men and women, gender (FEMALE) is also included. Access to labor and credit markets are measured with two variables—UNEMPLOYED and MORTGAGE. These two variables report whether the individual was unemployed at any point during the previous year and whether the individual, if a home owner, had a mortgage on the home. Because industries with larger average-size firms have less potential for entrepreneurial activity, the variable SIZE, measuring the average number of workers per firm in detailed industry groups, is included. Of course, a potential entrepreneur's choice of industry may depend on both ease of entry and potential for growth, the latter of which may be greater in industries with larger firms.

Several variables attempt to capture the relationship between race and race-related phenomena and the likelihood that an individual will be an entrepreneur. A-A indicates that the individual is African Amer-

**TABLE 1-9   Logit Estimates of the Probability of Being an Employer**

| Variable | 1:Pooled Data | 2:White outside agriculture | 3:A-A outside agriculture | 4:White in agriculture | 5:A-A in agriculture |
|---|---|---|---|---|---|
| N | 128,391 | 76,311 | 11,056 | 25,804 | 14,004 |
| Intercept | −1.61 | −1.61 | −2.69 | −4.93 | −3.79 |
| Age | 0.07 | 0.05 | 0.05 | 0.10 | 0.08 |
| Literacy | 0.57 | 1.26 | 0.63* | 0.90 | 0.38 |
| Female | −1.85 | −1.78 | −0.60* | −1.37 | −2.70 |
| Home | 0.29 | 0.67 | 0.98 | 0.02* | −0.77 |
| Mortgage | 0.22 | −0.13* | −0.09* | 0.48 | 0.59 |
| Unemployed | −2.81 | −2.39 | −3.17* | −3.71 | −2.42 |
| SIZE | −5.60 | −5.20 | −4.64 | | |
| Agriculture | 0.58 | | | | |
| South | 0.49 | 0.21 | 0.18* | 0.68 | 2.12 |
| A-A | −0.80 | | | | |
| Asian | −0.98 | | | | |
| COUNTY | 0.42 | | −0.15* | | 0.65 |
| INDUSTRY | 2.51 | | −2.91 | | −5.03 |
| Home * A-A | −0.92 | | | | |
| Mortg * A-A | 0.26* | | | | |
| Unemp * A-A | 0.38* | | | | |

*Not significant at the 99% level. All unmarked coefficients are significant at greater than 99% confidence levels.

ican (Negro or mulatto) and ASIAN that he or she is Chinese, Japanese, or Hawaiian. Two variables designed to pick up the effects of occupational and residential segregation are included. The first (COUNTY) measures the percentage of the county population that is African American. The second (INDUSTRY) measures the percentage of total employment in a detailed industry group that is African American. In the regressions in which African Americans and whites are pooled, I include variables interacting the unemployed, home, and mortgage variables with the African American race variable, to determine whether the relationship between those variables and entrepreneurship is different for African Americans and whites. The regressions are run separately for agriculture and nonagriculture.

In every specification of the regression in which the data was pooled from individuals of different races, the coefficients on AFRICAN AMERICAN and ASIAN were negative, suggesting that, given the other things controlled for, African Americans and Asians were less

**TABLE 1-10   Logit Estimates of the Probability of Being Self-Employed**

| Variable | 1:Pooled Data | 2:White outside agriculture | 3:A-A outside agriculture | 4:White in agriculture | 5:A-A in agriculture |
|---|---|---|---|---|---|
| N | 130,056 | 80,884 | 12,966 | 25,850 | 12,048 |
| Intercept | 1.13 | 1.42 | 0.32* | −3.82 | −2.54 |
| Age | 0.06 | 0.05 | 0.03 | 0.08 | 0.06 |
| Literacy | 0.56 | 0.11* | 0.17 | 0.80 | 0.51 |
| Female | −0.65 | −0.37 | 1.15 | −1.80 | −2.27 |
| | | | | | |
| Home | 0.29 | 0.43 | −0.17* | 0.00* | −0.08* |
| Mortgage | 0.04 | −0.17 | 0.36 | 0.23 | 0.05* |
| Unemployed | −2.38 | −2.10 | −1.58 | −2.96 | −1.73 |
| | | | | | |
| SIZE | −7.73 | −7.46 | −6.28 | | |
| Agriculture | −0.64 | | | | |
| South | 0.35 | 0.33 | 0.84 | 0.43 | 0.61 |
| | | | | | |
| A-A | −2.97 | | | | |
| Asian | −0.99 | | | | |
| COUNTY | 0.51 | | 0.35* | | 0.25* |
| INDUSTRY | 8.95 | | 3.45 | | −5.38 |
| Home * A-A | −0.34 | | | | |
| Mortg * A-A | 0.04* | | | | |
| Unemp * A-A | 0.99 | | | | |

*Not significant at the 99% level. All unmarked coefficients are significant at greater than 99% confidence levels.

likely than whites to be entrepreneurs. Because I have not controlled for wealth and other important determinants of entrepreneurship, this should be interpreted cautiously. For example, much of this negative effect may reflect the lower average wealth levels of African Americans and Asians. As would be expected from the discussion earlier, being female was also generally associated with a decreased probability of being an entrepreneur. The one exception (Table 1-10, column 3) was the case of African Americans outside agriculture, where women were significantly more likely than men to be self-employed. The "human capital" variables behave as expected—older, literate people are more likely to be entrepreneurs—but the literacy variable is frequently insignificant, especially in the self-employment regressions.

In the pooled regressions (Table 1-9, column 1 and Table 1-10, column 1) and in most of the nonagricultural regressions (Table 1-9, column 2 and Table 1-10, column 2), owning a home was associated with an increased likelihood of being an entrepreneur. But in other cases, the coefficient is negative and insignificant. This effect seems to be driven by a large number of tenant farmers and sharecroppers who are self-employed or employers. There are two ways to think about this result. One is that home ownership may be a reasonable proxy for wealth outside agriculture, but not within agriculture. The other is to accept that home ownership is correlated with wealth but that wealth is less important to entrepreneurship in agriculture than outside it, because there were institutional mechanisms that allowed those with little wealth to acquire—through tenancy or sharecropping—the inputs necessary to engage in business. African Americans in agriculture were actually significantly less likely to be employers if they owned a home (Table 1-9, column 5). This may suggest that African Americans who have moved their way up the agricultural ladder sufficiently to own their home may also be in a position to diversify their crop plantings outside of cotton in a way that decreases their need for labor outside the family.

Having a mortgage (visible evidence of access to credit and of indebtedness) was usually positively associated with entrepreneurship. The variable is insignificant in several regressions, however, apparently being less important for those who were self-employed than employers, and somewhat more significant in agriculture than outside it. Again, this may well reflect the patterns of tenure on agricultural land used for different crops or cultivated at different scales.

Previous unemployment strongly and significantly decreases the probability that an individual will be an entrepreneur. This is true for both whites and African Americans. The results are stronger in the employer than in the self-employed regressions. In all the self-employed regressions, the absolute value of the coefficient is smaller for African Americans than whites; in the pooled, self-employed regression the variable interacting race and previous unemployment is positive and significant (Table 1-10, column 1). These results suggest that there was some "falling into," as opposed to "opting into," self-employment, and that there was somewhat more of it among African Americans than among whites. But overall, both African American and white entrepreneurs were more likely to have been continuously employed. African American entrepreneurs may have left wage labor because discrimination limited opportunities, but those individuals who had found wage labor, perhaps with unsatisfactory conditions, were more likely to become entrepreneurs than those who had been excluded from wage labor.

Across a variety of specifications, African Americans living in a county with a larger percentage of African Americans (COUNTY) were more likely to be entrepreneurs. This provides some support for "enclave" explanations of ethnic business, which argue that ethnically homogeneous residential communities can provide a market or other forms of support for ethnic businesses. A similar measure, INDUSTRY, was designed to pick up the effect of a large African American presence, and a pool of African American workers who were potential entrepreneurs, within detailed industry divisions. It gave very inconsistent results. In three of the African American–only regressions, the INDUSTRY coefficient was negative and significant. Thus, African American employers, and the self-employed in agriculture, were less likely to be in industries with a heavily African American workforce. This reflects the concentration of African American workers in industries with few African American entrepreneurs. The industries where African Americans located were ones in which a large proportion of the workforce was entrepreneurial, and those were not the industries that had large proportions of African American workers. In contrast, in the nonagricultural, self-employed African American regression (Table 1-10, column 3), the coefficient on INDUSTRY is significant in positive. This reflects the large number of African American women in services, a sector that also employed a large number of African American workers.

## CONCLUSION

This chapter has found that overall rates of entrepreneurship—defined here simply as working in one's own business, with employees or not, were roughly equal between whites and African Americans in 1910. This average equality masks important differences. These differences are not obviously explained by the oft-referred-to lack of entrepreneurial values on the part of African American culture or institutions. On the other hand, the differences in patterns of entrepreneurship during this period may help to explain the decline, over the first three quarters of the twentieth century, of African American entrepreneurship. The most important feature of African American entrepreneurship that one can draw from this study is the heavy concentration in agriculture, and for African American women, agriculture and personal services. One can speculate that as these sectors declined over the course of the century, so did African American entrepreneurship.

Although the results of the regression analysis presented here must be treated very carefully, because of the limited nature of the data, they do suggest two important findings. First, most African American employers were truly entrepreneurs in the sense of "opting" rather than "falling" into entrepreneurship. The African American self-employed included a small, but significantly greater proportion of the previously unemployed than did the white. Second, African American entrepreneurs were more likely to be located in counties with a higher percentage African American population. This provides tentative support for enclave explanations of African American entrepreneurship, before the creation of large urban ghettos. All that this chapter cannot answer points to the importance of further research to understand the historical context of African American entrepreneurship. This research should also shed light on the process of entrepreneurship in the United States more generally. If competitive forces have not led to convergence, but rather divergence, in the entrepreneurial behavior of African Americans and whites, a re-examination of the variety of networks that support entrepreneurship among the majority ethnic group is also in order.

## NOTES

The author acknowledges the very helpful research assistance of Anne Young and Gema Ricart-Moes, and comments from Skipper Hammond, Warren Whatley, and participants in seminars at the University of Michigan, UCLA, Caltech, and the 1995 Business History Conference.

1. Following standard use among sociologists and economists (Butler, 1991; Meyer, 1990), I define an "entrepreneur" as one who runs his or her own business. I do not restrict my study to those who were particularly innovative in their business activities or transformed the industries in which they participated.

2. Extrapolating from the sample suggests that there were 1.25 million African American "entrepreneurs" in agriculture and not quite half a million outside agriculture.

3. Differences in the use of employed labor in northern and southern agriculture do help to create the different patterns observed. White men in southern agriculture were more likely to be employers than were their northern counterparts (33.64 percent compared to 27.21 percent). Only 10 percent of (the very few) African Americans in northern agriculture were employers, a much lower proportion than either whites in the North or African Americans in the South.

## REFERENCES

Butler, John Sibley. (1991). *Entrepreneurship and self-help among black Americans: A reconsideration of race and economics.* Albany, NY: SUNY Press.
Fairlie, Robert W., and Bruce Meyer. (1994). The ethnic and racial character of self employment. (National Bureau of Economic Research Working Paper No. 4791).
Light, Ivan. (1972). *Ethnic enterprise in America.* Berkeley: University of California Press.
Meyer, Bruce. (1990). Why are there so few black entrepreneurs? (National Bureau of Economic Research Working Paper No. 3537).
Washington, Booker T. (1969). *The Negro in business.* Boston: Hertel, Jenkins and Company.
Work, Monroe N. (1912). *Negro year book 1912.* Tuskegee, AL: Tuskegee Institute.

# 2

# Black Entrepreneurs, 1970–1990: A Demographic Perspective

*Hayward Derrick Horton*

Self-employment is a major component of the historical development of the United States. Many sociologists have noted that immigrants and minorities have led the way in entrepreneurship—often as a sole means of survival in a relatively discriminatory labor market (Bonacich & Modell, 1980). One exception to this general trend has been black Americans (Light, 1979). Whereas historical and socio-cultural approaches to the study of black entrepreneurship have shed some light on the subject (Butler, 1991), only recently have demographic approaches been applied to the topic (Horton & De Jong, 1991). Accordingly, this study builds on earlier efforts to study black entrepreneurs from a demographic perspective. Specifically, three questions are addressed: (1) To what extent has the population of entrepreneurs changed over the 1970–1990 period? (2) What are the relative effects of race, social, and demographic factors in determining entrepreneurship among blacks? (3) What are the policy implications in the changes in the patterns of black entrepreneurship?

## THEORETICAL EXPLANATIONS FOR BLACK ENTREPRENEURSHIP

Over the years, several scholars have presented theoretical arguments to explain entrepreneurship for immigrants and minorities in the United States. For instance, Light (1979) offered disadvantage theory as an explanation for minority patterns of self-employment. He argued that minorities turn to self-employment as a response to discrimination in the labor force. Bonacich (1972) offered a theory of middleman minorities to explain the phenomenon of Asian entrepreneurship (Bonacich & Modell, 1980). Portes and Bach (1985) used ethnic enclave theory to explain entrepreneurship and economic development among Cuban Americans. However, one of the limitations of these and similar approaches has been their inability to explain black entrepreneurship.

The most comprehensive theory of *black* entrepreneurship was presented by Butler (1991). In his classic *Entrepreneurship and Self-Help among Black Americans* he introduces the concept of the economic detour to explain why levels of black entrepreneurship tended to be lower than those of other groups. Jim Crow laws and general practices of racial exclusion, including violence, were employed to limit the opportunities for blacks in American society. Butler (1991) notes:

> Throughout the nation, Afro-American businesses were forced to concentrate into race-specific business districts. They were forced to move businesses which had served the community for years from the central point of town. When Afro-American businessmen arrived in a city, they had to settle in the Afro-American district. It was simply against the law to settle their businesses in the developing downtown district of a major section. (p. 145)

Butler (1991) documents that neither Japanese, Chinese, Mexicans, Cubans, nor any other group has had to "go it alone" as blacks have had to. He introduced the concept of the truncated Afro-American middleman to explain this phenomenon.

Horton and De Jong (1991) approached the study of black entrepreneurship from a demographic perspective. This framework focuses on the population of self-employed persons in an attempt to predict the social and demographic characteristics of black entrepreneurs. Using 1970 data and 1980 data from the U.S. Census, they found that those factors that determine social mobility in general likewise increase the likelihood that one will be self-employed. The current study builds on that analysis by examining the patterns of self-employment for black labor force participants from 1970 to 1990.

## DATA AND METHODS

### Data

The data from this study are the 1970, 1980, and 1990 Public Use Microdata Samples (PUMS) data from the U.S. Bureau of the Census. The PUMS data are collected on the long form of the decennial census questionnaire by approximately 5 percent of the total population. The data yield detailed population and housing characteristics for representative samples of the entire U.S. population. Hence, these data allow for the cross-tabulation of variables that are not generally found in printed form. The sample sizes for the 1970, 1980, and 1990 samples are 27,663, 10,348, and 10,397 respectively.

Only non-farm, labor force participants are included in this analysis.

### Operationalization of the Variables

*Entrepreneurial Status.* The dependent variable in the analysis, this variable was created by combining self-employed workers with workers who were employees of their own corporations. The codes are 0 for non-entrepreneurs and 1 for entrepreneurs.

*Sex.* Male is coded 0, and female is coded 1.

*Age.* A series of dummy variables with the categories 25–34, 35–44, 45–54, and 55–64; 65 and over is the reference category.

*Married.* Not married is coded 0, and married is coded 1.

*Education.* Represented as actual years of schooling.

*Region.* A dichotomy with non-South as 0 and South as 1.

*Industry.* This variable has the codes 0 for nontraditional and 1 for traditional.

*Occupation.* This dichotomy is coded 0 for blue-collar and 1 for white-collar.

### Methods

Logistic regression is the multivariate technique used for this study. It is appropriate when the dependent variable is dichotomous. Logistic regression models predict the log odds of being in one category of the dependent variable (in this case, entrepreneur) as opposed to the other (nonentrepreneur). Log odds of 0 indicate no effect; positive log odds indicate that a given variable increases the likelihood of entrepreneurship; negative log odds represent a decreased likelihood of the same.

## RESULTS

### Descriptive Analysis

Table 2-1 presents the cross tabulations of entrepreneurship with race and several of the variables of the analysis. These data show that the proportion of self-employed black workers has remained relatively low over the two-decade period. In 1970, 3.4 percent of all blacks in the labor force were self-employed. There was decline in 1980 to 2.6 percent. In 1990, the figure rose again: 4.1 percent of all black labor force participants were self-employed.

The white patterns of self-employment are different from those for blacks. Not only were white proportions greater, their levels remained stable over the 1970–1980 period (9.8 percent and 9.9 percent, respectively). In 1990 the percentage of white, self-employed labor force participants rose to 11.8 percent. This figure is nearly three times the comparable figure for black self-employment for that year.

**TABLE 2-1   Percentage Self-Employed for Blacks and Whites for Selected Social and Demographic Indicators, 1970–1990**

|  |  | Blacks | | | Whites | | |
|---|---|---|---|---|---|---|---|
|  |  | 1970 | 1980 | 1990 | 1970 | 1980 | 1990 |
| Total |  | 3.4 | 2.6 | 4.1 | 9.8 | 9.9 | 11.8 |
| Sex: | Male | 5.0 | 3.7 | 4.0 | 12.9 | 13.5 | 14.8 |
|  | Female | 1.3 | 1.4 | 4.1 | 4.4 | 4.7 | 7.9 |
| Age: | 25–34 | 2.1 | 1.4 | 3.3 | 5.9 | 8.8 | 7.8 |
|  | 34–44 | 3.0 | 2.2 | 3.1 | 11.3 | 12.2 | 11.5 |
|  | 45–54 | 5.4 | 5.6 | 5.0 | 12.7 | 12.5 | 13.3 |
|  | 55–64 | 5.6 | 3.7 | 3.3 | 16.2 | 15.7 | 16.6 |
|  | 65+ | 11.2 | 15.4 | 14.0 | 28.4 | 24.0 | 23.2 |
| Region: | South | 3.8 | 3.0 | 4.1 | 10.7 | 10.9 | 13.4 |
|  | NonSouth | 3.0 | 2.3 | 4.1 | 9.4 | 9.5 | 11.4 |
| Industry: | Traditional | 3.4 | 6.7 | 6.3 | 14.8 | 12.7 | 14.7 |
|  | Nontraditional | 2.5 | 1.9 | 3.7 | 6.2 | 9.2 | 11.2 |
| Occupation: | White Collar | 3.6 | 1.3 | 2.8 | 10.8 | 9.3 | 10.9 |
|  | Blue Collar | 2.6 | 2.9 | 4.2 | 5.7 | 7.4 | 10.4 |
| N |  | 15,668 | 1,056 | 908 | 11,995 | 9,262 | 9,489 |

An examination of the sex variable shows substantive change over time among black labor force participants. In 1970, 5.0 percent of black males were self-employed compared to 1.3 percent of black females (Figure 2-1). In 1980, there was a narrowing of the gap because of the decline in the level of black male self-employment. The figures are 3.7 percent and 1.4 percent for males and females respectively. By 1990, there had been an increase for both groups. However, the increase had been most dramatic for black females. In fact, black females had gained parity with black males by 1990. Their level of 4.1 percent self-employment was in fact modestly higher than that for black males (4.0 percent).

However, sex-parity in entrepreneurship did not occur for whites over the period. In 1970, the levels of self-employment for white males was 12.9 percent compared to 4.4 percent for females. The 1980 levels were 13.5 percent for white males and 4.7 percent for white females. In 1990, the comparable figures were 14.8 percent for males and 7.9 percent for females. It is important to note that despite the persistent gender differences in self-employment for whites, white females tend to have levels of entrepreneurship that are higher than that of black males or females. Moreover, the patterns over time are different. Both white males and females experienced steady increases over the two-decade period. This pattern is at variance with the decline for black males and no change for black females during the 1970–1980 decade. The sum of these race-sex differences suggests that for blacks, race is more important than sex in determining entrepreneurship.

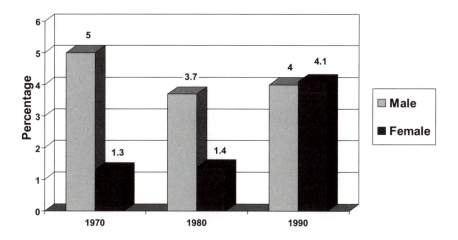

**Figure 2-1**  Entrepreneurial status by sex for blacks, 1970–1990.

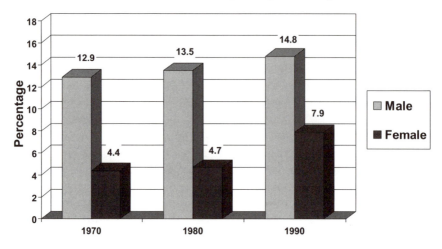

**Figure 2-2**  Entrepreneurial status by sex for whites, 1970–1990.

The patterns for race and entrepreneurship by age generally support those found by Horton and De Jong (1991). Blacks in older age categories tend to have higher percentages of self-employed workers than those in younger categories. (See Figure 2-3.) In addition, these patterns persisted over time. In 1970, 2.1 percent of blacks in the 25–34 age category were self-employed. The 35–44, 45–54, and 55–64 age catego-

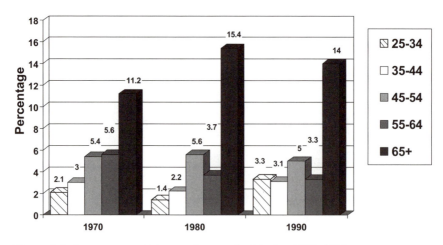

**Figure 2-3**  Entrepreneurial status by age for blacks, 1970–1990.

ries had percentages of 3.0, 5.4, and 5.6 respectively. However, 11.2 percent of the 65-and-over age category were self-employed. Similar patterns were found for blacks across age categories in 1980 and 1990. In 1980, the youngest age category had a percentage self-employed of 1.4; the percentage for the oldest was 15.4. In 1990, 3.3 percent was the percentage for labor force participants in the youngest age category, and 14.0 percent was the figure found among the oldest. In short, for blacks entrepreneurs, age matters.

However, age also matters for white self-employed labor force participants. In 1970, the percentage self-employed for whites ranged from 5.9 in the 25–34 category to 28.4 in the 65 and over category. In 1980, the figures ranged from 8.8 percent for the youngest to 24.0 percent for the oldest of the white self-employed. Comparable figures in 1990 were 7.8 percent and 23.2 percent for the youngest and oldest whites respectively. Nevertheless, it is important to note that in no age category, for any year, does the level of black self-employment equal that of comparable whites.

The patterns of self-employment for blacks do not vary substantially across regions. (See Figure 2.5.) This trend seems to have held over the two-decade period. In 1970 the levels of self-employment for blacks in the South and non-South were 3.8 percent and 3.0 percent in that order. The self-employment percentages were 3.0 percent in the South and 2.3 percent in the non-South in 1980. Those figures for 1990 were 4.1 percent in both categories.

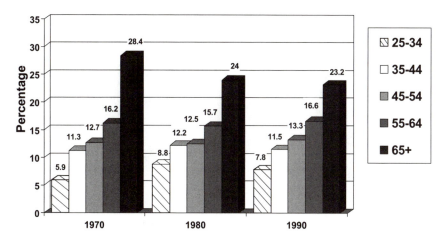

**Figure 2-4**  Entrepreneurial status by age for whites, 1970–1990.

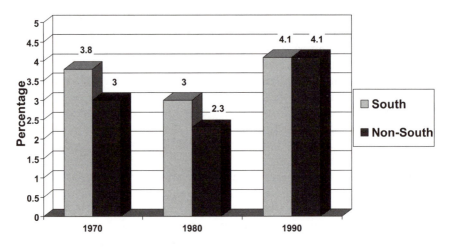

**Figure 2-5**  Entrepreneurial status by region for blacks, 1970–1990.

The regional patterns for whites were similar in the sense that the percentage of self-employment was slightly higher in the South and non-South for all years. (See Figure 2.6.) However, as has been the case for other variables, the white levels of self-employment were consistently 2 to 4 times greater than for comparable blacks.

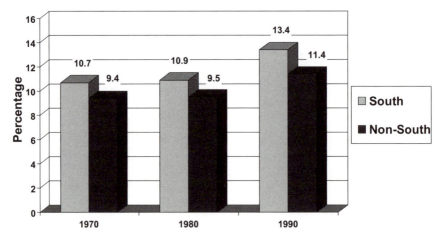

**Figure 2-6**  Entrepreneurial status by region for whites, 1970–1990.

The patterns for industry for the black self-employed are again consistent with the earlier study by Horton and De Jong(1991). Blacks tended to have higher percentages of the self-employed in traditional industries. (See Figure 2-7.) In 1970, there were 3.4 percent self-employed in the traditional area compared to 2.5 percent in nontraditional industries. In 1980, the two categories changed in opposite directions. The traditional category increased in its percentage of self-employed to 6.7 percent. The nontraditional area decreased to 1.9 percent. Finally, the figures for 1990 were 6.3 percent and 3.7 percent in the traditional and nontraditional categories in that order.

The level of self-employed among whites in the traditional area was 14.8 percent in 1970 (Figure 2-8). The nontraditional area had a figure of 6.2 percent for that year. In 1980, 12.7 percent were found in the traditional and 9.2 percent in the nontraditional industries. The 1990 levels of self-employment for whites across industries were 14.7 percent for traditional and 11.2 percent for nontraditional categories. The overall pattern for whites is similar to that for blacks in that higher percentages are found in the traditional category for each year. However, in no instance does the black percentage exceed that for whites.

The final variable of consideration in the descriptive analysis is occupation. For blacks, the self-employed represented 3.6 percent of all labor force participants in the white-collar category (Figure 2-9). In the blue-collar category, the percentage is 2.6 percent. For 1980, the white-collar category decreased to 1.3 percent, and 2.9 percent represents

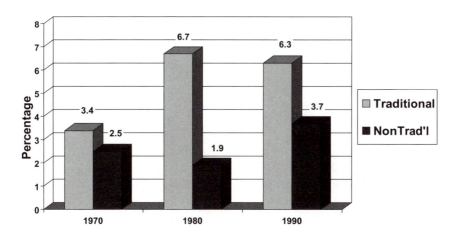

**Figure 2-7** Entrepreneurial status by industry for blacks, 1970–1990.

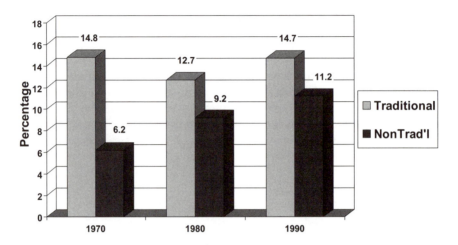

**Figure 2-8**  Entrepreneurial status by industry for whites, 1970–1990.

relative stability for the blue-collar area. By 1990, both categories in-creased with 2.8 percent among the white-collar labor force partici-pants, and 4.2 percent among those in the blue-collar area. In short, over the two-decade period there was a reversal in the occupational trends in self-employment for blacks. In 1970, white-collar workers had a higher percentage. By 1990, blue-collar workers had the higher level of self-employed among their ranks.

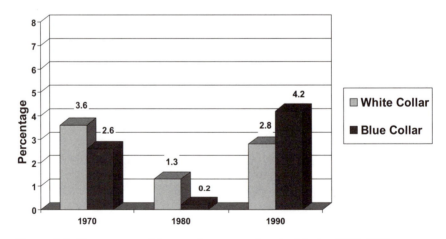

**Figure 2-9**  Entrepreneurial status by occupation for blacks, 1970–1990.

The patterns of self-employment by occupation were different for whites. White-collar workers had higher or equal levels of self-employment throughout the two-decade period. (See Figure 2-10.) In 1970, the figures were 10.8 percent for the white-collar and 5.7 percent for the blue-collar categories. In 1980 the levels were 9.3 percent and 7.4 percent respectively for the two areas. By 1990 the categories were essentially equal: 10.9 percent for white-collar labor force participants and 10.4 percent for blue-collar workers. These patterns echo those found for other variables: Despite intragroup differences, in no occupational category does the black level of self-employment equal that for whites.

In summary, these descriptive patterns demonstrate the extent to which black self-employment varies across categories of social and demographic factors. Whereas there has been a modest increase in the overall level of self-employment for blacks, this increase has been greatest for black females. Black females went from lower than 2 percent self-employment in 1970 to gain parity with black males by 1990. Moreover, an examination of age differences revealed dramatically high levels of self-employment for blacks who are 65 and over. In fact, the oldest category of blacks had higher or equal levels of self-employment than whites in the youngest to middle-age categories.

However, in all other categories, the general pattern was that blacks trailed whites in levels of self-employment. Even blacks who were 65 and over had levels that were considerably lower than those of whites in the same category. In short, these patterns suggest that race is a major

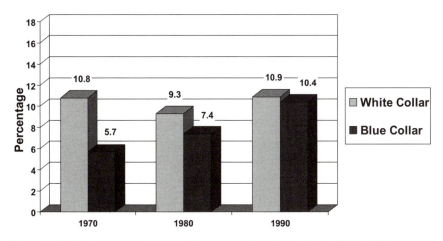

**Figur 2-10**  Entrepreneurial status by occupation for whites, 1970–1990.

determinant of self-employment. Moreover, the effects of race on self-employment appear to persist over time.

### Multivariate Analysis

Table 2-2 and Table 2-3 present the results of the logistic regression analysis. In Table 2-2, the main effects models are presented. The primary focus here is to assess the net effect of race. However, a secondary goal is to determine the effects of other social and demographic variables hypothesized to impact upon entrepreneurial status.

Thus, the primary question: Does race still matter relative to self-employment once controls for social and demographic factors are introduced? The answer is yes, even when one controls for age, sex, region, marital status, education, occupation, and industry. Moreover, the direction of the effect is unchanged over time. All things being equal, blacks are less likely than whites to be self-employed. Moreover, the effects for 1970–1990 are all significant at the p <.001 level.

An examination of the net effects of the other variables reveals other interesting results. For instance, women consistently are less likely than men to be self-employed. For each year, the effect is negative and significant at the p <.001 level.

**TABLE 2-2   Logistic Regression Models Predicting the Log Odds of Entrepreneurial Status by Race Net of Other Sociodemographic Factors, 1970–1990**

| Independent Variables | 1970 | 1980 | 1990 |
|---|---|---|---|
| Race (Black) | −.873*** | −1.168*** | −1.017*** |
| Sex (Female) | −1.423*** | −1.098*** | −.653*** |
| Age:   25–34 | .138 | −.202* | −1.308*** |
| 35–44 | .889** | .142 | −.891*** |
| 45–54 | 1.231*** | .247* | −.675*** |
| 55–64 | 1.460*** | .955*** | −.484** |
| South | .213** | .148 | −.013 |
| Industry (Traditional) | 1.004** | .791*** | .555*** |
| Occupation (White Collar) | .343*** | −.014 | −.236** |
| Married | .685*** | .879*** | .383*** |
| Educations | .055*** | .075*** | .066*** |
| Constant | −4.518*** | −3.907*** | −1.905*** |
| −2 Log Likelihood | 6748.508*** | 5699.887*** | 6808.533*** |
| N | 25,473 | 10,317 | 10,397 |

* p < .05        **p < .01        p < .001

**TABLE 2-3  Logistic Regression Models Predicting the Log Odds of Entrepreneurial Status for Blacks and Whites with Interaction Effects, 1970–1990**

| Independent Variables | Blacks | | | Whites | | |
|---|---|---|---|---|---|---|
| | 1970 | 1980 | 1990 | 1970 | 1980 | 1990 |
| Sex (Female) | -1.946*** | -1.767* | .129 | -1.753*** | -1.368*** | -.760*** |
| Age: 25–34 | .602* | -.538 | -1.401* | .044 | .411 | -1.287*** |
| 35–44 | .982*** | -.105 | -1.534* | .805*** | .803*** | -.892*** |
| 45–54 | 1.660*** | .842 | -1.043 | 1.007*** | .858*** | -.696*** |
| 55–64 | 1.714*** | .284 | -1.518* | 1.301*** | 1.183*** | -.440** |
| South | .318* | .174 | -.068 | .164 | .162* | -.022 |
| Industry (Traditional) | .379* | 1.28* | .441 | .939*** | .677*** | .310** |
| Occupation (White Collar) | .641*** | -.644 | -.627 | .244* | -.223 | -.259** |
| Married | .505** | .958* | .452 | .792*** | .584*** | .386*** |
| Education | .037* | .039 | .043 | .070*** | .083*** | .068*** |
| Female x Industry | .900* | 1.345 | .015 | .907*** | .677*** | .428* |
| Constant | -5.249*** | -4.625*** | -2.528** | -4.612*** | -4.243*** | -1.878*** |
| -2 Log Likelihood | 2,312.018*** | 217.345 | 295.823 | 4,388.583*** | 5,154.458*** | 6,112.919*** |
| N | 14,304 | 1,056 | 908 | 11,169 | 9,262 | 9,489 |

*p< **p < .01  ***p < .001

The net effects of the age variable are at variance with the descriptive patterns observed. In 1970 and 1980 all age categories, except the youngest group, are more likely than the elderly to be self-employed. However, the directions of the effects change in 1990. In that year, all age groups are less likely than the 65 and over category to be self-employed. These findings are consistent with those of the Horton and De Jong study (1991).

The region variable was significant only in 1970. Being in the South instead of the non-South increased the likelihood of self-employment.

Industry was highly significant and positive throughout the two-decade period. Entrepreneurs are more likely to be found in traditional rather than nontraditional industries.

Occupation was significant and positive in 1970, not significant in 1980, and significant but significant and negative in 1990. Being white-collar increased the likelihood of self-employment at the beginning of the period. However, by the end, blue-collar workers were more likely than white-collar workers to be self-employed.

Marital status was consistent in its effect on entrepreneurial status over time. Being married increased the likelihood of self-employment. The effect was significant at the p <.001 level for all years.

Finally, education increases the likelihood of being self-employed. The effects for education are positive at the p <.001 level for each year of the analysis.

Table 2-3 presents separate logistic regression models for blacks and whites for 1970, 1980, and 1990. The focus here is to assess the effects of various independent variables on black entrepreneurship over time. The models for whites are here solely as a basis for comparison.

These results reveal considerable change in the nature of black entrepreneurship over the two-decade period. For instance, net the effects of social and demographic variables, gender declined in significance in predicting black self-employment. In 1970 and 1980, black females were significantly less likely than black males to be self-employed (p <.001 for both years). However, in 1990 black females were just as likely to be self-employed as black men. The effect for that year is not statistically significant. It should be noted that white females had not received parity with white males over the period.

The effect of age on black entrepreneurship changed between 1970 and 1990. In the beginning decade, blacks who were under 65 years of age were more likely to be self-employed than those above 65. However, in 1980 the effects were nonsignificant. By 1990, all age categories with the exception of one were less likely to be self-employed than the 65 and over group. The effect for the 45–54 age category was not significant. Similar patterns are observed for whites over the two-decade period.

Region likewise changed in its effect on black self-employment. Being in the South increased the likelihood of being self-employed for blacks in 1970. However, the effects for 1980 and 1990 were not significant. This would suggest that opportunities for self-employment for blacks outside of the South increased over the period. For whites, being in the South changed from increasing to decreasing the likelihood of self-employment between 1970 and 1990.

Finally, industry, occupation, marital status, education, and the interaction between sex and industry follow a similar pattern: Each is significant in 1970, but not so in 1990. However, each remains significant for whites.

This analysis suggests that the factors that are hypothesized to affect self-employment operate differently for blacks and whites. Given the unique history of blacks in American society, and the level of structural inequality that they still face (Wilson, 1987; Butler, 1991; Massey and Denton, 1993; Omi and Winant, 1994), this finding is not surprising. However, it stands to reason that efforts to increase the population of self-employed blacks must likewise be structural, rather than individual, in nature. The following is an example of such an effort.

## THE BLACK ORGANIZATIONAL AUTONOMY (BOA) MODEL

Horton (1992) introduced the first sociological model of black community development, the Black Organizational Autonomy (BOA) Model. According to this model, viable black communities are those that have or emphasize the following: (1) economic autonomy; (2) emphasis on history and culture; (3) internally developed and controlled data sources; (4) socially inclusive leadership; and (5) the development and incorporation of females in leadership roles.

It is important to note that black community development is defined as "the establishment and perpetuation of indigenous social, cultural and economic institutions to address the needs and concerns of the black community" (Horton, 1992). In this context, black entrepreneurship is consistent with black community development. Indeed, given the current political environment, black community development may be the only viable means of increasing the population of entrepreneurs. At this writing, the U.S. Congress is responding to a growing mood of political intolerance by attempting to dismantle many of the programs that were designed to facilitate equal opportunity to disadvantaged minorities—including dismantling the Small Business Administration. It is clear that the impetus for increasing black entrepreneurship must come from within the black community. The BOA model is well suited to meet this challenge.

One example of the application of the principles of the BOA model is the black community of Waterloo, Iowa. In 1977, this community established a community-owned radio station. Realizing that the white power structure would attempt to impede their efforts, the community leaders used their own resources to incorporate the business in Washington, DC. The community was determined to be independent of external funding because that resulted in external control. Thus, fish fries were held as fund-raising activities. Once established, the radio station became a community center that provided tutorial services and internship opportunities for youth; an incubator for small businesses in the area; and food cooperatives via its ownership of farm properties. As an information source, the community center could mobilize the community almost immediately around some issue of community concern. The station gave the grassroots people a voice. Its historical and cultural programs helped to unify a community that was divided by social class. Political forums are often held so that leaders of different philosophical orientations can meet to address common concerns. Most important, it initiated and supported black entrepreneurship because black business development was at the heart of the goals of the community-owned radio station. Finally, it is important to note that most of the initiators and entrepreneurs associated with this effort were black women. The organization recognized that in order to be successful, the best talent available had to be utilized. As often is the case in the history of black America, much of the very best talent was female.

## CONCLUSION

The purpose of this chapter is threefold. First, an assessment was made of the nature of change in the population of black entrepreneurs over the 1970–1990 period. Second, a determination was made of the relative effects of social and demographic variables on black entrepreneurship. Finally, the policy implications of the findings were addressed.

The findings revealed that there was a modest increase in the level of entrepreneurship for black labor force participants. However, the results of the logistic regression analysis revealed that blacks continued to be less likely than whites to be self-employed throughout the two-decade period. Moreover, by 1990 black women were just as likely as black men to be self-employed—a finding that was at variance with the trend for whites. On the other hand, the age pattern for blacks was similar to that for whites relative to entrepreneurship. The elderly of both groups were the most likely to be self-employed. Finally, several variables hypothesized to impact upon self-employment were distinct in their effects for blacks and whites: education, marital status, industry, occupation, and the interaction of sex and industry. None of these factors significantly affected black entrepreneurship, but they were highly significant for whites. One implication of these findings is that successful strategies to increase the population of black entrepreneurs must be distinct from those employed to increase white entrepreneurship. Structural, rather than individual, approaches are most likely to be successful. Given the current political environment, those structural efforts may have to originate from within the black community—as historically has been the case for black Americans.

## NOTES

1. In this study, entrepreneurship is defined as self-employment, as opposed to simply business ownership.

2. The files for each year are different in important, but substantively insignificant, ways. The 1970 file is a combination of two separate files for that year: the 1/10,000 sample for blacks and the 1/100,000 sample for whites. This file was created in the early 1980s for the purpose of a multivariate analysis of crosstabulated dated (logit analysis) of black entrepreneurs. The 1980 file is the 1/1000 sample for both groups. The 1990 file is the 1/10,000 sample for blacks and whites. To reiterate, given the quality and size of these samples, and the multivariate nature of this analysis, these differences are not expected to have measurable effects on the analysis.

3. The emphasis of this analysis is on the population of entrepreneurs rather than on businesses. Thus, by combining the self-employed category with those employees of their own corporations (incorporated self-employed workers), it is argued, a true measure of entrepreneurship is obtained. In other words, printed census data on the self-employed tend to underestimate the size of the entrepreneurial population. Similarly, a focus on the number of businesses as a measure of entrepreneurship may be equally as misleading. In contemporary times, self-employed individuals, particularly the better educated, are more likely than in the past to incorporate. In the case where there are two or more incorporators, there is only one business reported. The incorporators are categorized as employees of the corporation. Thus, it is possible to have a decrease in the number of businesses but an increase in the number of entrepreneurs (assuming that in times past, the incorporators would have more than likely established separate and independent businesses).

4. For an explication of the BOA model, readers should consult Horton (1992). Also, the forthcoming book by Horton and Lundy-Allen, *Rebuilding Black Communities: Black Community Development in Contemporary America,* provides an in-depth discussion of the model with case studies.

## REFERENCES

Bonacich, Edna. (1972). A theory of middleman minorities. *American Sociological Review,* 38, 583–594.

Bonacich, Edna, & John Modell. (1980). *The economic basis of ethnic solidarity: Small business in the Japanese American community*. Berkeley: University of California Press.

Butler, John Sibley. (1991). *Entrepreneurship and self-help among black Americans*. Albany: SUNY Press.

Horton, Hayward Derrick. (1992). A sociological approach to black community development: Presentation of the Black Organizational Autonomy Model. *Journal of the Community Development Society*, 23, 1–19.

Horton, Hayward Derrick, & Gordon F. De Jong. (1991). Black entrepreneurs: A sociodemographic analysis. *Research in Race and Ethnic Relations*, 6, 105–120.

Light, Ivan. (1979). Disadvantaged minorities in self-employment. *International Journal of Comparative Sociology*, 20, 31–45.

Massey, Douglas, & Nancy Denton. (1993). *American apartheid: Segregation and the making of the underclass*. Cambridge, MA: Harvard University Press.

Omi, Michael, & Howard Winant. (1994). *Racial Formation in the United States: From the 1960s to the 1990s*. 2nd edition. New York: Routledge.

Portes, Alejandro, & Robert L. Bach. (1985). *Latin journey*. Berkeley: University of California Press.

Wilson, William J. (1987). *The truly disadvantaged*. Chicago: University of Chicago Press.

# 3

# The Role of the Enclave Economy in Immigrant Adaptation and Community Building: The Case of New York's Chinatown

*Min Zhou*

Chinese Americans are by far the largest subgroup of Asian Americans. As a direct result of the liberalization of the U.S. immigration law in 1965, which abolished the national quotas system, they have experienced rapid population growth. Over the past 50 years, the Chinese American population has increased more than 15 times, from 150,005 in 1950 to 1,645,472 in 1990, and to approximately 2.5 million at the dawn of the new millennium. Much of this growth was attributed to immigration. According to the U.S. Immigration and Naturalization Service (1991), a total of 1,261,445 immigrants were admitted to the United States from China, Hong Kong, and Taiwan as permanent residents between 1951 and 1998. The 1990 U.S. Census also attests to the big part played by immigration: Foreign-born persons accounted for 70 percent of Chinese Americans nationwide and almost 80 percent in New York City.

Parallel to the increase in sheer numbers is the changing face of America's Chinatowns from bachelors' societies to full-fledged immigrant communities. Most visible has been the phenomenal growth of ethnic enterprises in and out of Chinatowns. From 1977 to 1987, the U.S.

census reported that the number of Chinese-owned firms grew by 286 percent, compared to 238 percent for Asian-owned firms, 93 percent for black-owned firms, and 93 percent for Hispanic-owned firms. Overall, there was approximately 1 ethnic firm for every 18 Chinese, but only 1 ethnic firm for every 71 blacks and 1 for every 53 Hispanics. From 1987 to 1997, the number of Chinese-American–owned businesses continued to grow at a rate of 180 percent (from less than 90,000 to 252,577). As of 1997, there was approximately 1 ethnic firm for every 9 Chinese, compared to 1 ethnic for every 11 Asians, 1 for every 42 blacks, and 1 for every 29 Hispanics. Chinese-American–owned business enterprises made up 9 percent of the total minority-owned business enterprises nationwide, but 19 percent of the total gross receipts (U.S. Bureau of the Census 1991, 1996). This paper explores what enables Chinese immigrants to go into business and how ethnic entrepreneurship has affected immigrant adaptation and community building, based on the case of New York City's Chinatown.

## ETHNIC ENTREPRENEURSHIP: A SURVIVAL STRATEGY VERSUS A CHOSEN MEANS FOR SOCIAL MOBILITY

The creation of entrepreneurial communities by certain immigrant groups and the question of whether these communities represent an involuntary strategy for survival or a chosen means for social mobility have received considerable attention in the past (Bailey & Waldinger, 1991; Butler, 1991; Hurh & Kim, 1984; Light, 1972, 1984; Light & Bonacich, 1988; Min, 1995; Portes & Zhou, 1992, 1996; Zhou, 1992; Zhou & Logan, 1989). Why are some groups more inclined to entrepreneurship than others? Is entrepreneurship a result of social conditions of the host society unfavorable to immigrant groups, of unique immigrant group characteristics, or of the interaction between the two? Three theoretical approaches of ethnic entrepreneurship provide insight.

### The Middleman Minority

The middleman-minority approach has been used to describe ethnic minority groups that are in intermediate positions between the ruling elite and the people they rule. The middleman-minority theory posits that the sojourning orientation of ethnic group members, ethnic solidarity, and the hostile environment in the host society contribute to the rise of middleman minorities. Bonacich (1973) has argued that the sojourning orientation of immigrants, interacting with their marginal status as foreigners in the host society, leads them into businesses or occupations that allow them to avoid direct competition with native majority group members. For survival in a hostile new world, sojourners are inclined toward small entrepreneurship in businesses where money can be raised relatively quickly and assets can be easily turned into cash and in areas where businesses may be acquired relatively cheaply and with minimum competition, such as poor minority neighborhoods. As the sojourning entrepreneurs profit from sales to the underprivileged, they are likely to encounter resentment from those around them. The hostility that they encounter at the local and societal levels intensifies their sense of solidarity and the necessity to band together to defend one another, leading to greater cooperation and stronger institutional support, such as the willingness to lend one another money and rotating credit associations.

Bonacich's middleman-minority explanation seems to fit some Chinese business operations, such as fast-food takeout restaurants, and many Korean businesses, such as grocery, liquor, and other retail stores, in poor minority neighborhoods where owners have no intention to reside. As outsiders, they tend to distance themselves from the people they serve and to retain a strong sense of their own cultural identity. Their role as middleman minorities is explicit: They serve as an effective buffer between absentee white capitalist owners and nonwhite residents living in poor urban areas. Meanwhile, they are either stereotyped by the mainstream society as a "model minority" in denying that racism or racial discrimination adversely affects conomic success (Hamamoto, 1992), or blamed for exploiting the urban poor and draining money from poor neighborhoods. The resentment developed through direct contact between middleman business owners and members of minority groups has often escalated into intense interethnic conflicts. The Los Angeles Riots of 1992, for example, caused the loss of about 850 Korean-owned businesses, over half of all business losses, at a cost of $300 million. The conflict between middleman minorities and minority residents in urban ghettos in general, and the Korean-Black conflict in particular, is not so much a cultural misunderstanding as it is "at bottom a displacement of the more fundamental problem: the profoundly disruptive effects of economic inequality" (Hamamoto, 1992). Overall, the middleman minorities tend to use ethnic entrepreneurship as a survival strategy to make quick money and then move out of the middleman position to pursue other, more viable endeavors.

## The Ethnic Market Niches

A second theoretical approach has used the idea of market niches to account for immigrant entrepreneurial activity. There are three basic elements to an attempt to understand immigrant business from the point of view of market niches: opportunity structures, group characteristics, and ethnic strategies (Aldrich & Waldinger, 1990). Opportunity structures are the forms of opportunities presented to an ethnic group by the economy of the host country. Aldrich and Waldinger (1990) point out that there must be a demand for a business's services in order for the business to arise. The ethnic market may be seen as a "niche," a position in the economic environment where immigrant businesses have an adaptive advantage.

An ethnic community provides a demand for goods and services that immigrant businesses are uniquely qualified to provide, because immigrant businessmen know the tastes and buying preferences brought from their homeland. The ethnic niches that provide culturally specific products in the ethnic community become the protected sector of ethnic economies (Zhou, 1992). These ethnic market niches are mostly in labor-intensive, low-profit businesses that are shunned by natives, or in unstable businesses that must meet continually changing demands that large, well-established mainstream firms cannot easily handle, such as the garment industry. Other market niches may be those that are not adequately served by the larger mainstream economy, such as inner-city neighborhoods from which large grocery stores, drugstores, and other services have withdrawn, matching the description of the middleman-minority phenomenon. Still other market niches correspond to the demand of the host society for exotic goods, such as ethnic food, clothing, or other goods. These niches are similar to the ones in ethnic enclaves, but larger, because such a demand provides an opportunity to sell goods to a non–co-ethnic clientele.

Though special niches and paths of access are open and created for potential business entrepreneurs, group characteristics are important in answering the question of why particular ethnic groups are so disproportionately concentrated in small business. Group characteristics pertaining to ethnic entrepreneurship include financial capital, human capital, and social capital. Financial, or material, capital—money and properties—is a crucial prerequisite for ethnic entrepreneurs. Many ethnic enterprises are small in size and may be engaged in middleman occupations because they generally require small amounts of initial capital and minimum labor, which can be mobilized within the family and the ethnic community, through family savings, community-based rotating credits and overseas money, and the available pool of cheap co-ethnic labor. Some immigrants may be predisposed to enter business because they possess the education, skills, or cultural traits that incline them to business activities. Others may do well in entrepreneurial activities because they can mobilize resources from their family and social networks and depend on high levels of cooperation within the ethnic community.

Ethnic strategies are developed from a particular combination of opportunity structures and group characteristics. Earlier middlemen, such as Jews, have withdrawn from the inner city after they have been assimilated into mainstream society over the course of several generations, with each of the succeeding generations less and less interested in small business. As an adaptive strategy, some immigrant group members go into business as a way to avoid low-wage menial labor, to prevent the depreciation of their human capital, and to preserve their pre-immigration standard of living (Hurh & Kim, 1984). How effective entrepreneurship is as an adaptive strategy depends on how well potential entrepreneurs are able to develop patterns of trust and cooperation among themselves, and how well they are able to mobilize resources from existing family and ethnic networks that enabled them to obtain sufficient capital and labor to fill the vacant market niches. Consequently, the concentration of certain ethnic groups in particular market niches of successful pioneers may lead to the entry and successful performance of later arrivals. The referral of kin and co-ethnics for these established ethnic businesses, in turn, strengthens intangible ethnic networks and builds a wall around the ethnic labor market against the entry of outsiders. Once an ethnic niche is in place, "the immigrant sector has grown as a self-feeding process. Newcomers take up work in immigrant firms, and workers who have gained skills and experience working for coethnic owners set up a new business of their own" (Bailey & Waldinger, 1991, p. 443).

## The Enclave Economies

A third theoretical approach incorporates some major elements of the middleman-minority theory and the ethnic market-niche thesis. The enclave-economy theory consists of both structural and cultural components. On the one hand, it conceptualizes the enclave as an ethnic labor market distinct from the larger labor market, where immigrants are provided with potential benefits, such as opportunities for self-employment and social advancement. On the other hand, it perceives the enclave as an integrated cultural entity maintained by bounded solidarity and enforceable trust—a form of social capital necessary for ethnic entrepreneurship (Portes & Zhou, 1992). Within the enclave, immigrant entrepreneurs and workers are organized around the symbols of a common nationhood, familiar cultural environment, and densely knit networks.

A key feature of the enclave economy is the co-ethnicity of entrepreneurs and workers. An enclave is defined as a spatial concentration of ethnic firms with a wide variety of economic activities (Logan, Alba, & McNulty, 1991; Portes, 1987; Zhou & Logan, 1989). The economic enclave provides co-ethnic members with privileged access to a particular supply of raw materials or finished goods, to jobs that require unusual skills, and to a low-wage, reliable co-ethnic workforce. Economic activities in the enclave can include both productive industries and community-based goods and services. In an earlier work, I identified an "enclave protected sector" and an "enclave export sector" in the Chinese enclave economy in New York (Zhou, 1992). The protected sector arises within the ethnic community itself. It represents a captive market, oriented toward ethnic-specific goods and services that are not easily accessible outside the enclave and toward solutions to various adjustment and settlement problems relating to immigration. The enclave export sector contains a nonethnic market characteristic of leftover niches of the larger secondary economy, such as the garment industry, but generates income to be circulated back into the ethnic markets and reinvested in both sectors (pp. 110–116). All immigrant groups may likely create a few businesses to serve their own cultural needs, but the rise of full-fledged ethnic enclaves represents an exceptional phenomenon (Portes, 1995).

The enclave economy approach goes beyond the middleman-minority theory and the ethnic market-niche thesis to focus on the implications and social consequences of ethnic entrepreneurship on immigrant adaptation. Although ethnic entrepreneurship may still be motivated by self-interest, it cannot be successful without its roots in the ethnic community bounded by group solidarity and the enforcement capacity of the community. Bounded solidarity and enforceable trust enable employers in ethnic enclaves to demand greater discipline and effort from co-ethnic workers, who, in turn, receive preferential treatment from owners in terms of job offers, promotions, and business training. Although ethnic enclaves may be short-lived and may seldom last beyond the second generation, they create unique opportunity structures to enable group members to incorporate into mainstream society intergenerationally and thus are an effective alternative and a chosen "mobility path compensating for lingering labor market disadvantage" (Portes & Zhou, 1992).

Portes and Zhou (1996) conclude, based on data from the 1980 census and their own surveys, that entrepreneurship represents a major path for individual and collective economic mobility among ethnic minorities. This conclusion is based on four facts: (1) the consistently higher average earnings of the self-employed over employees of the same ethnic background, on both an hourly and yearly basis; (2) the resilience of a positive net self-employment effect on earnings, even after controlling for relevant human capital variables; (3) the finding that insignificant or negative self-employment effects on earnings in regression models employing a logarithmic transformation of earnings is seemingly due to the suppression of positive outliers (high earners), the vast majority of whom are self-employed; (4) historical evidence indicating that the most entrepreneurial immigrant groups in the past have had above-average rates of educational and occupational intergenerational mobility and that their descendants enjoy individual and family incomes superior to the national averages (Portes & Bach, 1985; Portes & Jensen, 1989; Portes & Zhou, 1992, 1996).

In general, there has been an emerging sociological consensus that ethnic entrepreneurship represents both an important phenomenon and a viable path for economic mobility. Next, I use Chinatown as an example to illustrate how ethnic entrepreneurship affects the adaptation of immigrant Chinese and how Chinatowns have been impacted by the growing enclave economy.

## IMMIGRATION AND CHANGES IN CHINATOWN: FROM A BACHELORS' SHELTER TO A FULL-FLEDGED ETHNIC ENCLAVE

Chinese-American entrepreneurship dates back to the 19th century and has its roots in the segregation of immigrant Chinese from other American ethnic groups. The Chinese first came to California as sojourning laborers from the coastal province of Guangdong (Kwangtung) in the late 1850s in the hope of finding gold in the Gold Mountain to take back to China. Between 1851 and 1860, some 41,000 Chinese arrived in the United States. Upon arrival, they were sent to work in different gold fields in the Sierra Nevada foothills. After surface deposits of gold mines were depleted, forcing white miners to quit mining, Chinese miners remained in these mining areas, working for companies that attempted harder methods of digging for gold. The 1860 U.S. census recorded that almost all Chinese in the United States were concentrated in the state of California, and within the state, 84 percent were in mining counties (Chan, 1991). In the late 1860s, the Central Pacific Company started to recruit Chinese miners and contract laborers from China to work on the western section of the first continental railroad. During this period, 64,000 more Chinese arrived in the United States; about 40,000 came between 1867 and 1870 (Chan, 1991).

Despite the fact that by 1860 the Chinese made up 25 percent of the labor force of California, their distinct physical appearance, dress, and religious and cultural practices kept them identifiably different from the European ethnic groups of the majority population. Although prejudice against Chinese immigrants had always existed, after the Civil War, as the building of the railroads ended and as the United States slipped into an economic depression in 1873, competition for jobs made economic discrimination and pressures for the segregation of the Chinese particularly intense. Because the Chinese often worked for relatively low wages, they were perceived as threats to the growing American labor movement, and skilled craft workers began to adopt the slogan "Chinamen must go!" in their efforts to rally white working people and achieve political power (Saxton, 1971). The 1870s and 1880s were marked by anti-Chinese riots and massacres throughout California and in other places in the American West (Chan, 1991). Chinese were generally barred from obtaining American citizenship. In 1882, the U.S. Congress passed the Chinese Exclusion Act, barring the immigration of Chinese laborers. As a result of the widespread mob violence, discrimination, and legal exclusion, the Chinese began to take refuge in their own communities in large towns on the West Coast. Chinatowns in New York City and other large Northeastern cities grew as they absorbed those fleeing the extreme persecution in California (Lee, 1960; Lyman, 1974; Zhou, 1992).

Early Chinatowns were essentially products of exclusion. Although Chinese immigrants were legally excluded from the "gold mountain," they continued to be motivated by a sojourning goal of making a fortune in America and returning home with gold. In keeping their gold dream alive, they left their families behind in China and were drawn to this community by extensive kinship networks. During the time when legal and institutional exclusion set barriers and when American society made available few options of life to these Chinese sojourners, they had to isolate themselves socially in Chinatown and to work at odd jobs that few Americans wanted. Because they had no families with them and had no intention to stay a long time, they built Chinatown initially as a place of refuge that resembled home.

Chinatown took root in New York City as excluded workers moved eastward in the hope of fulfilling their gold dream. By the 1940s, this Chinatown, still a bachelors' shelter with a sex ratio of 603 men per 100 women, had grown into a 10-block enclave, accommodating almost all Chinese immigrants in the city. In old Chinatown, immigrant workers could speak their own language, eat their own food, play their own games, exchange news from home, and share common experiences with fellow countrymen day in and day out. For the Chinese, it appeared that small businesses grew out of two main reasons. On the one hand, legal exclusion and labor market discrimination prohibited them from being hired in the mainstream economy and thus pushed them into pursuing small businesses in their own enclave and seeking occupational niches unwanted by natives. On the other hand, ethnic concentration created a tremendous demand for goods and services from the excluded co-ethnics and also an availability of low-wage labor to supply to the emerging ethnic economies. Thus, small businesses grew to meet the needs of the bachelors' society by creating jobs that would enable both Chinese owners and workers to avoid competition with the larger society. The Chinese laundry business and restaurant business emerged from this situation: Early twentieth-century Chinese went into the laundry business in such large numbers that by 1920 well over a third of Chinese workers in New York (37.5 percent) were occupied in laundry work, and over 300 restaurants and tea houses had opened in the 10-block area of Chinatown by the late 1950s, serving meals for Chinese laborers, most of whom had no families with them, as well as exotic food to non-Chinese tourists (Zhou, 1992). These business establishments opened up a unique structure of opportunities that corresponded to the goals of the sojourning Chinese and strengthened the social basis of the ethnic community.

The repeal of the Chinese Exclusion Act in 1943 and the passage of the War Bride Act in 1945 caused the bachelors' society to dissolve. Chinese women, who made up more than half of the postwar arrivals from China, were allowed into the United States to join their husbands and families. However, the number of Chinese immigrants entering the United States each year between 1945 and 1965 was quite small because the annual quota was set at 105 (Sung, 1987). After 1965, when Congress amended the immigration law abolishing the national origins quota system, the number of Chinese in the United States increased manyfold. Together with their native-born co-ethnics, the number of ethnic Chinese in New York City grew more than 6 times in just three decades, from 33,000 in 1960 to 239,000 in 1990, and to an estimate of nearly one half million in 1998. The sudden surge of Chinese immigration has been accompanied by a remarkable change: Rather than being trapped in Chinatowns, Chinese-Americans have begun to show levels of educational and occupational achievement and median household income higher than the national average and to be applauded as a model minority. The change does not appear to be associated with the disappearance of Chinatowns, which have actually grown and expanded in new directions, taking over decaying adjacent neighborhoods. New satellite Chinatowns or "ethnoburbs" (a term used to describe suburban Chinese middle-class communities—see Li, 1997) have sprung up outside inner cities and into the suburbs (Fong, 1994; Li, 1997; Zhou, 1992).

Unlike the old-timers who were uniformly unskilled laborers, recent Chinese immigrants have come from more diverse socioeconomic backgrounds. For a variety of reasons, they have been disproportionately drawn from the highly educated and professional segments of the sending societies. Immigrant Chinese from Taiwan, for example, have displayed the highest levels of educational attainment and occupational achievement compared to their counterparts from mainland China and other parts of the world. The 1990 Census showed that foreign-born Chinese at productive ages (ages 25 to 64) attaining four or more years of college education were almost twice as common as U.S.-born non-Hispanic whites (42 percent versus 21 percent). Foreign-born Chinese holding professional occupations were more common than U.S.-born non-Hispanic whites (35 percent versus 27 percent).

Recent immigrant Chinese are not only more diverse than earlier arrivals, they also come with goals that are vastly different from those of the old-timers, who were here to sojourn with an intention to return to China eventually rather than to settle and to eventually assimilate. They are characterized by their strong desire to become integrated into the mainstream society and to make America their new home. Many of them have immigrated to the United States to secure their already well-established lives, and more important, to provide their children with a future without fear and uncertainty, in which the children can realize their full potential.

Despite the much higher qualifications of the new immigrants, their willingness to assimilate into American society, and the more open society that they encounter, many Chinese still tend to concentrate in Chinatown or to invest in new Chinatowns. Language is a major barrier, as over half of the newcomers speak broken English or no English at all. Another barrier may be the lack of suitable networks linking them to the mainstream society. These initial barriers turn many Chinese immigrants to Chinatowns where they can take advantage of pre-existing community ties and resources to secure a foothold in their new country. Recent studies of Chinatowns and ethnoburbs show that both small business owners and wealthy investors from Hong Kong, Taiwan, and China tend to invest in Chinatowns and ethnoburbs (Li, 1997; Zhou, 1992). Prospective ethnic entrepreneurs often have inadequate information about, and limited access to, mainstream labor and consumer markets, and they also presume racism and fear discrimination in dealing with unfamiliar situations and institutions. Consequently, immigrant entrepreneurs and overseas Chinese investors concentrate their business activities in old Chinatowns or build up certain local areas into the status of new ethnic enclaves, such as Flushing's new Chinatown and Sunset Park's Chinatown in New York, and Monterey Park in Los Angeles. Some of the extraordinary development in New York's Chinatown have attracted the attention of mainstream media. For example, the Wing Ming Building, an 11-story full-service office tower at the core of Manhattan's Chinatown was constructed by a Hong Kong businessman at a cost of over $6 million (Tobier, 1979; Wang, 1979); The East West Tower in Chinatown, a $21 million, 143-unit project, was entirely financed by overseas Chinese capital from Hong

Kong and the Middle East (*New York Times*, September 20, 1981). In the past 30 years, Chinatown's enclave economy has experienced steady growth despite several recession cycles that affected the city. Today, various sources of financing in Chinatown, combined with the experience, human capital, and family ties of new Chinese immigrants, have made it possible for immigrants of diverse socioeconomic background, including those of modest class status, to try their hand at entrepreneurship, which has broadened the base for economic development. As a result, ethnic economies in the enclave have become diversified, ranging from traditional services such as restaurants, labor-intensive manufacturing, to various professional services. Illustrated in Table 3-1 is the growth of Chinese-owned businesses in the New York metropolitan area and in a satellite Chinatown in Flushing.

Significant changes can be seen in the growth of restaurants, a traditionally strong ethnic business, and the replacement of laundries with garment factories, a rapidly growing industry in Chinatown. Noticeable also is the diversification of economic activities. Services that rely on an ethnic clientele, such as accounting, insurance, real estate agencies, travel agencies, doctors (including herbalists), beauty salons and barber shops, and entertainment facilities, have experienced tremendous growth since the late 1950s. In Flushing's Chinatown, the development of ethnic economies is on a similar scale, if not larger. According to a 1982 survey, there were only five grocery stores, three restaurants, one real estate agency, one professional building, one drug and herbal store, and one beauty salon that were owned by the Chinese. Just 10 years later, the area was booming with Chinese-owned businesses.

The numbers presented in Table 3-1 were inconclusive, as they were based on Chinese telephone directories and a small market survey in 1990. Nevertheless, they indicated a trend of ethnic entrepreneurship among Chinese immigrants. Most of these ethnic establishments, except for restaurants, were concentrated in Chinatowns in Lower East Manhattan and Flushing. The actual number in the New York area was much larger. As reported in the Economic Censuses, there were 10,864 Chinese-owned business enterprises based in the New York metropolitan area (accounting for 86 percent of these Chinese-owned firms in the state of New York) in 1987, and that number increased to 19,537 in 1992. In 1987, the enterprises with employees averaged $308,638 in annual sales, a figure comparable to that for all Asian-owned firms in the city, but exceeding by more than $50,000 those of other minority-owned enterprises nationwide (U.S. Bureau of the Census 1991, 1996). The 1990 Census data also revealed that self-employed Chinese workers were distributed in a wide range of economic activities, but with a concentration in retail trade (40 percent of the ethnic labor force), particularly in the restaurant business, and professional services (18 percent). These

**TABLE 3-1   Selected Chinese-Owned Businesses: Chinatowns In Lower East Manhattan and Flushing**

| Businesses | 1958[1] | 1988[1] | Flushing[2] 1990 |
|---|---|---|---|
| Restaurants | 304 | 781 | 53 |
| Restaurant equipment | 0 | 92 | na |
| Garment factories | 0 | 437 | 11 |
| Laundries | na | 20 | na |
| | | | |
| Accountants | 3 | 107 | 17 |
| Banks[3] | 2 | 39 | 22 |
| Import/export firms | 9 | 164 | na |
| Insurance, real estate agencies, and stockbrokers | 4 | 320 | 54 |
| Law firms | 12 | 186 | 27 |
| Travel agencies | 2 | 115 | na |
| | | | |
| Doctor offices and pharmacies | 38 | 574 | 123 |
| | | | |
| Bakeries | 4 | 46 | 20 |
| Grocery stores and other food stores | 75 | 303 | na |
| | | | |
| Beauty salons and barber shops | 7 | 111 | 33 |
| Florists, gift shops, and jewelry shops | 76 | 179 | na |
| | | | |
| Bookstores | 0 | 8 | na |
| Educational and training centers | na | na | 31 |
| Newspapers and periodicals | 5 | 24 | na |
| Photo labs and studios | 4 | 19 | na |
| Television and radio stations | 0 | 12 | na |
| Theaters and cinemas | 5 | 7 | na |
| Video rentals | 0 | 41 | na |
| | | | |
| Total | 550 | 3,585 | 391 |

*Notes:*
1. Adapted from Table 5-1 in Zhou (1992).
2. Adapted from Schuman S. Tu (1990), Market survey and market potential in Flushing, *World Journal* (December 16).
3. Including non-Chinese bank branches located in Manhattan's Chinatown, which employ a disproportionate number of Chinese-speaking employees.

data suggest that, unlike traditional ethnic businesses, which are small in scale and middleman in nature, Chinese entrepreneurship has undergone significant changes, encompassing the rise of a new range of capital- and knowledge-intensive services such as banking, insurance, real estate, and medical/health services. In fact, Chinatowns, both old and new, have become full-fledged ethnic enclaves—more enticing places for entrepreneurs to do business because of their densely knit networks, familiar cultural environment, and cheap but reliable source of labor.

## SOURCES OF ETHNIC ENTREPRENEURSHIP

What enables immigrant Chinese to become entrepreneurs? Part of the answer to this question may be found in the advantages that Chinese immigrants have over other ethnic groups in establishing small enterprises. Among these advantages are the possession of human capital, that is, education and skills; financial capital, or the money needed to establish business enterprises; and social capital, or patterns of cooperation among group members that provide resources. Chinese immigrants have either brought with them these major forms of capital or acquired them after arrival in the United States.

The first source of advantage is human capital, including education and work experience. Having group members with high levels of education and specialized skills can help the group gain information on ethnic economies as well as the larger economy, to accumulate knowledge about markets and government regulations, and to choose the best strategies possible in a situation of limited options. Moreover, having clear intentions to settle in America and to achieve success for themselves and for their families enables the group to make long-term investment decisions. In old Chinatowns, immigrant Chinese did not gravitate to laundries and restaurants by nature, as was often believed at the time. They entered these marginal economic activities mainly as a temporary means to cope with, and survive in, a very difficult environment. Because they had no intention to incorporate into the larger society, they had been depicted for many years as "the unassimilable," being trapped in a dead-end situation. Today, the demands of new immigrants for speeding up the process of assimilation have brought about important changes in the economic structure of Chinatown, which are seen in the diversification of the enclave economy.

A second source of ethnic entrepreneurship is financial capital, which consists mainly of lifelong savings and foreign capital. Family savings are an important source of financial capital, and they are made possible primarily on frugality. Chinese immigrants, like immigrants from Europe, generally share the value of thrift and delayed gratification. They tend to perceive their present frugality as a means to fulfill future goals. Thus, it is not unusual to find that immigrants spend only on basic things such as housing and food without much on leisure and luxury, and that adult children turn in their income to their parents for family savings. This way, even for some low-income immigrant families, starting up a small business does not seem to be a remote, unreachable goal. However, family savings are barely enough. Other traditional ways of mobilizing resources have been important for small business development in the past and have continued to function as the enclave economy expanded in recent years. One such tradition is the rotating credit associations, which are organized through community-based organizations and kinship associations to be widely used for capital mobilization and for social needs (Light, 1972; Light & Bonacich, 1988; Wong, 1984, 1998).

In Chinatown's enclave economy, small family-run businesses, which require low start-up capital and low operation cost and may be easily liquidated, have still constituted the majority. Start-up costs for small business, such as small garment factories, and grocery stores, range from $2,000 to $30,000, which can possibly be pooled from family savings. Larger businesses, such as banking, insurance, real estate, and upscale restaurants, cannot possibly be financed by pooled family savings or traditional rotating credit associations but have to rely on the influx of wealth and capital from abroad. Funds from economically fast-growing parts of East Asia (Hong Kong and Taiwan, in particular) have poured into investments in the United States. In New York, listed Chinese-owned banks, insurance agencies, and real estate agencies grew by 8,000 percent from 1958 to 1988. Capital from Taiwan has turned Flushing, New York, into a wealthy Chinatown, and Monterey Park, California, into Little Taipei, where modern buildings and shopping malls with bilingual signs offer testimony to the impact of Chinese on the city. Monterey Park has now become the only U.S. city in which over half of the population is Asian (mostly Chinese).

In addition to human and financial capital, a third source of ethnic entrepreneurship is social capital in the ethnic community. Social capital is embedded in the structure of social relations. Chinese entrepreneurs raise capital and mobilize resources to establish businesses not simply through family savings or overseas investment, but also through close relations to the ethnic community, including sentimental and instrumental ties to the social structures of the ethnic enclave and the access to family labor and coethnic labor. Immigrants create bounded solidarity by virtue of their shared cultural bonds and shared experiences of being treated as foreigners, which in turn heighten awareness of common symbols, values, and obligations and foster enforceable trust among immigrants. Bounded solidarity and enforceable trust, however, do not inhere in the moral conviction of the individual or the culture of origin; rather, they interact with structural factors in the host society to help immigrants organize their social and economic lives in disadvantaged or adverse situations (Portes & Zhou, 1992). Enclave entrepreneurs conducting economic activities within their own community can avoid intense interethnic conflicts that occur inevitably in middleman phenomena because shared cultural affinities allow coethnic consumers, workers, investors, and entrepreneurs to operate in protected consumer, labor, and capital markets.

Access to family labor and coethnic labor is also crucial for ethnic entrepreneurship. Many immigrant enterprises, especially labor-intensive grocery and food stores, restaurants, and garment factories, depend on unpaid family labor and low-wage immigrant labor. The access to low-cost co-ethnic labor gives ethnic entrepreneurs a clear competitive edge. From the point of view of co-ethnic workers, ethnic businesses offer material and symbolic compensations that cannot be accounted for simply in dollar terms. Although jobs in ethnic enterprises are characterized by low wages, long working hours, and poor working conditions, immigrant workers are provided with a familiar work environment in which they are effectively shielded from deficiencies in language, education, and general knowledge of the larger society. They can obtain first-hand information on employment and business opportunities through their family members, kin, and co-ethnics to avoid the expensive cost of time and effort involved in finding good jobs in the larger market. They are able to work longer hours to quickly accumulate family savings for future plans. They can gain access to rotating credit, clan associations, and the family for financial support and resource mobilization. Finally, they can get job training and cultivate an entrepreneurial spirit at work and, possibly, be prepared for eventual transition to self-employment (Bailey & Waldinger, 1991). It is found that many garment factory and restaurant owners built their businesses on family savings accumulated from wages earned in the garment industry (Zhou, 1992).

For many new immigrants, low-paid menial work is a part of the time-honored path toward economic independence and upward mobility of their families in America. It is the ethnic solidarity and mutual trust between co-ethnic workers and entrepreneurs, combined with human and financial capital, that facilitate ethnic entrepreneurship among Chinese Americans. Next, I examine both positive and negative consequences associated with ethnic entrepreneurship.

## CONSEQUENCES OF ETHNIC ENTREPRENEURSHIP

### Beneficial Consequences for Co-Ethnic Members

Without doubt, ethnic entrepreneurship can create job opportunities for immigrant group members to compensate for many of their disadvantages as newcomers to American society. The disadvantages associated with immigrant status, such as lack of English, transferable education and work skills, lack of access to employment networks in the larger society, and racial prejudice and discrimination, often block immigrant workers from entering the labor market of the mainstream economy. Whereas immigrants who have strong human capital may be able to choose to participate in or out of Chinatown, ethnic economies have opened up a viable option with ample financial capital, housing, and employment opportunities for immigrant Chinese and subsequent arrivals, especially for those without adequate human capital. Since the 1980s, Chinatown's garment industry, for example, has provided jobs for more than 20,000 immigrant Chinese, mostly women. It is estimated that three out of five immigrant Chinese women in Chinatown work in the garment industry. Although the garment industry showed signs of decline in the 1990s, it continued to serve an important source of entrepreneurship and employment for Chinese immigrants. The restaurant business, another backbone industry in Chinatown, has employed at least 15,000 immigrant Chinese workers (Zhou, 1992) and has continued to be the most important component of the enclave economy.

For immigrants with either sufficient human capital and/or financial capital, self-employment is their best strategy to adapt to their new country by minimizing the possibility of downward social mobility: to avoid low-wage menial labor, to prevent depreciation of their capital accumulated before immigration, and to preserve their already established socioeconomic status. Moreover, through ethnic entrepreneurship, immigrants can effectively fight the loss of pride, self-value, and sense of achievement associated with immigrant status and eventually enter the mainstream society with dignity, self-esteem, and a sense of identity. Further, immigrant entrepreneurs can bypass the harmful psychological and social consequences of racial discrimination by creating conditions for their own economic mobility: the improvement of the economic status of families and family savings for purchasing homes or starting up businesses. Table 3-2 shows the median earnings, household incomes, rates of home ownership, and rates of unemployment among self-employed and salaried workers by race or ethnicity, based on 1990 census data.

The data indicate that self-employed workers of all racial/ethnic groups show an absolute earnings advantage over their salaried co-ethnics. In terms of economics status of the family, self-employed workers have higher median household incomes than their salaried co-ethnics, except for U.S.-born blacks; and without exception, self-employed workers are much more likely than their salaried co-ethnics to live in their own homes regardless of race or ethnicity. These figures coincide with results

**TABLE 3-2 Mean Earnings, Median Household Incomes, Rates of Home Ownership, and Rates of Unemployment among Self-Employed and Salaried Workers by Nativity and Race/Ethnicity: 1990**

| Race/Ethnicity | Mean Earnings ($) | Median Household Income ($) | Home Ownership (%) | Unemployment (%) |
|---|---|---|---|---|
| Foreign-Born | | | | |
| Chinese workers | 24,945 | 47,751 | 66.1 | 3.3 |
| Chinese entrepreneurs | 36,132 | 51,900 | 82.5 | 1.4 |
| | | | | |
| Non-Hispanic black workers | 20,911 | 39,000 | 44.9 | 6.1 |
| Non-Hispanic black entrepreneurs | 24,693 | 40,562 | 55.8 | 6.0 |
| | | | | |
| Non-Hispanic white workers | 28,962 | 47,700 | 69.8 | 4.0 |
| Non-Hispanic white entrepreneurs | 40,011 | 51,131 | 80.2 | 2.0 |
| | | | | |
| U.S.-Born | | | | |
| Chinese workers | 33,268 | 61,000 | 77.1 | 1.9 |
| Chinese entrepreneurs | 47,765 | 69,360 | 83.0 | 1.1 |
| | | | | |
| Non-Hispanic black workers[2] | 19,185 | 32,820 | 58.0 | 6.9 |
| Non-Hispanic black entrepreneurs[2] | 22,167 | 32,590 | 66.5 | 6.1 |
| | | | | |
| Non-Hispanic white workers[3] | 25,946 | 41,500 | 75.9 | 3.7 |
| Non-Hispanic white entrepreneurs[3] | 34,354 | 44,300 | 83.9 | 1.8 |

Notes:
1. Including all workers age 25 to 64 and in the labor force.
2. A 10 percent random sample from the 1990 5%-PUMS.
3. A 60 percent random sample from the 1990 5%-PUMS.

Source: U.S. Census of Population and Housing: 1990 PUMS.

reported a decade earlier, based on the 1980 Census data (Portes & Zhou, 1996). Noticeable, however, is the fact that both Chinese workers and entrepreneurs, regardless of nativity, have surpassed their non-Hispanic white counterparts in average earnings and household incomes, indicating the successful incorporation of the Chinese beginning in the 1980s.

Ethnic entrepreneurship may also account in part for the particularly low unemployment rates among foreign-born Chinese workers. For those who are in the labor force, the unemployment rate for foreign-born Chinese workers was only 3.3 percent, compared to 6.9 percent for U.S.-born non-Hispanic black workers, and 4.0 percent for U.S.-born non-Hispanic white workers. It appears that ethnic entrepreneurship benefits not only the self-employed but also immigrant workers, especially those who lack English language ability, transferable education, marketable skills, formal employment networks, and even legal standing to compete in the larger labor market. In large cities where immigrants are disproportionately concentrated, the job situation is often paradoxical: Whereas U.S.-born minority workers are hardest hit by declining manufacturing and eroding employment opportunities, immigrant workers in the same cities have experienced growing economic opportunities. Some analysts argue that immigrants have taken jobs away from U.S.-born minorities. However, a more realistic picture reflects that immigrants simply respond to industrial downsizing by creating their own match between available opportunities and ethnic resources (Light, 1972; Sassen, 1988; Waldinger, 1989). A prime example is the role of Chinatown's garment industry in creating job opportunities for immigrant Chinese women. In New York City, where the decline of the manufacturing sector has caused severe unemployment among minority workers, immigrant Chinese women, who have little proficiency in English, poor education, and little work experience, display exceptionally high rates of labor force participation. Three quarters of the Chinese women are employed full-time in the labor force, as compared to only 22 percent of Puerto Rican women, who were overrepresented in garment manufacturing before the industry's decline. More than half of these Chinese women work in Chinatown's garment industry. Without Chinatown's garment industry, many immigrant workers might simply be jobless (Zhou & Nordquist, 1994).

Ethnic entrepreneurship, finally, contributes to the accumulation of social capital rooted in the ethnic community and also to community building. Entrepreneurship directly brings about economic prosperity in ethnic enclaves, which in turn feeds into the social structures of the community, as seen in the changing role of traditional social organizations and new establishments of various types of community-based organizations to facilitate immigrant adaptation. By glancing at one of the Chinese business directories in New York, for example, one can easily come up with a list of over 100 voluntary associations, 61 community service organizations, 41 community-based employment agencies, 16 daycare centers, 27 career training schools, 28 Chinese and English language schools, and 9 dancing and music schools (Chinatown Today Publishing, 1993. *Note:* The actual number of community organizations in Chinatown was approximately twice as many as this list because many were not listed in this particular directory). Most of these organizations are located in Manhattan's Chinatown; some are located in new satellite Chinatowns in Flushing and Sunset Park (Zhou, 1997). These community-based organizations do not function merely to meet the basic needs of fellow countrymen, such as helping workers obtain employment and offering different levels of social support, and to organize economic activities, but also to provide services associated with a wide range of resettlement and adjustment issues, such language and job training, after-school programs, family services, and counseling.

If ethnic communities are interpreted in terms of social capital, it becomes possible to suggest a mechanism by which the adherence to community-based support systems and positive cultural orientations can provide an adaptive advantage for immigrants and their offspring as they strive to achieve their goals in American society. On the one hand, jobs made available in ethnic economies and goods and services provided by the community tend to tie immigrant Chinese and their offspring to Chinatown despite spatial dispersion. These ties have directly or indirectly broadened the base of ethnic interaction and thus increased the degree of ethnic cohesion, which in turn sustains a sense of identity, community, and ethnic solidarity. On the other hand, despite the low wages and long working hours typical of many jobs in China-town, immigrants take pride in being able to work and support their families. The work ethic and the capacity for delayed gratification in parents is explicitly or implicitly passed on to children, who are expected by their parents to appreciate the value of schooling as a means to move out of Chinatown. The networks of support and social control mechanisms in Chinatowns, for example, facilitate upward mobility of young Chinese Americans by enabling families to reinforce community values and standards in children and to accumulate funds for education to give the younger generation a jump-start into the American economy. In a recent study on the second generation growing up in Chinatown, I demonstrated the lasting impact of enclave economies on the adaptation of immigrant Chinese and their offspring (Zhou, 1997).

In sum, both co-ethnic workers and employers benefit from a reciprocal relationship. They are both bound by sentiment, trust, and face (implying ethnic obligations) in pursuing each other's goals. It is true that workers in co-ethnic firms generally work at lower pay. However, they are by no means willingly accepting low wages; rather, they view it as an alternative to possible joblessness, so that they can surmount structural obstacles and lift themselves and their families up socioeconomically.

### The Downside of Ethnic Entrepreneurship

The downside of ethnic entrepreneurship may be relative to the issue of interethnic relations and ethnic incorporation. The first problem of business growth in Chinatowns relates to costs that usually have to be incurred by both residents in Chinatown and nonethnic residents in surrounding neighborhoods. The familiar growing pains in rapidly expanding business activities in Chinatowns include traffic congestion, skyrocketing real estate prices, overcrowding, and the displacement of the urban poor. Many longtime residents in new Chinatowns, such as Monterey Park, California, and Flushing, New York, fear that their neighborhoods are turning into microcosms of Hong Kong and Taipei, which are among the most crowded and polluted cities in the world. Longtime residents also sometimes feel that they are being priced out of their homes and businesses by soaring rents and heavy influx of investment funds from Asia.

Relations with other American minority groups pose another problem. Immigrant Chinese and many immigrants from Asia tend to penetrate into declining white working-class or lower-middle-class communities in cities. Because a sizable Chinese concentration is often accompanied by a concentration of ethnic businesses, longtime residents, mostly whites, tend to perceive incoming Chinese as outsiders interested in making money but not in local affairs. The high presence of entrepreneurship in a neighborhood paralleled by poor participation in local politics and community-based affairs by immigrants adds to the tensions and fuels interethnic antagonism (Fong, 1994).

For Chinese businesses that are operated in poor inner-city minority neighborhoods in which Chinese try to avoid residence, the interethnic relations are even more fragile, though the Chinese case may not be as visible as the Korean case. When ethnic entrepreneurs play the role of the middleman minorities, their foreignness and success may be resented by the disadvantaged groups they serve, because they are perceived as invading strangers who do not make special efforts to establish close links with the communities of their customers. When significant numbers of ethnic businesses penetrate into neighborhoods that contain members of other American minorities, ethnic entrepreneurship on the part of entrepreneurs can also lead to friction between the haves and the have-nots, and this friction may be intensified by ethnic allegiances, as is often documented in the literature.

A third problem associated with ethnic entrepreneurship may be ethnic exclusion. Until recently, immigrant Chinese, as well as most Asian immigrants, have been portrayed as indifferent to U.S. politics and uninterested in assimilation. This differs sharply from other immigrant groups, such as Cuban Americans. Most immigrant Chinese have remained instead closely connected with events at home and are doing business with their country of origin. The resulting political isolation reinforces the stereotype of Chinese as selfish and clannish. This political isolation tends to be accompanied by a social and psychological isolation. Chinese entrepreneurs often consciously retain a sense of being "Chinese." Because of their intense involvement in their own businesses and their businesses largely depend on bounded solidarity, they may be seen as having no desire to hire nonethnic workers and no desire to incorporate into the mainstream economy, despite the fact that their lives and livelihoods become inseparable from the new land.

## CONCLUSION

Ethnic entrepreneurship among Chinese Americans may fit in part the situation of middleman minorities, or that of ethnic market niches, or that of enclave economies. The different theoretical approaches that I have laid out may be seen as emphasizing different reasons that opportunities for ethnic entrepreneurship exist. The middleman-minority theory draws attention to the fact that immigrant group members, as foreigners, often find positions between relatively privileged and relatively underprivileged groups of Americans and tend to develop high levels of cooperation that enable them to survive in a foreign and often hostile economic environment. The ethnic market-niche thesis examines how the characteristics of immigrant groups may correspond to unmet demands in the economy of the host country. The enclave-economy theory looks at how shared ethnicity may be the basis for a small economy and how small ethnic economies may grow in size and power.

Each of these theoretical approaches provides some of the reasons that immigrant group members may be inclined to business. However, the evidence indicates that ethnic businesses are not simply marginal activities that many immigrants are forced into because of their status as newcomers and members of minorities. Despite the downside, they are composed of a crucial alternative route to upward mobility in American society for immigrant group members. What is more important, then, is the role of entrepreneurship in facilitating immigrant adaptation. In the case of the Chinese, ethnic entrepreneurship is played out in the context of ethnic communities.

Although there is some basis to the stereotypical view of Chinese businesses as small, family firms concentrated mainly in Chinatown, many Chinese-owned businesses have grown in size and diversity in recent years. The Chinese have gone beyond laundries and restaurants to enter a wide variety of fields of endeavor. Although restaurants do remain an important source of self-employment for Chinese entrepreneurs, many Chinese-owned businesses have become more incorporated into the larger economy and more commonly associated with the majority American population.

As an alternative path to social mobility, both ethnic workers and entrepreneurs may receive benefits from ethnic businesses. For employers, the relatively inexpensive labor of other members of their ethnic group can provide a competitive advantage. Although the self-employed may benefit more from this situation than employees, ethnic businesses do provide newly arrived immigrants with a starting place in America and help them to avoid unemployment. They also give new immigrants a familiar work environment, in which the immigrants can amass savings, develop skills, and prepare children for upward mobility. As the Chinese-American population grows, the number, size, diversity, and importance of ethnic businesses in America will also grow, and this growth will be expected to strengthen the ethnic community, which continues to function as a source of support for entrepreneurship and immigrant adaptation.

## NOTE

An earlier version of this chapter was presented at the Conference on Immigrant and Minority Entrepreneurship: Building American Communities and Economies, Austin, TX, March 14–16, 1995. This chapter was written while the author was in residence at the Russell Sage Foundation (1994–1995), whose support is gratefully acknowledged.

## REFERENCES

Aldrich, Howard E., & Roger Waldinger. (1990). Ethnicity and entrepreneurship. *American Review of Sociology, 16,* 111–35.

Bailey, Thomas, & Roger Waldinger. (1991). Primary, secondary, and enclave labor markets: A training system approach. *American Sociological Review, 56,* 432–445.

Bonacich, Edna. (1973). A theory of middleman minorities. *American Sociological Review, 37,* 547–59.

Butler, John S. (1991). *Entrepreneurship and self-help among black Americans.* Albany: State University of New York Press.

Chan, Sucheng. (1991). *Asian Americans: An interpretive history.* Boston: Twayne Publishers.

Chinatown Today Publishing. (1993). *Chinese-American life guide.* Hong Kong: Chinatown Today Publishing.

Fong, Timothy P. (1994). *The first suburban Chinatown: The remaking of Monterey Park,California.* Philadelphia: Temple University Press.

Hamamoto. (1992). Black-Korean conflict in Los Angeles. *Z Magazine* (July/August), 61–62.

Hurh, Won Moo, & Kwang Chung Kim. (1984). Korean immigrants in America: A structural analysis of ethnic confinement and adhesive adaptation. Cranbury, NJ: Associated University Presses.

Lee, Rose Hum. (1960). *The Chinese in the United States of America.* Hong Kong: Hong Kong University Press.

Li, Wei. (1997). *Spatial transformation of an urban ethnic community from Chinatown to Chinese ethnoburb in Los Angeles.* Doctoral dissertation, Department of Geography, University of Southern California, Los Angeles.

Light, Ivan H. (1972). *Ethnic enterprise in America: Business welfare among Chinese, Japanese and blacks.* Berkeley: University of California Press.

Light, Ivan H. (1984). Immigrant and ethnic enterprise in North America. *Ethnic and Racial Studies,* 7 (2): 195–216.

Light, Ivan, & Edna Bonacich. (1988). *Immigrant entrepreneurs: Koreans in Los Angeles, 1965–1982.* Berkeley: University of California Press.

Logan, John R., Richard Alba, & Tom McNulty. (1991). Identifying ethnic enclave economies in the United States. *Social Forces,* 72 (3).

Lyman, Stanford M. (1974). *Chinese Americans.* New York: Random House.

Min, Pyong Gap. (1995). *Ethnic business, intergroup conflicts, and ethnic solidarity: Koreans in New York and Los Angeles.* Princeton, NJ: Princeton University Press.

Portes, Alejandro. (1987). The social origins of the Cuban enclave economy of Miami. *Sociological Perspectives,* 30, 340–472.

Portes, Alejandro. (1995). Economic sociology and the sociology of immigration: A conceptual overview. In Alejandro Portes (Ed.), *The economic sociology of immigration—Essays on networks, ethnicity, and entrepreneurship* (pp. 1–4). New York: Russell Sage Foundation.

Portes, Alejandro, & R. Bach. (1985). *Latin Journey.* Los Angeles: University of California Press.

Portes, Alejandro, & L. I. Jensen. (1989). The enclave and the entrants: Patterns of ethnic enterprise in Miami before and after Mariel. *American Sociological Review,* 54 (6), 929–949.

Portes, Alejandro, & Min Zhou. (1992). Gaining the upper hand: Economic mobility among immigrant and domestic minorities. *Ethnic and Racial Studies,* 15, 491–522.

Portes, Alejandro, & Min Zhou. (1996). Self-employment and the earnings of immigrants. *American Sociological Review,* 61 (2), 219–230.

Sassen, Saskia. (1988). *The mobility of labor and capital.* New York: Cambridge University Press.

Saxton, Alexander. (1971). *The indispensable enemy: Labor and the anti-Chinese movement in California.* Berkeley: University of California Press.

Sung, Betty Lee. (1987). *The adjustment experience of Chinese immigrant children in New York City.* New York: Center for Migration Studies.

Tobier, Manuel. (1979). The new face of Chinatown. *New York Affairs,* 5 (3), 66–76.

U.S. Bureau of the Census. 1990 PUMS. *Census of population and housing, 1990: Public UseMicrodata samples (A) [MRDF].* Washington: U.S. Bureau of the Census [producer and distributor].

U.S. Bureau of the Census. (1991). *Survey of minority-owned business enterprises, 1987, MB87-1 to 4.* Washington: U.S. Department of Commerce.

U.S. Bureau of the Census. (1996). *Survey of minority-owned business enterprises, 1992, MB92-1 to 4.* Washington: U.S. Department of Commerce.

Waldinger, Roger. (1989). Structural opportunity or ethnic advantage: Immigrant business development in New York. *International Migration Review,* 23 (1), 48–72.

Wang, John. (1979). Behind the boom: Power and economics in Chinatown. *New York Affairs, 5* (3), 77–81.

Wong, Bernard. (1984). *Patronage, brokerage, entrepreneurship and the Chinese community of New York City.* New York: AMS Press.

Wong, Bernard. (1998). *Ethnicity and entrepreneurship: The new Chinese immigrants in the San Francisco Bay Area.* Boston: Allyn and Bacon.

Zhou, Min. (1992). *Chinatown: The socioeconomic potential of an urban enclave.* Philadelphia: Temple University Press.

Zhou, Min. (1997). Social capital in Chinatown: The role of community-based organizations and families in the adaptation of the younger generation. In Lois Weis and Maxine S. Seller (Eds.), *Beyond black and white: New voices, new faces in the United States schools,* pp. 181–206. Albany: State University of New York Press.

Zhou, Min, & John R. Logan. (1989). Returns on human capital in ethnic enclaves: New York City's Chinatown. *American Sociological Review, 54,* 809–820.

Zhou, Min, & Regina Nordquist. (1994). Work and its place in the lives of immigrant women: Garment workers in New York City's Chinatown. *Applied Behavioral Science Review, 2* (2), 187–211.

# 4

# Building Community through Entrepreneurship: Lessons from the United States and Vietnam

*Stephen J. Appold and John D. Kasarda*

This chapter reports on a continuing research program examining the relationship between entrepreneurship and communities. The studies included are based on original small-scale survey data collection in the United States and Vietnam. The seemingly diverse studies share a concern for a mismatch between the supply of labor and the supply of jobs. Specifically, we consider the strengths and limitations of policy tools rooted in a conception of an "entrepreneurial society" to address that mismatch by generating additional employment and wealth.

Rather than highlight the differences between the situations in each country, we focus on the commonalities and ask three related questions about the relationship between entrepreneurship and community. First, do small neighborhood businesses benefit residential communities? Our answer is yes, but there are limitations. We base our answer on a survey of 110 small businesses located in a balanced sample of predominantly white and predominantly black Pittsburgh neighborhoods. Second, can community (or more exactly social capital, the resources of your friends and family) aid in the creation of small businesses? Our answer is yes, but there are limitations. We base our answer on a survey of 124 small manufacturing enterprises located in Hanoi, Vietnam. Third, can formal help substitute for the absence of community (again, more exactly, social capital)? Our answer is yes, but there are limitations (mostly in our data). We base our answer on in-depth structured interviews with 28 recent or nascent black and white entrepreneurs in the greater Pittsburgh area.

Before addressing each of these three questions, we first outline our broader concern for the labor-employment mismatch with illustrative U.S. and global data. We then outline two opposing job creation paradigms and describe how the character of the labor market can facilitate or frustrate policies rooted in the conception of an entrepreneurial society. We conclude by identifying some of the gaps in our knowledge.

## THE LABOR-EMPLOYMENT MISMATCH

There is a tremendous labor-employment mismatch in the national and global economies that has the power, if unchecked, to devastate human lives and destroy communities. We define the labor-employment mismatch as a structural imbalance between numbers of jobs and the numbers of persons that could potentially occupy those jobs. The magnitude of this mismatch is difficult to judge because many individuals may be so discouraged that they remove themselves from an active search for employment. Although employment dislocations may be the perhaps normal and inevitable result of the evolution of a healthy economy, when concentrated in geographic and social space, the disruptions are not equally shared. There is, therefore, an immense need for entrepreneurial ventures that create employment opportunities.

In the United States that labor-employment mismatch is perhaps most visible in the older industrial cities of the Northeast and Midwest, where manufacturing employment has declined and information processing functions have increased in relative importance. Hovering around 20 million, there has been little change in the number of manufacturing jobs in the United States while the economy added close to 55 million additional jobs in other sectors since 1970. That employment growth, however, has been unevenly distributed with much faster employment growth in the South and West than in the Northeast and Midwest. Moreover, the aggregate employment trends in the Northeast and Midwest masked a continuing decline in manufacturing employment in those regions. Manufacturing job loss has been greatest in the central counties of metropolitan areas with populations of 150,000 or more in those two regions (Kasarda, 1995).

A comparison of Philadelphia and Dallas, two archetypical but not extreme cities, over the past two decades highlights the domestic U.S.

trends (see Table 4-1). Philadelphia's employment has eased downward from 772,000 in 1970 to 611,000 in 1990, whereas Dallas's employment has almost doubled from 584,000 to 1,100,000 in the same time period. More telling, however, is Philadelphia's drop in manufacturing jobs from 257,000 in 1970 to 85,000 in 1990. Dallas's manufacturing employment actually grew modestly from 171,000 to 181,000. The implications of the trends for the labor force can be seen even more clearly by examining the education level of those employed in the two cities. In Philadelphia, opportunities for those with 13 or more years of education increased 13 percent between 1970 and 1990, whereas the number of jobs held by those with fewer than 12 years of schooling declined by 48 percent. Meanwhile in Dallas, jobs for those with less than 12 years of education increased 39 percent and jobs for those with a high level of education increased 312 percent. Job creation for those with little schooling has not kept pace with job creation for those with many years of schooling (Kasarda, 1993). Nor has employment for those with little schooling been sufficient to absorb job seekers.

A similar pattern repeats itself in city after city, creating stress in the labor market for those with low educational credentials. Sectoral changes, primarily in the Northeast and Midwest, have exacerbated that stress, often resulting in pockets of concentrated poverty. In 1960, approximately 16 percent of the poor in both Dallas and Philadelphia lived in areas (Census tracts) of "extreme poverty."[1] By 1990, that percentage had increased modestly in Dallas but had almost doubled in Philadelphia. Moreover, while the proportion of the poor blacks in "extreme poverty" areas had remained approximately the same over time, that proportion increased by almost 10 percentage points in Philadelphia. In fact, in 1990, 22 percent of Philadelphia's poor blacks lived in the so-called "underclass"[2] areas; only 6 percent of Dallas's poor blacks did.

**TABLE 4-1 U.S. Labor-Employment Mismatch: Philadelphia and Dallas**

|  | Philadelphia | | Dallas | |
|---|---|---|---|---|
|  | 1970 | 1990 | 1970 | 1990 |
| Total employment (000) | 772 | 611 | 584 | 1,111 |
| Manufacturing employment (000) | 257 | 85 | 171 | 181 |
| Employees with < 12 yrs. edu. | 430 | 226 | 337 | 468 |
| Employees with 13+ yrs. edu. | 205 | 231 | 107 | 334 |
| Population living in poverty (000) | 294 | 313 | 119 | 178 |
| Poverty population in "extreme poverty" census tracts | 15.9% | 29.8% | 18% | 23% |

The large-scale disequilibrium between labor demand and labor supply may now finally be beginning to subside in the United States. Interregional migration is becoming less dramatic, and the decline in central city populations is slowing and, in some cases, reversing. However, as discussed earlier, concentrations of poverty promise to remain in many metropolitan areas, leading to a concern for the health of central city, particularly minority, neighborhoods. Future economic participation may not be equitable if concentrated poverty cuts some individuals off from meaningful opportunity. We examine Pittsburgh, a city that has experienced dramatic employment dislocations resulting in a shift in its employment base, to investigate the contributions of small neighborhood businesses to community vitality and to investigate the effectiveness of interventions in the entrepreneurial process.

The global employment situation is less immediate to U.S. observers but perhaps of larger long-term significance. Tremendous gains in labor-force size have occurred and are expected throughout the Third World over the next several decades (see Table 4-2). The majority of the world's population lives in what are broadly termed the developing countries (DCs). Population growth rates are approximately 1.89 percent per year in the developing countries, whereas they average approximately .56 percent in the more developed countries (United Nations, 1994). In 1950, the more developed countries (MDCs) accounted for approximately one third of the world's population. By the end of this decade, they will be home to only about one fifth. Moreover, in 1950, although only half as many people lived in MDCs as DCs, MDCs accounted for about 1.5 times as large a nonagricultural labor force as the developing countries. Since the late 1970s, over half of the global supply of nonagricultural labor has been in the DCs. That nonagricul-

**TABLE 4-2  Global Population and Non-Agricultural Labor Force Trends**

| Year | | Developed Countries | Developing Countries | |
|------|------|------|------|------|
| 1950 | Population | 832 | 1,683 | 2,515 |
| | | 33% | 67% | |
| | Non-Agricultural Labor force | 241 | 154 | 395 |
| | | 61% | 39% | |
| 2000 | Population | 1,300 | 4,800 | 6,100 |
| | | 21% | 79% | |
| | Non-Agricultural Labor force | 290 | 560 | 850 |
| | | 34% | 66% | |
| | | | | (in millions) |

tural labor force is estimated to be growing at about 3.5 percent per year and, by the year 2003, approximately two thirds of the world's nonagricultural labor will be in the developing countries.

Earlier demographic concern was directed toward the question of population growth and the adequacy of available resources. A good deal of the earlier policy and academic discussion revolved around the division of wealth within families, that is, the effects of dependency ratios—the dependents usually being young but now increasingly old. The concern with labor force growth is similar but perhaps more acute. Each individual must establish a claim on societal wealth. Dependents, young and old, do this through family ties. Yet, aside from the diminishing number of subsistence farmers, each household must establish a claim through work outside the household.

The labor-employment mismatch in the developing world is perhaps most visible in the growing cities of South America, Africa, and Asia. Population growth and migration strain the ability of the formal economy to generate sufficient employment. The great numbers of people who are entering and will continue to enter the labor force require employment opportunities for their subsistence. Vietnam, one of the poorest but most promising economies in the world, sustains a high rate of labor force growth yet still labors under inflexible formal economic institutions. Accordingly, we look to Hanoi to investigate the role of community in facilitating entrepreneurship.

## AN "ADMINISTERED" SOCIETY OR AN "ENTREPRENEURIAL" SOCIETY

A top-down policy approach may not be sufficient to address contemporary job creation needs. There may be a need to shift between two, very different, models of employment generation. The first is rooted in the concept of an "administered society," epitomized by Galbraith (1972), where large enterprises and direct governmental effort are central in generating employment opportunities. For the most part, individuals are seen as directly dependent upon existing, powerful institutions to create new employment opportunities. Until recently, a good deal of the policy discussion about job creation has centered around this type of top-down approach to job creation, certainly in Vietnam but also in the United States. Negotiation among government and business elites combined with the manipulation of business costs through macroeconomic interventions, such as money supply adjustments and fiscal policy, on the national level, and microeconomic interventions, such as the use of tax abatements and subsidy, on the local level, were viewed as sufficient to guide the creation of employment.

As late as the 1970s, maintaining full employment and regional equity was a stated goal of the governments of many industrialized nations.

These policies appear to have been largely ineffective. Circumstances may have overstressed economic institutions. Businesses may engage in strategic behavior in their interactions with national and local governments, waiting for expansionist policy interventions rather than immediately responding to market conditions. Local employment generation focused heavily on industrial recruitment—the big "elephant hunt"—and retention through financial incentives. The costs of local employment creation were high and led to no aggregate improvement in economic welfare, pointing to the need for a different style of policy intervention. Moreover, the failure of the administered society model of economic production is all but inevitable. Three relevant problems plague all organizations, whether large or small, publicly or privately owned. Internal vested interests (Selznick, 1957), unclear environmental signals (March & Olsen, 1976), and skill shortages inhibit businesses' ability to routinize innovation, respond to market needs, and control implementation performance.

A second model of economic production is based on the idea of an entrepreneurial society. Though large firms and organizations may continue to play a role, new firms provide the bulk of future employment. This type of bottom-up approach, with decentralized decision-making and responsibility, is probably best exemplified by the discussion over the informal sector. The contemporary policy debate may be shifting from a question of how central institutions can create employment to how private individuals will create their own claims on societal wealth and in so doing (i.e., through entrepreneurial activities) expand societal wealth.

Entrepreneurship is the social mechanism of the second chance. In fact, the entrepreneurs who succeed in accomplishing a task frequently have had a failure experience while employed as managers attempting the same task. They were able to learn from their mistakes but were unable to get their former employers to adapt. The problems of organizational rigidity could be seen in the command economies of the former Soviet bloc, but they were, ironically, visible much earlier in the mixed economies of Western Europe and North America.

The potential impact of entrepreneurship on the resurgence of local and, by extension, national economies can be seen in Figure 4-1. We graph the number of jobs (private nonfarm employment) and the number of business establishments in Allegheny County (the location of Pittsburgh) using County Business Pattern data. Employment in the county drops between 1980 and 1984. This was the era of large-scale employment losses in the steel and other heavy manufacturing sectors. During this same period, however, the number of establishments actu-

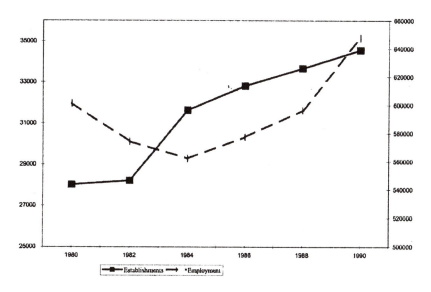

**Figure 4-1** Allegheny County: employment and establishments.

ally increases despite the dramatic employment loss. Subsequently, as a portion of the establishments become increasingly successful, employment growth begins to accelerate. The figure illustrates the "sow and grow" potential of entrepreneurship for generating employment and rejuvenating economies.

Relying on studies performed in Pittsburgh and Hanoi, we address three concerns about the contribution of entrepreneurship to community and on the contribution of community to entrepreneurship.

### The Community Benefit of Small Businesses: A Lesson from Pittsburgh's Neighborhoods

The social health of communities and the human development of their residents, on the one hand, and the vitality of the neighborhood small business sector, on the other, are frequently thought to be closely tied. Small business owners may be neighborhood residents, so local businesses can be taken as an indication of the community's leadership capabilities. Small business ownership is a frequent route for upward social mobility. Small neighborhood businesses may also increase the local demand for labor and add to the available economic opportunity by employing nearby residents. Proximate employment is particularly important for young people just entering the labor force. Further, to the extent that the neighborhood business owners and employees reside locally, patronage keeps money in the community. This is a sensitive issue in some neighborhoods; buying from local businesses is seen as an act of community building.

Local businesses do, in fact, provide valued amenities to localities. The services they offer make neighborhoods more attractive. But businesspeople also have a vested interest in neighborhood upkeep and community improvement. They, therefore, may frequently serve in community organizations, often taking leadership roles in fighting off crime, cajoling the municipal administration into performing services, and attracting other businesses. These community-building organizations, providing tangible benefits to the public, are sometimes referred to as growth machines.

In order to measure the benefit of entrepreneurship to communities, and minority communities in particular, we surveyed 110 small businesses located in the commercial districts of nine Pittsburgh area neighborhoods; five neighborhoods were predominantly white, four black.[3] Most neighborhoods are in or adjacent to the central city and within a few miles of Pittsburgh's Golden Triangle. However, in order to better balance the sample design by including a low-income white area, one neighborhood in a former mill town was included. We report on the 110 businesses owned by blacks or whites.

The businesses are about evenly split between the white and black neighborhoods. Approximately 70 percent of the business owners are white. Our sample design included businesses with 50 or fewer employees. Almost all the businesses are retail establishments; 91 are independently owned and operated businesses; the remaining 19 are franchisees or members of a chain. The businesses averaged approximately 10 years of operation at the time of the survey—but those with white owners averaged 19 years, those with black owners averaged 8.5 years. White-owned businesses in black neighborhoods averaged 22.6 years of operation, those in white neighborhoods 17.4 years. The degree of stability is not surprising given the pattern of population change in Pittsburgh. Central city population has declined, and several of the neighborhoods included in the survey shifted during the 1970s from predominantly white residents to black.

Although the types of business they engage in are roughly equivalent, only 10 percent of the white businesses are owned by women. Almost half the black-owned businesses are.

Our most striking finding is the effect of the interaction between race of owner and racial composition of the neighborhood on the racial composition of employment, shown in Table 4-3. In predominantly white neighborhoods, 89 percent of the employees are white and 11 percent black. In the predominantly black neighborhoods, 40 percent of

**TABLE 4-3  Percentage of Small Firm Labor Force that is Black, by Selected Pittsburgh Neighborhoods and Race of Owner**

| Predominant race of neighborhood | Race of Owner | | |
|---|---|---|---|
| | White | Black | |
| White | 11% | — | 11% |
| Black | 27% | 96% | 60% |
| | | | N = 101 |

the employees are white and 60 percent black. Those last figures, however, mask substantial differences between white- and black-owned businesses. Among the white-owned businesses in predominantly black neighborhoods, 73 percent of the employees are white and 27 percent are black. This last distribution approximates the citywide racial composition. Among the black-owned businesses in those same neighborhoods, 96 percent of the employees are black. Thus we find a clear effect of employer characteristics on employment opportunities.

We asked a series of questions investigating owner recruitment mechanisms. Of the 86 establishments for which we have data,[4] 75 percent used referrals from friends, business associates, or employees in preference to advertisements, job services, and other public mechanisms. However, 84 percent of the businesses in black neighborhoods favored referrals, compared to 62 percent in white neighborhoods.

Table 4-4 shows that the effect of race on employee recruitment does not, however, necessarily imply local benefit. In 62 percent of the cases, the last person hired was a resident of the neighborhood. This did not vary appreciably by race of owner or by the racial composition of the neighborhood. However, 70 percent of the white employers in black neighborhoods hired their last employee from the neighborhood, surpassing black employers in those same neighborhoods (50 percent) and white employers in white neighborhoods (58 percent). Although we found that owners who reside near their place of business are more likely to hire locally, local residence is not the norm. Only 21 percent of

**TABLE 4-4  Percentage of Small FirmsThat Hired the Last Employee Locally, by Selected Pittsburgh Neighborhoods and Race of Owner**

| Predominant race of neighborhood | Race of Owner | | |
|---|---|---|---|
| | White | Black | |
| White | 58% | — | 58% |
| Black | 70% | 50% | 65% |
| | | | N = 86 |

the owners live in the neighborhood where they did business. However, a greater proportion of the black owners (28 percent) live in the neighborhood where their business is, whereas only 17 percent of the white owners are local residents. The effect of local residence on recruitment does not vary substantially by race.

Because many of our sample firms are family-operated, only half of the respondents had ever hired a manager. Only 36 percent of the most recently hired managers were neighborhood residents. Black business owners, however, hire managers from the local labor pool twice as frequently as white owners do.

Almost two thirds (62 percent) of the business owners surveyed participate in a community service organization. At 78 percent, the participation rate among black business owners is higher than that of white owners. Three factors may explain the participation gap. First, race differences between owners and neighborhood residents may discourage participation; the participation of white owners operating in black neighborhoods is two thirds that of white owners in white neighborhoods. Second, community development corporations supplying assistance to small business owners are more common in the black neighborhoods. Third, community and ethnic awareness may be higher among black owners; 53 percent of the black owners felt that their race was of some benefit in running their business, whereas only 26 percent of the white owners, operating in predominantly white neighborhoods, shared that sentiment.

Our results indicate that minority entrepreneurship provides important contributions to minority communities. Black business owners do hire blacks more often than do white entrepreneurs, and social networks play a significant role. Furthermore, these ties are more important in minority neighborhoods than they are in white neighborhoods. These benefits, however, are not necessarily neighborhood based. White owners in predominantly black neighborhoods hire nearby residents most often. In fact, one black respondent in a predominantly black neighborhood claimed to specifically avoid hiring neighborhood residents. Our evidence suggests, however, that place-based business development strategies, such as enterprise zones, would probably not be effective. There is too much spatial leakage in hiring among both black and white entrepreneurs.

### Social Capital in the Creation of Entrepreneurship:
### A Lesson from Hanoi

Large changes in the external and internal environment, including the near-collapse of an international support network centered in the former Soviet Union and rapid domestic labor force growth, has placed great stress on Vietnam's centrally planned economy. Regulatory changes, increased spending brought about by renewed economic growth, and employment dislocation stemming from the downsizing of some large state-owned enterprises have resulted in the growth in the number of small-scale manufacturing establishments. These enterprises tend to locate in specialized clusters in cities and their immediate suburbs.

The literature on small-scale enterprise frequently emphasizes the role of noneconomic relationships in the determining economic behavior, particularly in situations where markets are imperfect and where official regulatory mechanisms only insufficiently protect creditors, business partners, and workers. That is, social capital is important in facilitating entrepreneurship.

Anthropological accounts of the survival strategies of the poor in developing countries (Hart, 1982) often stress the social nature of material exchanges wherein family members are often the parties to the exchange. Similarly, Stack (1974) illustrates how fictive kinship ties were sometimes created to mask what are, essentially, economic pooling arrangements. Granovetter (1985) suggests that these real or fictive kinship ties are used to create a sense of obligation and contain the inclination toward opportunism. That is, social ties cement the norm of reciprocity and thereby reinforce mutual commitments. Powell (1990) suggests that the mixture of social ties and economic exchanges makes a new organizational form, network organizations, possible. That form gives small businesses enhanced competitiveness.

Our data in examining the role of social capital in firm-formation are the products of a survey of 124 small-scale enterprises in Hanoi.[5] We sampled 27 aluminum formers, 27 iron workers, 44 clothing manufacturers, and 26 furniture makers. The interviews were informal and exploratory. The entrepreneurs contacted were eager to participate, and a completion rate of approximately 94 percent (8 refusals) was obtained.

Producers in these particular sectors are known to cluster near other firms in the same sectors. Most of the workplaces are open-fronted, and passersby can easily examine the wares, observe the amount of activity, and watch the work being performed. Work is often performed on the sidewalk or in the street. These agglomerations are well defined and known to consumers. The aluminum utensil manufacturers use aluminum sheets imported from India or made domestically from recycled cans and presses to form the flat sheets into useful shapes. The ornamental ironworkers produce primarily for the construction industry, and in fact many are located near an area known for the supply of building materials. Most of the production is devoted to decorative, yet protective, window and door bars. The clothing manufacturers surveyed are oriented toward a range of activities. They custom manufacture clothing for individuals and wholesale orders but also retail ready-to-wear clothing made in other plants. Furniture makers work almost exclusively with wood. They manufacture tables, chairs, beds, and stand-alone kitchen cabinets satisfying the basic needs of households. These same enterprises also manufacture doors and supply other wooden construction materials.

The median age of the businesses was approximately 5.5 years at the time of the interviews, implying that the majority of the enterprises were not founded until several years after the official instigation of economic restructuring in 1986 but were founded before the laws on private ownership began to be clarified. We did find, however, that approximately 23 percent of those surveyed were formed before 1986 and a few dated from the 1960s.

The entrepreneurs themselves had a mean age of 35.0 at the time of the business founding, although some may have inherited the business from their parents. This is remarkably similar to results of other surveys performed in different countries with very different circumstances. The entrepreneurs are overwhelmingly male, constituting approximately 75 percent of the sample. Those in the clothing sector are somewhat younger than those in other sectors and, at 50 percent of those sampled, much more likely to be female.

Formal capital markets are poorly developed in Vietnam. Informal relationships have the potential to ameliorate the shortcomings of the official institutions. Almost all capital needed to start businesses comes from personal savings, the family, friends, suppliers, or customers. Just over half of our respondents relied on family help to buy the equipment needed to start their business. One tenth received capital from a friend. One eighth received help from a material supplier, and 5 percent obtained aid from a customer. Family help clearly dominates as a source of start-up capital; 37 percent of the respondents received help from their families and no other source. At the same time, however, 41 percent of the entrepreneurs received no outside help at all and relied exclusively on their own savings. Despite the geographic clustering of the enterprises, few of the capital sources were nearby. Only 10 percent of the capital sources were located in the neighborhood of the business; the majority of those appear to be family members.

Those not receiving any outside start-up capital tend to be younger and in the clothing sector. Approximately 40 percent of the sample received no outside help in gathering the necessary start-up capital, 61 percent of those in the clothing sector received no help. Aluminum formers (18 percent) and ironworkers (30 percent) were the least likely to not receive any outside funds. (See Table 4-5 for a summary.)

Enterprises require operating, as well as start-up, capital. In fact, all but 4 percent of the enterprises rely on outside sources for some amount

**TABLE 4-5   Capital Source and Firm Performance: Small Hanoi Manufacturers**

| |
|---|
| Where does start-up capital originate? |
|     50+ percent receive capital from family members |
|     37 percent receive capital from family members only |
|     10 percent receive capital from friends |
|     41 percent receive no outside capital |
| Who receives family funds? |
|     Older, male entrepreneurs |
|     Those with fathers who were professionals |
|     Those who were professionals themselves |
| Effect of family funds |
|     Larger facilities, more employees |
|     More successful |

of operating capital. Family members remain a principal source of operating capital, supplying help to 55 percent of the sample. Friends decrease even further as a source of help, giving aid to 5 percent of those surveyed. The prevalence of help from business relationships, however, increases dramatically. Material suppliers supply capital for the purchase of materials to 82 percent of the enterprises; customers lend funds to buy supplies to 46 percent of the sample. Only 8 percent of the enterprises rely solely on family help in purchasing materials.

Although there is no overall relationship between helping out one's family as a motivation for entrepreneurship and receiving help from them in the form of start-up funds, it is at least ironic that entrepreneurs in the clothing sector were the most likely to identify "helping family finances" as a motivation for going into business but the least likely to receive help from them. Clothing makers are also the least likely to receive family funds for operating expenses. Perhaps these are the families least able to supply capital.

The sources of capital appear to be independent of each other. We found, in particular, only a modest relationship between friends and family as sources of start-up capital and no relationship for operating capital. That is, there is little tendency to rely on social ties versus business ties in seeking funds. There is, however, a tendency to receive both start-up and operating funds from family members if their help is received at all. A similar relationship is found for friends also.

There is a weak relationship between gender and the ability to raise capital from particular sources. Men appear to be better able to raise start-up capital and operating capital from family members than women. Gender makes no difference in raising start-up capital from friends, suppliers, or customers, but women are somewhat more likely to be able to raise operating capital from suppliers and customers than men. Although only a small minority of enterprises gathered any of their start-up capital in their geographical neighborhood, women were much more likely than men to do so.

The age of the entrepreneur may partially explain the higher success of men in winning family support. The men in the sample are significantly older than the women, and age is significantly correlated with the ability to raise start-up and operating capital from family sources. Age is correlated with the ability to raise start-up capital from material suppliers but a bit more strongly correlated with the ability to raise start-up and operating capital from family sources.

Almost 70 percent of the entrepreneurs from professional families received help with the start-up capital from their family members, whereas only 40 percent of those whose fathers were in crafts received such help. Similarly, those whose previous job was in the professions were more likely to receive help from their families, 65 percent, whereas those who previously worked in crafts were much less likely, 43 percent, to receive such help. That is, 43 percent of those with previous experience in the field of business received start-up capital from their families, whereas 58 percent of those with no experience did so.

This pattern does not imply that those receiving family help are smaller, less promising businesses. Businesses receiving family help are larger in terms of floor area and in terms of total number of employees. And, although our measure is subjective, we have tentative evidence that the enterprises receiving family help are more successful than those that do not. Receiving start-up capital from a friend appears to result in a greater number of nonfamily workers, a greater number of total workers, and a larger number of machines.

Agglomerations of small-scale manufacturing enterprises are often seen in industrialized countries as a promising route to industrial revival (Piore & Sabel, 1984) and to industrialization in developing countries, such as Vietnam. Social, especially family, ties are hypothesized to play a significant role in economic transactions in these agglomerations.

We find partial support for these contentions. In particular, we find that whereas the situation varies by sector and although purely business contacts become more prevalent as sources of operating funds, friends and mainly family are important sources of start-up capital. Moreover, social capital sources appear to buy into the firm by contributing to the workforce.

Although we have no formal test of adequacy, social support appears to help ameliorate the low supply of funds in the formal capital market for these sectors. Moreover, social capital appears to be a factor in business success as well. On the other hand, the availability of that support appears to be limited. Those receiving start-up capital from family sources are older and more likely to be male. Further, family background determines whether support is received; experience in the sector does not have a positive effect. The family funds are not so much overcoming information imperfections in the capital market about the talents of particular individuals but investments only the well-placed are able to make. Therefore, although there appear to be substantial social benefits in the form of greater product availability and employment creation, entrepreneurship at this level may have only limited application as an income redistribution mechanism. Social capital accrues mainly to those with other personal resources. To the extent that human capital is necessary to gain social capital and social capital is necessary for business success, entrepreneurship has only limited usefulness as a direct poverty-reducing policy tool but may be of indirect benefit by generating employment.

### Substituting Formal Channels for Social Capital:
### A Further Lesson from Pittsburgh

Because entrepreneurship is a route of social mobility for minority groups, the factors accounting for entrepreneurship among blacks has become a point of central interest among policy analysts interested in understanding income inequality. We might expect entrepreneurship to be high among blacks; it is not. Pittsburgh is somewhat of an extreme case. African American entrepreneurship is below the national average in Pittsburgh. Furthermore, investigations of the relatively high levels of entrepreneurship found among some Asian immigrant groups reveal that education and financial capital may not be as important as a cooperative community structure.

In Allegheny County, the rate of business ownership among blacks is just over one third that among whites (1.7 versus 4.9 percent). Given the importance of minority business ownership for minority employment, described in an earlier section, the question of whether steps can be effectively taken to enhance the level of minority entrepreneurship takes on policy significance. The importance of social capital in firm-formation and success was described in the previous section. Here we examine differences in personal resources social capital between white and black entrepreneurs and investigate how those differences affect the entrepreneurship process.

We interviewed 28 black and white entrepreneurs in the greater Pittsburgh area at critical stages of the business gestation process: a pre-opening or nascent stage, a recently opened stage (within approximately two years of initial opening), and a recently failed (after no more than two years of operation) stage.[6] Figure 4-2 illustrates the points in the gestation process from which our sample was drawn. Of the 28 businesses, 10 were still in the process of formation, 15 were open, and 3 had recently closed. Because we were interested in businesses at these critical stages, we worked through intermediaries to locate these entrepreneurs. We are unable to judge the representativeness of our small sample, but although the number of cases is small, the data set does have a balanced design, allowing comparisons to be made. Much of the research, which attempts to measure the effects of entrepreneurial help, reports only the perceived benefit of those who received aid.

We asked detailed questions about several steps in the entrepreneurial gestation process, about enterprise operations and, in the cases where applicable, the reasons for and conditions surrounding closing. We also asked about personal attributes and resources and about sources of formal and informal help for each of the several gestational steps. The heart of the analysis that follows is centered on the steps leading to opening day. These include solidifying the business idea, writing the business plan, performing a marketing survey, obtaining a business site, cultivating a supplier base, developing a clientele, securing the necessary licenses, recruiting a workforce, and acquiring financing.

The sample contained an equal number of black and white entrepreneurs. The types of business activities were roughly comparable across racial categories. The black-owned and white-owned businesses were about equally successful on a series of measures.

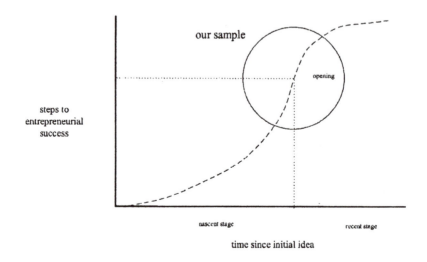

Figure 4-2  Entrepreneurial gestation.

We found no large racial differences in the personal resources the entrepreneurs brought to their present ventures. Whites were slightly older, in their late 40s, on average, and thus had more work experience. Whites had slightly higher education than blacks, averaging about a bachelor's degree. Blacks and whites had about the same amount of formal education in business and about the same amount of work experience in management. Half the sample had previously owned and operated another business, but there were no racial differences in having that experience. We did find, however, that blacks more frequently had formal education in their field of business (85 percent versus 50 percent).

We found little difference in self-reported measures of psychological traits between our black and white entrepreneurs. Both blacks and whites reported a high to very high level of persistence. Both reported a high level of confidence in their business venture (at least while it was open). Black entrepreneurs, however, reported a higher level of personal self-confidence than the whites.

We found few differences in the level of social capital. Both blacks and whites reported about the same level of confidence on the part of close family and friends. That level of confidence, however, is considerably lower than what the entrepreneurs report for themselves. Approximately the same number of black and white entrepreneurs report having family members who have owned businesses. However, 93 percent of the white entrepreneurs report having personal friends who own businesses, whereas only 71 percent of the black entrepreneurs do.

Having friends in business is important because it is one of the few components of personal resources that has a relationship with business success. Only 20 percent of those without friends in business achieve our measure of success, but 57 percent of those who have friends do. Success is defined here as remaining open and breaking even or achieving a net profit any time by the third year of operation (depending on how old the business was at the time of interview).

We found a positive relationship between the entrepreneur's age and business success. Previous business experience appeared to have no effect on entrepreneurial success. The entrepreneur's self-reported persistence and self-confidence had no measurable effect.

Given the great overall similarities in the personal resources of the black and white entrepreneurs in our sample and in their level of success, one might ask whether significant differences exist between the two groups. We find that they do and that they are to be found in the need for assistance in the entrepreneurial process and in the sources of that assistance. Whites are apparently more easily able to proceed through the several gestational steps than blacks without outside aid. Moreover, blacks are more likely than whites to use formal, rather than informal, channels of help, such as community development corporations, the Small Business Development Center of Duquesne University, the Urban Redevelopment Authority, and the Minority Enterprise Corporation of Southwestern Pennsylvania, when searching for aid.

For example, approximately 55 percent of our entrepreneurs sought outside help when searching for a business site. That was 36 percent of the whites but 71 percent of the blacks in the sample. Of those who sought outside help, 50 percent of the whites could rely on friends or family. Only about 10 percent of the blacks could.

One might hypothesize that the number of organizations meant to aid minority entrepreneurs could predispose black entrepreneurs to use formal help channels more than whites. We find no evidence in support of that contention. Blacks are more likely to report asking for help from a formal organization and being refused than the whites in our sample. We conclude that black entrepreneurs are forced to rely on formal organizations even though those organizations are not always receptive. (See Table 4-6 for a summary.)

Blacks and whites come approximately equally prepared to the entrepreneurial process; they achieve approximately equal levels of success, but blacks have more apparent difficulty along the way. Black entrepreneurs are, therefore, more likely to seek aid from both informal and formal sources. Having less social capital, they rely more heavily than whites on formal help organizations. It appears that formal entrepreneurial aid organizations are able to compensate for deficits in social capital.

Most government efforts at supporting small business are meant to affect the financial viability of those businesses by easing credit restrictions or reserving markets. These policies are both politically threatened and of questionable effectiveness. They may come too late in the gestational process. Therefore, we examined the early stages of entrepreneurship, the time before and immediately after opening. We investigated whether formal organizations could aid entrepreneurs without adequate social capital address questions of Who and How. We found

**TABLE 4-6   Sources of Help: Selected Nascent and Recent Pittsburgh Entrepreneurs**

| |
|---|
| Little black-white differences in resources |
| Little black-white differences in psychological characteristics |
| Whites have more friends in business |
| Having friends in business is correlated with success |
| Blacks more likely to need outside help |
| Blacks more likely to need to rely on formal sources |

that they could. Moreover, that sort of business support might be cost-effective.[7]

## CONSIDERATIONS AND LIMITATIONS

Programs to create employment that are rooted in the model of an entrepreneurial society hold the promise of relatively inexpensive interventions in the employment-generation process by sacrificing control over the content of those jobs. That is, rather than target particular industries for development, as many national industrial policies and local recruitment efforts do, entrepreneurship-based policies recognize that contemporary opportunities are often found in very narrowly circumscribed market niches best visible to those with direct experience. We believe, however, that even though such an approach to job generation holds much promise, there may also be severe constraints on the ability of these efforts to generate quality employment. Entrepreneurial activities are situated in context, which affects their efficacy. Perhaps chief among the societal level constraints is the character of the prevalent job allocation system.

Building on work that is primarily focused on the developed world, concerning job generation (Birch, 1979), the absorption of the baby boom (Easterlin, 1976) and organizational demography (Keyfitz, 1973), we see two contrasting ideal type models of job allocation. The first, following the U.S. pattern, could be called an occupational attainment model; the second, more readily seen in Canada and much of Northern Europe, could be termed an income attainment model. The income attainment model may be associated with what Olson (1982) has termed rigid distributional coalitions, whereas the other model would be characterized by a continuing process of change in social institutions.

The occupational and income attainment models stand as polar opposites. Figure 4-3 illustrates the differences in entrepreneurship patterns under the two models of job generation. Under the occupational attainment model, wages are soft in the face of an expanding supply of workers while opportunities to do various sorts of work are comparatively open (albeit at relatively low wages and requiring an additional willingness for individuals to invest in their own futures). This model hypothesizes both flexible wages and substitution between capital and labor—that is, a range of available technologies. Stickiness in either area would characterize the income attainment model. The income attainment model is characterized by relatively limited productive employment opportunities but attractive wage development for those fortunate enough to gain employment. Excess labor waits in a queue, redirected toward educational establishments, retirement, and the home or open unemployment.

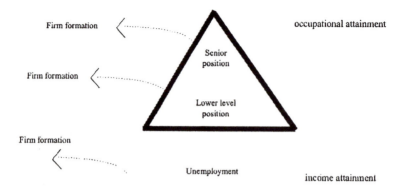

**Figure 4-3**  Career timing of entrepreneurship.

Because most practical human capital at all levels of skill and education is gained on the job, job allocation regimes may have a serious effect on the type of self-generation of employment—entrepreneurship—in a country and its ability to generate new wealth. Under an income attainment regime, those most distressed are the young, new arrivals and the least well endowed. They will most often be forced to create their own employment. Although possibly eager to make the personal investments required, they will, however, probably lack the prerequisites to perform meaningful services and may be forced to do subsistence work or possibly engage in illegal activities. Even those with high levels of education are unlikely to be fully aware of the potential opportunities in their fields.

Those disadvantaged under an occupational attainment regime will not be the young or least qualified—for them the employment system is relatively open. Because labor market entry is open, the trajectory of income attainment throughout a career may be somewhat flat. If dissatisfaction occurs at a later stage of life, when entrepreneurs are more likely to have garnered a store of human capital gained through work experience, built up a network of social contacts, and command a supply of family labor, the ventures formed are more likely to be productive and oriented toward wider or more distant markets. We would therefore expect the transitions to self-employment later in life to involve more skill to generate more employment and wealth.

The efficacy of entrepreneurship as an employment and income policy is therefore determined, in part, by the character of the supply of entrepreneurs. In each of our studies, older (middle-aged) entrepreneurs appear to be more successful than those who are younger. In order to address the problem of structural imbalances between labor and employment and reduce the level of dislocation, policies rooted in a conception of an entrepreneurial society will need to produce sufficient numbers of the somewhat older entrepreneurs who can mobilize both product market niches and labor.

In the first study discussed, we focused specifically on very local niches because we were concerned with neighborhood well-being. Figure 4-4 summarizes the possible general collective outcomes of entrepreneurial mobilization of product and labor markets. If minority entrepreneurs are unable to mobilize new product niches but are able to tap otherwise underutilized labor, the distribution or the burden of the labor-employment mismatch may become more evenly distributed. The underclass phenomenon, visible in many cities, may be reduced or eradicated by redistributing poverty, even without creating new wealth. If, however, entrepreneurs are able to find new market niches but are unable to mobilize a new labor source, possibly because the many unemployed do not have appropriate technical skills, their efforts may result in rising wages among the employed and sustained joblessness among those who are not, resulting in exacerbated divergence. If entrepreneurs are unable to mobilize new markets or labor, their efforts are largely wasted, and policies to support entrepreneurial ventures would be misplaced in a bottomless pit. This, of course, is the criticism of programs to support small business in general. If, however, entrepreneurs are able to mobilize both new markets and new sources of labor, sustained prosperity would be the result. Entrepreneurship in sectors where market niches have the potential to grow offers the most promise.

Mobilize product markets

|  | Yes | No |
|---|---|---|
| Mobilize new labor — Yes | reduction of dislocation | redistribution of poverty burden |
| Mobilize new labor — No | labor shortage and unemployment | no contribution |

Figure 4-4  Outcomes of entrepreneurial process.

These considerations temper our enthusiasm for the universal applicability of the encouragement of entrepreneurship as a policy tool. The contribution of entrepreneurship to the creation of quality employment might vary from situation to situation.

## CONCLUSION

Business ownership has always been considered a hallmark of personal success in the United States and throughout the world. Ownership of a successful business often yields a comfortable income. More important, perhaps, is the feeling of personal independence many business owners report. Furthermore, business owners are often accorded a high level of prestige within the community. Entrepreneurship—the process of finding a market, mobilizing resources, and actually starting a business—is often seen as a route to personal fulfillment.

Not only is entrepreneurship an indicator of personal accomplishment, it is a measure of group prosperity closely watched by social commentators. Entrepreneurship is a route of social mobility, which becomes particularly important for those facing discrimination and other barriers whose paths are blocked by the normal channels of career development.

We began with a concern for the employment-labor mismatch and the ability of entrepreneurial policies to address that mismatch. We find that small businesses do create benefits for local neighborhood communities; that social capital does help in the creation of entrepreneurial ventures; and that formal help mechanisms can be effective.

We find, however, important gaps in our knowledge of the connections between entrepreneurship, employment, and community. We briefly mention a few here. Before making informed recommendations on entrepreneurial policies, we need to know more about the relationship between neighborhood businesses, crime, and residential stability. To the extent that neighborhood businesses reduce street crime and provide amenities, they may serve to strengthen inner-city neighborhoods and thereby aid in the redevelopment of many of the country's industrial cities. Further, we need to know more about the spillover effects of community-saving interventions such as crime fighting. It is possible that police actions to reduce drug marketing actually exacerbate the situation by creating new employment vacancies in illegal organizations. We also need to know more about the job search/employee recruitment, promotion, and retention behavior of individuals and firms. The relationship between black entrepreneurship and black employment may not be straightforward. Essentially, we need a map of local labor markets to find the critical points for intervention. Finally, we need to know the extent of discrimination in employment. Clearly, the greater the level of labor market discrimination, the greater the potential impact of minority entrepreneurship on minority employment.

## NOTES

An earlier version of this chapter was presented at the conference on "Immigrant and Minority Entrepreneurship: Building American Communities and Economies," Austin, TX, March 14–16, 1995.

1. "Extreme poverty" areas are defined as Census tracts where 40 percent or more of the households have incomes below the official poverty level (Kasarda, 1993).
2. "Underclass areas" are defined as Census tracts with disproportionately high rates of joblessness, female-headed families, teenage school dropout, and welfare receipt (Ricketts and Sawhill 1988).
3. The results reported in this section rely heavily on Tita and Hamilton (1992).
4. The remaining businesses have not hired an employee recently.
5. This section is adapted from Appold, Le, Nguyen, and Kasarda (1995).
6. The results reported in this section rely heavily on McLoughlin and Shimanuki (1993) and Lewis (1993).
7. Our interviewees already had a high level of commitment to the venture. We wonder about what the effectiveness of such organizations would be if they could intervene earlier in the gestational process.

## REFERENCES

Appold, Stephen J., Le Ngoc Hung, Nguyen Quy Than, and John D. Kasarda. 1995. Family and friends in small-scale businesses: An exploratory study of industrial districts in Vietnam. Paper presented at the Southern Sociological Society Meetings, April 6–8, Atlanta.

Birch, David. (1979). *The job generation process*. Cambridge: MIT Program on Neighborhood and Regional Change.

Easterlin, R. A. (1976). The conflict between aspirations and resources. *Population and Development Review, 2*, 417–426.

Galbraith, John. (1972). *The new industrial state*. New York: Houghton Mifflin.

Granovetter, Mark. (1985). Economic action and the problem of embeddedness. *American Journal of Sociology, 91*, 481–510.

Hart, Keith. (1982). *The political economy of West African agriculture*. New York: Cambridge University Press.

Kasarda, John D. 1993. Cities as places where people live and work: Urban change and neighborhood distress. In Henry G. Cisneros (ed.), *Interwoven destinies: Cities and the nation*, 81–124.

Kasarda, John D. (1993). Inner-city poverty and economic access. Chapter 4 in Jack Sommer and Donald A. Hicks (eds.), *Rediscovering urban America: Perspectives on the 1980s*. Washington: Department of Housing and Urban Development.

Kasarda, John D. (1995). Industrial restructuring and changing job locations. In Reynolds Farley (ed.), *State of the Union: America in the 1990s*, 215–267. New York: Russell Sage Foundation.

Keyfitz, Nathan. (1973). *Applied mathematical demography.* New York: John Wiley and Sons.

Lewis, Myron. (1993). Assets, liabilities and success: An investigation of black and white entrepreneurial ventures. Heinz School, Manuscript.

March, James G., & Johan P. Olsen. (1976). *Ambiguity and choice in organizations.* Bergen: Universitetforlaget.

McLoughlin, Kathleen, & Suzanne Shimanuki. (1993). Determinants of entrepreneurial success amongst small business owners and nascent entrepreneurs in Pittsburgh by race. Heinz School, Manuscript.

Olson, Mancur. (1982). *The rise and decline of nations: Economic growth, stagflation and social rigidities.* New Haven: Yale University Press.

Piore, Michael J., & Charles F. Sabel. (1984). *The second industrial divide: Possibilities for prosperity.* New York: Basic Books.

Powell, Walter W. (1990). Neither market nor hierarchy: Network forms of organization. *Research in Organizational Behavior, 12,* 295–336.

Ricketts, Erol and Isabel Sawhill. (1988). Defining and measuring the underclass. *Journal of Policy Analysis and Management* 7:316–325.

Selznick, Philip. (1957). *Leadership in administration: A sociological interpretation.* Evanston, IL.: Row, Peterson.

Stack, Carol B. 1974. *All our kin: Strategies for survival in a black community.* New York: Harper and Row.

Tita, George E., & Eric Hamilton. (1992). The benefits of small business: A case study of Pittsburgh-area neighborhoods. Heinz School Working Paper, presented at the 1992 American Sociological Association meetings, Pittsburgh.

United Nations. (1994). *World demographic estimates and projections, 1950–2025.* (ST/ESA/SER.R/70). New York: United Nations.

# 5

# Fitting In: The Arab American Entrepreneur

*Samia El-Badry*

## BACKGROUND AND INTRODUCTION

Though Arab Americans are the least studied ethnic group in the United States, they receive considerable publicity associated with political and economic events that usually occur overseas. These may be of grave political and diplomatic importance, but they overshadow Arab Americans' financial and social impact in the United States. The majority of Arab Americans are U.S. citizens, much like other Americans, except younger, better educated, more affluent, and more likely to own businesses.

The Arab ancestry groups include Algerian, Egyptian, Libyan, Moroccan, Tunisian, North African, Bahraini, Iraqi, Jordanian, Transjordanian, Kuwaiti, Lebanese, Saudi Arabian, Syrian, Yemeni, Omani (including Muscan, Trucial states, Trucial Oman, Qatar, and Bedouin), Kurdish, Palestinian (including Palestine, Gaza Strip, Gazan, and the West Bank), South Yemen (including People's Republic of Yemen, Aden, and Aden Protectorate), and United Arab Emirates. Because U.S. Arabs come from so many different countries and have different religious and cultural backgrounds, there is no one Arab American community; common to all Arab immigrants, however, is the Arabic language. (See Figure 5-1.)

To examine this population, we have conducted a topographical study, first briefly describing the basic socioeconomic characteristics of all Arab Americans and then focusing on the demographic and socio-economic features of entrepreneurs.

To place these data in context, we also examined other American entrepreneur groups, comparing them with their Arab American counterparts. To ensure sufficiently large samples, entrepreneurship data were analyzed by U.S. regions rather than by state or metropolitan area.

## ALL ARAB AMERICANS

The study data are derived from the 1 percent Public Use Microdata Samples (PUMS) of the 1990 United States Census. Our sample did not allow us to break down the total Arab American population into country of origin.

The 1990 Census found 870,000 Americans who list Arab as one of their top two ancestries. This census definition is inconsistent, however, and not necessarily reliable. Before 1920, census records lumped Arabs together with Turks, Armenians, and other non–Arabic-speaking people. Moreover, until recently, non-Syrian Asian Arabs were counted as "other Asians," and others were categorized as "other Africans." Palestinians, the main postwar group, were counted as refugees, Israelis, or nationals of their last country of residence. If the census undercount were adjusted and if Arab Americans filled out census forms, their numbers might be as large as 3 million.

Census data show that 82 percent of Arab Americans are U.S. citizens, with 63 percent born in the United States. Fifty-four percent of Arab Americans are men, compared with 49 percent of the total U.S. population. This is partly because men of all nationalities typically immigrate before women do.

- Algeria
- Egypt
- Iraq
- Jordan
- Kuwait
- Lebanon
- Libya
- Morocco
- Oman
- Palestine
- Qatar
- Saudi Arabia
- Syria
- TransJordan
- Tunisia
- UAE
- Yemen
- North Yemen
- South Yemen

**Figure 5-1** Reported countries of origin.

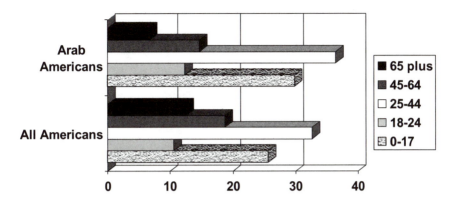

**Figure 5-2**  Arab Americans by age.

The Arab American population as a whole is quite young; again, probably because younger people are more likely to immigrate. Many Arab Americans are in their childbearing years, or are native-born children or teenagers (Figure 5-2). In general, Arab-Americans are better educated than the average American (Figure 5-3). More of them attend college, and they earn master's or advanced degrees at twice the average rate. Because they tend to be well educated and of working age, their workforce rates are high. Eighty percent of Arab Americans age 16 and older were employed in 1990, compared with 60 percent of all Americans. In addition, only 1.7 percent of Arab American entrepreneurs receive public assistance, compared with 7 percent of non–Arab American entrepreneurs.

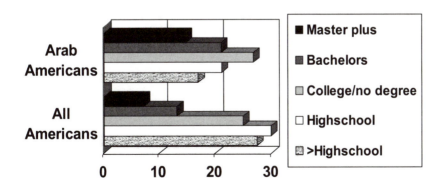

**Figure 5-3**  Education for Arab Americans.

In a volatile economy, with many large companies laying off people, Arab Americans—who often are entrepreneurs or self-employed (14 percent versus 8 percent)—may be less vulnerable to company layoffs.

## ARAB AMERICAN ENTREPRENEURS

### Description of Sample

The sample includes all entrepreneurs 16 years of age or older. The census defines entrepreneurs as people who report themselves to be "self-employed" in their "own incorporated" or "non-incorporated business," "professional practice," or "farm." The 1990 census data show 73,829 Arab American and 13,408,206 non–Arab American entrepreneurs. Sixty-four percent of self-employed Arab Americans own incorporated businesses, compared with only 27 percent of other entrepreneurs (Figure 5-4).

### Methodology and Operational Definitions

We make a distinction in our analysis between Arab American and non–Arab American entrepreneurs. Arab Americans claim membership in Arab ethnic groups or have an Arab ancestry. Ancestry refers to a person's ethnic origin or descent, roots, heritage; to his or her place of birth or that of his or her parents or ancestors before arrival in the United States. Respondents reported one or two ancestry groups; when either group was listed as Arab, that person was coded as an Arab American.

### Citizenship and Immigration

Most Arab American entrepreneurs are U.S. citizens, either by birth (47.0 percent) or naturalization (36.3 percent). Arab migration to the United States dates to the late nineteenth and early twentieth centuries. Early migrants typically were Syrian or Lebanese merchants pursuing

- Reported Arab American
    Self-Employed
        73,829 (14%)
- Reported Non–Arab American
    Self-Employed
        13,408,206 (8%)

**Figure 5-4**  PUMS 1 percent sample.

economic interests (Kayal, 1983). Legal and political restrictions, the Depression, and World War II curbed Arab migration between 1925 and 1948 (Naff, 1985) (Figures 5-5 and 5-6).

Arabs immigrating since World War II have tended to be from capitalist classes—landed gentry and influential urban-based families—replaced by new leadership in their various home countries. Many postwar immigrants were Palestinians displaced when Israel was established in 1948. Others were Egyptians whose land was appropriated by the Nasser regime, Syrians overthrown by revolutionaries, and Iraqi royalists fleeing the Republican regime. They often had attended Western or westernized schools, spoke fluent English, and identified themselves as members of a professional class (Elkholy, 1966; Haddad, 1985; El-Badry, 1987, 1994).

Immigration from the Middle East increased dramatically in the late 1960s (Reimers, 1992; El-Badry, 1985, 1987). By 1990, more than 75 percent of foreign-born Arab Americans in the United States had immigrated after 1964, compared with 52 percent of the total U.S. foreign-born population. The largest share (44 percent) of these arrived between 1975 and 1980, compared with 24 percent of all other foreign-born persons. Many Arabs immigrated during this period because of constant turmoil in the Middle East: The 1967 war, the civil war in Lebanon, the Kurd-Iraqi War of the 1960s, and the violence in Iraq and Iran after

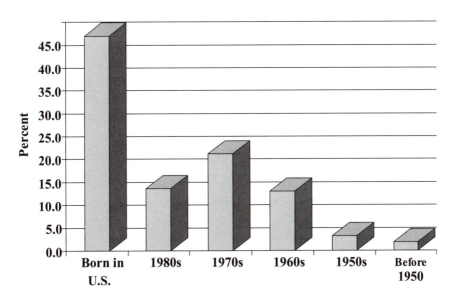

**Figure 5-5** Immigration of Arab American entrepreneurs (as of 1990).

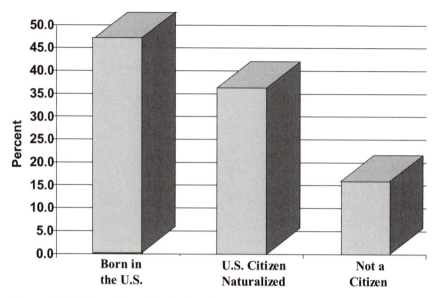

**Figure 5-6**  Citizenship of Arab American entrepreneurs.

1978 all were trigger points. These coincided with the Immigration Act of 1965, which ended the quota system favoring immigrants from Europe. Many in this migration flow were Moslem, with even higher educations and incomes than their predecessors. This group's socioeconomic attainment pattern also greatly surpassed that of other immigrant groups, and the American population as a whole (El-Badry, 1985, 1989, 1994; Zogby, 1991 [cited in Reimers, 1992]).

### Religion

Before 1960, as many as 90 percent of Arab immigrants were Christians, but recent immigrants are mostly Moslem. There were several prominent sects within the Christian population: Maronite Christians from Lebanon, Coptic Christians from Egypt, and Chaldeans from Iraq (Reimers, 1992, p. 119).

The new immigrants settled in or near established Arab American communities. The Detroit metropolitan region, especially Dearborn, attracted a steady stream of Arab immigrants after 1965 and may have the largest number of recent Arab immigrants. Most came from a variety of occupational backgrounds and found work in the auto industry or in other working-class employment, although not all Detroit Arabs sought such employment.

Christian Chaldeans, an Iraqi minority in a Moslem country, were among the first to take advantage of the 1965 Immigration Act. About

1,000 lived in Detroit before passage of the act. After 1965 their numbers increased, until by 1974 they accounted for approximately one seventh of Detroit's estimated 70,000 Middle Easterners. They opened grocery stores and established a reputation in that business similar to that of Korean greengrocers. By 1972 the Chaldeans were running about 278 stores in Detroit and assisting others in the United States. Another large Arab settlement in New York City, in Brooklyn, had attracted earlier Lebanese and Syrian migrations. Los Angeles lured many Coptic Christians from Egypt, part of the Egyptian immigrant wave after the 1967 Six-Day War (Reimers, 1992, p. 120).

### Where Do They Live?

Arab Americans, like many minority groups, are geographically concentrated. Over two thirds live in 10 states; one third in California, New York, and Michigan. They are also more likely than other Americans to live in metropolitan areas. Thirty-six percent of Arab Americans are found in 10 cities, primarily Detroit, New York, or Los Angeles.

Entrepreneurs in the United States, whether or not they are Arab American, most often live in the Pacific, South Atlantic, East North Central, or Mid-Atlantic regions. Entrepreneurs, regardless of ancestry, are least likely to live in the East South Central region. The regional distribution of Arab American entrepreneurs is similar to that of non–Arab American entrepreneurs (Figure 5-7).

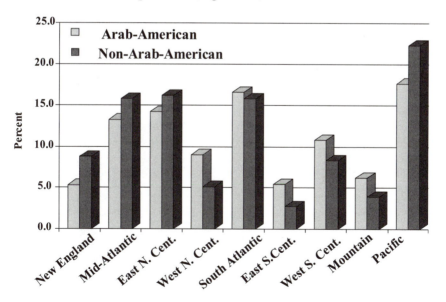

**Figure 5-7**  Where are the entrepreneurs?

## Age, Gender, and Marital Status

Both groups of entrepreneurs tend to be between the ages of 25 and 44, and their age distributions are similar, with Arab Americans generally younger than their non–Arab American counterparts in most age categories, which may reflect the large proportion of self-employed Arab workers. Studies of other ethnic groups show that businesses tend to be established by newer immigrants, and Arab immigrants are, for the most part, young (Figure 5-8).

Entrepreneurship in the United States is male-dominated. Regardless of ancestry, 67.4 percent of entrepreneurs are male, 32.6 percent female. The ratio of male to female entrepreneurs is slightly larger for Arab American than for non–Arab American entrepreneurs. Entrepreneurs of all ancestries in the United States are likely to be married (74.3 percent for non–Arab Americans and 73.6 percent for Arab Americans). It is interesting to note, however, that close to 16 percent of Arab American entrepreneurs are never-married singles (compared to 11.7 percent for non–Arab Americans).

## Education

In general, Arab Americans are better educated than the average American. A greater percentage attends college, and those who earn master's degrees or higher do so at twice the national average. Whereas most entrepreneurs in the United States have only a high school di-

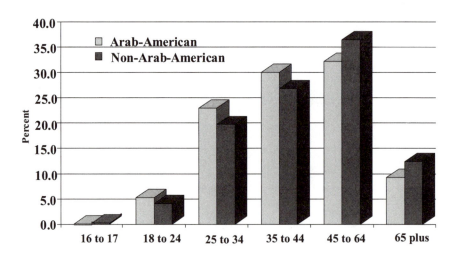

**Figure 5-8**  How old are entrepreneurs?

ploma or some college experience, Arab American entrepreneurs are more likely to attend college and have college and postgraduate degrees. These patterns remain the same when broken down by gender. Male entrepreneurs are more likely than females to have postgraduate degrees, however, and women entrepreneurs are more likely to have only a high school diploma or some college experience.

### Occupations

*Distribution.* The occupational distribution between Arab American entrepreneurs and their non-Arab counterparts is quite striking. The top five occupational categories for both groups are executive/administrative/managerial, professional specialty, sales, services (not personal domestic or protective), and precision repair. Sales comprises the largest percentage of both Arab American and non–Arab American entrepreneurs, although the rate of Arab Americans in sales (33.4 percent) is almost double that of non-Arabs (17.9 percent). Moreover, non–Arab American entrepreneurs are much more evenly distributed across other occupations such as farming, fishing, or forestry (Figure 5-9).

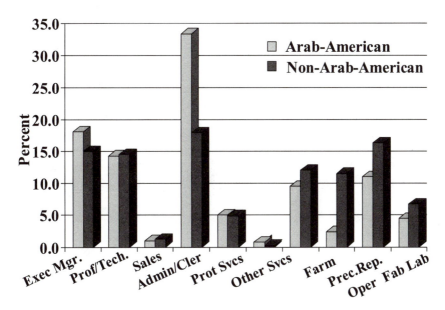

**Figure 5-9**  Occupation of entrepreneurs.

The top four industries attracting Arab and non–Arab American entrepreneurs are retail trade, construction, finance/insurance/real estate, and professional industries. Arab American entrepreneurs overwhelmingly work in retail trade (34.6 percent), followed by the professional industries (17.1 percent), whereas few are miners (0 percent) or public administrators (0 percent), or are engaged in entertainment/recreation (1.5 percent) or agriculture/forestry/fishing (2.6 percent). Non–Arab American entrepreneurs are more evenly distributed across industries, but most are also in the professions (19.5 percent) and retail trade (16 percent); the fewest work in entertainment/recreation (1.8 percent) and transport/commerce/utilities (3.7 percent) (Figure 5-10 and Figure 5-11).

*Region and Occupation.* This occupational and industrial distribution varies according to region. Arab American entrepreneurs in executive/managerial occupations concentrate in the Mid-Atlantic, Pacific, or South Atlantic regions (Figure 5-12), whereas those in the professions gravitate toward the East North Central and, less so, the Mountain regions (Figure 5-13). Arab Americans who are in sales favor the Pacific over other regions (Figure 5-14), whereas those in service occupations favor the East North Central and South Atlantic (Figure 5-15); and in

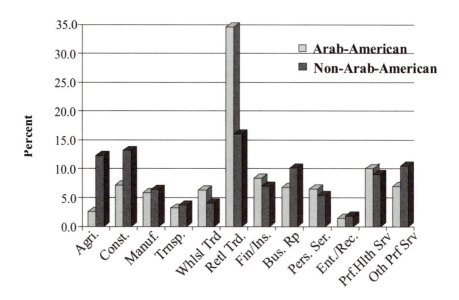

**Figure 5-10** Industries of entrepreneurs.

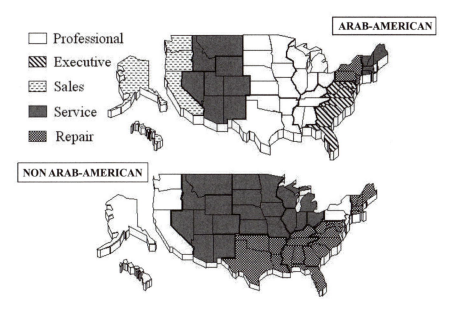

**Figure 5-11** Top regions by job type.

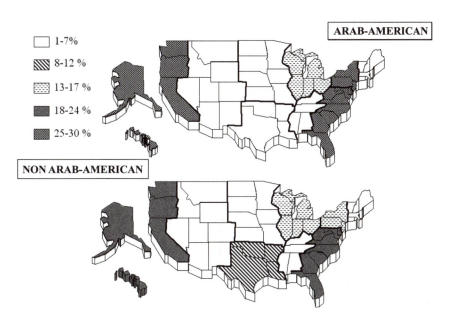

**Figure 5-12** Executive jobs.

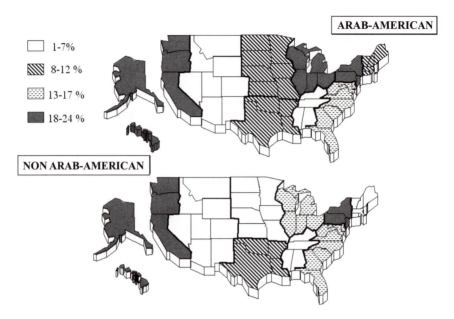

**Figure 5-13**  Professional jobs.

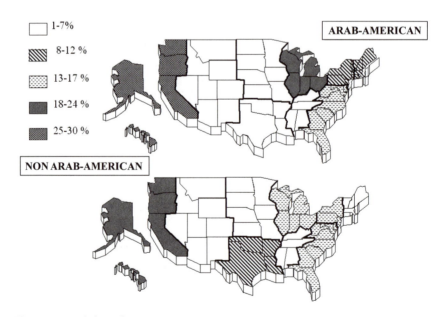

**Figure 5-14**  Sales jobs.

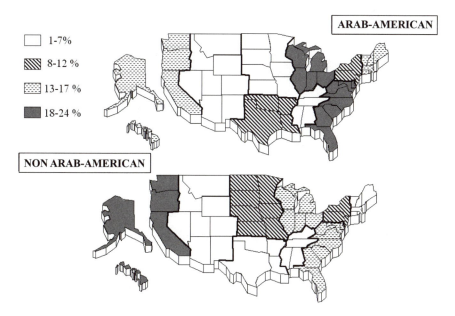

**Figure 5-15**  Service jobs.

precision repair, the Pacific and Mid-Atlantic regions are favored (refer to Figure 5-11). By comparison, non–Arab American entrepreneurs in executive/managerial occupations and sales typically live in the Pacific and South Atlantic (Figure 5-12), whereas those in professional occupations are most likely to be found in the Pacific and Mid-Atlantic regions (Figure 5-18), and those in retail trade tend to live in the South Atlantic and Pacific, and are least likely to live in the East South Central and New England regions (Figure 5-14).

The industries among the top four for Arab American entrepreneurs are distributed regionally as follows: Arab Americans in construction overwhelmingly locate in the Pacific, South Atlantic, and Mid-Atlantic regions, with the greatest concentration of non-Arabs in construction in the South Atlantic and Pacific, and a few in the Mountain region. The finance/insurance/real estate category is the only industrial arena where both groups, with similar proportions of workers, are most likely to live in the Pacific or South Atlantic regions and least likely in East South Central.

Among those industries not ranking in the top four for non–Arab American entrepreneurs, those in professional services are concentrated in the Pacific and Mid-Atlantic, with few in the Mountain and East South Central regions, but Arab American entrepreneurs in this industry reside primarily in the Pacific region and less often in the East

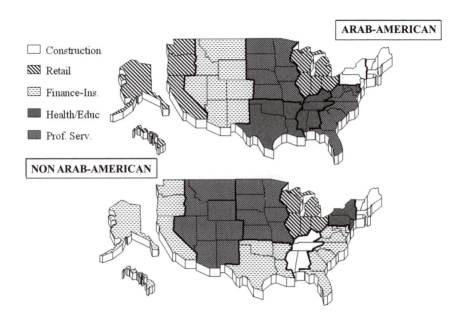

**Figure 5-16** Industry.

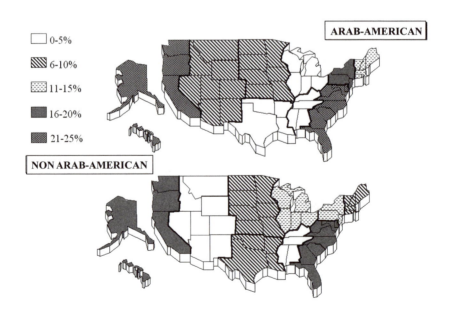

**Figure 5-17** Construction.

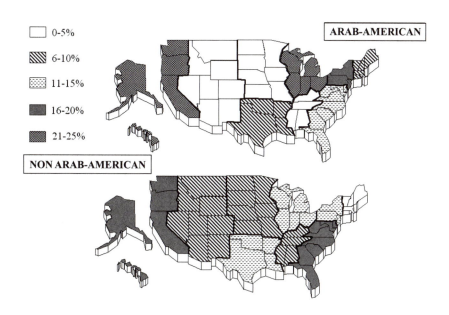

**Figure 5-18**  Retail trade.

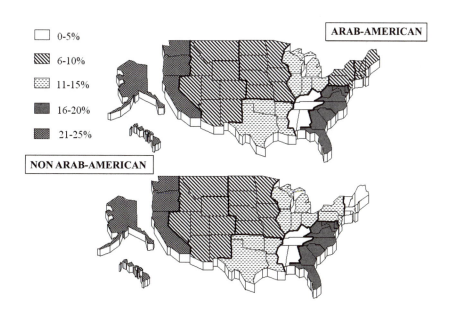

**Figure 5-19**  Finance, insurance, real estate.

South Central and New England (Figure 5-20). Similarly, most non–Arab American entrepreneurs in health and education can be found in the Pacific and Mid-Atlantic, with the fewest in the Mountain and East South Central regions, whereas Arab American entrepreneurs in these industries are concentrated in New England, the South Atlantic, and Mid-Atlantic (Figure 5-21).

*Education and Occupation.* The relationship between education and occupation is not surprising. Entrepreneurs in professional occupations often have postgraduate degrees. Close to 80 percent of Arab American entrepreneurial professionals 25 years of age and older have higher degrees (Figure 5-22), compared to nearly 55 percent of their non-Arab counterparts (Figure 5-23). Entrepreneurs of every ancestry in executive, precision repair, and sales occupations commonly have some college experience, whereas most in service occupations have not gone beyond high school.

Though the groups share similar patterns in education and industrial distribution, the variance between them is quite striking. For example, entrepreneurs in the professional health industries will more likely have postgraduate degrees, whereas those in finance/insurance/real estate usually have some college experience. But the proportion of Arab Americans holding degrees in both fields is at least 20 percent higher.

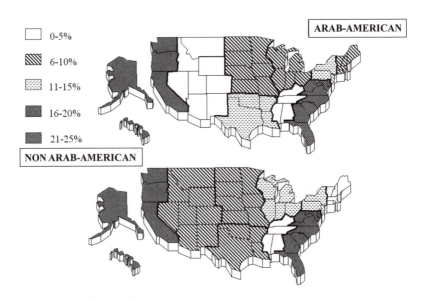

**Figure 5-20**  Professional services.

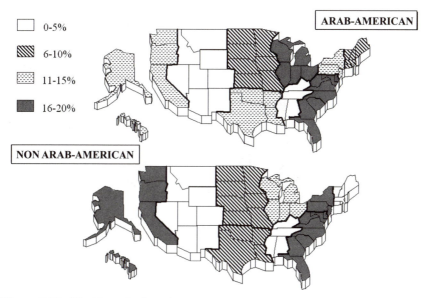

Figure 5-21  Health and education.

## Income

As occupation and industry vary, so does income. The average Arab American entrepreneur may have a higher personal and household income than a non–Arab American counterpart in most regions of the United States. Median household income is strikingly higher for Arab

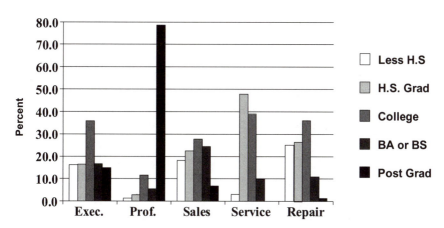

Figure 5-22  Education and occupation for Arab American entrepreneurs age 25 years and older.

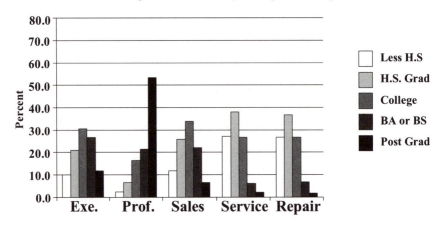

**Figure 5-23** Education and occupation for non–Arab American entrepreneurs age 25 years and older.

Americans in the Pacific, Northeast, New England, and South Atlantic regions, exceeding $50,000 per annum. Arab Americans in the Mountain region have higher household, but lower personal, incomes. In the Pacific region incomes of the two groups are similar, with non–Arab American entrepreneurs having lower household but slightly higher personal incomes. (See Figure 5-24.)

*Male/Female.* When median personal income is broken down by gender, many of the previously noted patterns are repeated. Arab American female and male entrepreneurs earn more than their non–Arab American counterparts in New England, West North Central, South Atlantic, and East South Central. Non–Arab American male and female entrepreneurs tend to have higher personal incomes in the Mountain region. All women, regardless of ancestry, earn very little, but Arab American female entrepreneurs typically earn more than non–Arab American females in all regions except West South Central and Mountain. Males of all ancestries typically earn more than females in every region. (See Figure 5-25 and Figure 5-26.)

## CONCLUSION

Arab Americans are numerous, affluent, and often misunderstood. Like many other ethnic or minority groups, they suffer from stereotyping and negative press. Yet they represent significant and distinct niche

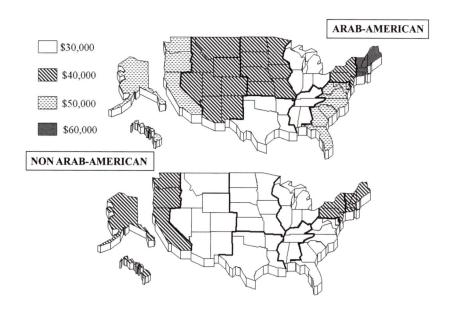

**Figure 5-24** Median household income.

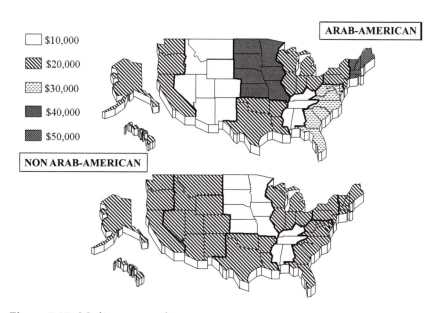

**Figure 5-25** Median personal income, men.

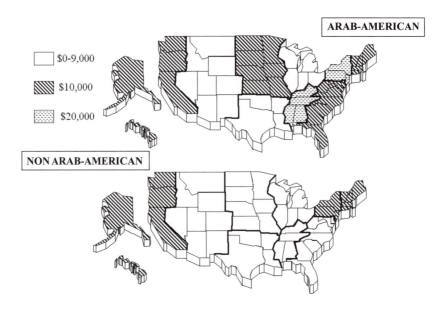

**Figure 5-26** Median personal income, women.

markets. Arab American entrepreneurship is as old as America, and has had to endure the traditional problems of inadequate capital, federal restrictions, and the failure of policy makers and educators to understand its importance in the community. A recent census estimates the receipts of Arab American entrepreneurs to be 1 percent of the U.S. total. This figure, however, is debated by many who say that the census is only looking at small companies. As a famous sociologist once said, "What is most important, however, is not the type or size of enterprise but the fact that business activity is again moving to the center" (Butler 1966, p. 10).

A glance through the advertising pages of Arab American publications reveals a mix of specialized and mainstream products and services, such as medical, legal, and educational services; literary works; foods; computer and electronic products. Like any other immigrant group, Arab Americans want to enjoy America's riches while preserving the important parts of their native culture. This is a beginning look at entrepreneurship from a diversity perspective, and diversity in entrepreneurship is a key foundation of American diversity.

## REFERENCES

Butler, John Sibley. 1996, winter. Entrepreneurship and the advantages of the inner city: How to augment the Porter Thesis. *Review of Black Political Economy* 24, Nos. 2–3, pp. 39–49.

El-Badry, Samia. 1985, October. *Variations in foreign labor supply: 15 developing countries, Latin America and the Middle East, 1975.* Presented at the Southern Regional Demographic Group Meeting, Austin, TX.

El-Badry, Samia. 1987. *Fitting in: An analysis of socio-economic attainment patterns of foreign-born Arab Americans and other nationalities in the United States, 1980.* Ph.D. Dissertation, The University of Texas at Austin.

El-Badry, Samia. 1989. *Gender and occupational attainment in the United States, 1980.* Tallahassee: Florida State University.

El-Badry, Samia. 1994. The Arab American market. *American Demographics.*

Elkholy, Abda A. 1966. Arab Moslems in the United States. New Haven, CT: College and University Press.

Haddad, Yvonne, Y. 1985. Arab Muslims and Islamic institutions in America: Adaptation and reform, in *Arabs in the New World.* Abraham and Abraham (eds.). Detroit: Center for Urban Studies, Wayne State University.

Kayal, P.M. 1983. Arab Christians in the United States, in *Arabs in the New World,* Abraham and Abraham (eds.) Detroit: Center for Urban Studies, Wayne State University.

Naff, A. 1985. *Becoming American, the early Arab immigrant experience.* Carbondale: Southern Illinois University Press.

Reimers, David M. 1992. *Still the golden door: The third world comes to America* (2nd ed.). New York: Columbia University Press.

United States Census Bureau. 1990. Census of the population, general social and economic characteristics, Part 1, U.S. summary, PC90, microdata samples (PUMS).

United States Census Bureau. 1990. Census of the population, socio economic characteristics of U.S. foreign born population, #CB84, Unpublished report.

Zogby, John. 1991. *Arab Americans today: A demographic profile of Arab Americans.* Washington: Arab American Institute.

# 6

# The Minority Community as a Natural Business Incubator

*Patricia Gene Greene and John Sibley Butler*

This study examines two methods of business implementation, the formal business incubator and a minority business community. A general picture of the business incubator is gathered from a review of business literature and compared to the initial results of a case study of the Ismaili Pakistani community in a midsize southwestern city. Major differences between the two implementation means are the motivations prompting the business initiations and some variety in services offered. Findings reinforce the necessity of understanding the institutional underpinnings of various types of business creation processes, as well as the continued importance of characteristics of the business founder. (*J. Busn. Res., 36* [1996], 51–58)

A collectivist perspective is used in order to compare two institutional means of implementing business enterprises—the formal business incubator, a facility designed to promote enterprise creation and success and the natural incubator, which has operated in minority communities within societies. Whereas the former is the subject matter of a growing body of research in the business literature, the latter is in need of more attention to the specificity of the process of the creation of economic organizations. We use a framework drawn from the middleman minority theory and institutional theory to show that minority communities develop the same kinds of support systems for their enterprises that are found in formal business incubators. We focus our study on a minority community defined by both religion and ethnicity, Ismaili Pakistani.

Although much of the research in entrepreneurship concerns characteristics of the founder, Gartner states that the more helpful emphasis should be on the process of business creation (Gartner, 1989). In this study, we suggest that in certain instances, as with group membership, the founder characteristics are inextricably bound with the creation process itself. We analyze this relationship by first discussing the concept of a business incubator as an institution that provides nourishment for new businesses. We then review middleman minority theory and describe the history of Ismaili Muslims from an institutional perspective. We conclude with an analysis of data from a case study of the enterprise creation process within a specific minority business community, the Ismaili Pakistani, in a midsized southwestern city.

## FORMAL BUSINESS INCUBATORS

One important consideration of the study of entrepreneurship is the means of implementing enterprises (Johannisson and Nowicki, 1992). The creative processes themselves are important to understand because of their potential contribution to the success or failure of an enterprise. The purpose of a business incubator is to provide some combination of necessary resources in order to nurture a new and/or growing business to some level of maturity.

Formal business incubators are designed to provide a nurturing environment, furnishing essential space, business assistance and support services that are crucial to the survival of the small business, especially during the initial stages of development (Allen and McCluskey, 1990). Whereas the origin of formal business incubators is rather ambiguous, the number of formal incubators in operation increased fourfold between 1980 and 1989 to reach a total of approximately 400 U.S. incubators (Rice and Abetti, 1992; NBIA, 1990; Allen and McCluskey, 1990).

The principal motivations underlying the formation of a formal business incubator are: (1) economic development efforts intended to stimulate the economy, create jobs, and diversify the local economic base; (2) the commercialization of research and the transfer of technology into new and different commercial applications; and (3) the enhancement of small business success (NBIA, 1990; Smilor and Gill,

1986). The incubators themselves vary not only by motivation of the sponsor, but also by such characteristics as the existence of plant or dedicated space, plant size, number and type of services provided, and number of tenants.

The heterogeneity of incubator forms is best conceptually organized by the use of a continuum or spectrum (Gatewood, Ogden, and Hoy, 1986). Allen and McCluskey (1990) employ the continuum concept with anchors of for-profit property development incubators and for-profit seed capital incubators. The former are concerned with the development of the incubator property per se, the latter with the development of profitable enterprises. Between the anchors lie points concerned with non-profit development corporation incubators and academic incubators. The non-profit organization is designed to encourage job creation and may be sponsored by the community or other governmental organization. The academic incubator is generally a collaborative effort between the academic institution and private industry. A hybrid incubator is a combination of any of the types given, e.g., a public-private partnership or a corporate incubator (Allen and McClusky, 1990).

Table 6-1 offers a summary of types of services available over a wide variety of incubators. The shared office services range between the rental of only physical space to more liberal provisions of office prod-

**TABLE 6-1   Examples of Incubator Services by Category**

| Shared Office | Management/Technical | Financing |
|---|---|---|
| Conference Room | Business plans | External aided |
| Photocopying | Marketing | Internally provided |
| Receptionist coverage | Accounting | Tenant revolving loan |
| Word processing/typist | Government grants and loans | Tenant seed capital |
| Security | Legal services | |
| Computer | Patent assistance | |
| Fax machine | Computer training | |
| Office equipment/furniture | International trade | |
| Business library | Government procurement | |
| Audio/visual equipment | Equity and debt financing | |
| Extra storage | Access to sophisticated | |
| Bookkeeping | computer processing | |
| Group health insurance | Access to other resources | |
| | outside the incubator | |
| | Research and development | |
| | Business taxes | |

*Source:* National Business Incubation Association, *The State of the Business Incubation Industry*, 1990, pp. 11–13.

ucts and services. The management and technical support also spans a wide variety of offerings, from the very general, e.g. basic accounting advice, to the very specific, e.g. computer processing and international trade. The range regarding the availability of financing goes from the usual case of no internal funds but help in searching for external funds to the exceptional case of the incubator organization providing tenant seed capital.

The incubator is designed to be the site of the initial stages of enterprise development, the birth and/or early growth stage of the tenant enterprise. The fledgling enterprise applies or is invited to apply for admission. If the enterprise meets the established criteria for admission, it establishes residency in the facility and begins to use whatever services are offered. Hopefully, the enterprise will thrive, and upon reaching some predetermined threshold, e.g., size, sales, or time, graduates from the incubator and physically moves into the outer environment.

Spitzer and Ford (1989) offer an interesting critique of incubator research, claiming that the majority of the research is done from the perspective of the incubator, rather than that of the tenants. These authors claim that changing perspective changes the services considered important. Respondents representing the incubator organization considered most important the provision of physical goods. However, respondents representing the tenant enterprises considered the atmosphere and moral support the most important provision. Along those lines, Rice and Abetti (1992) found the incubator manager as the most important intervention tool for tenant success. The role of the incubator manager is described by Campbell (1989) as that of "impresario" or "great man". This role, like every other aspect of incubators, varies greatly between incubators, but includes a selection of responsibilities such as networking, counseling, providing emotional support, and providing expertise in diverse areas as marketing, business operations, finance, and accounting (Rice and Abetti, 1992; Smilor and Gill, 1986).

Campbell (1989) describes the role of formal business incubators as "change agents" in economic development. Incubators address many marketplace failures, including problems of high information costs, low service levels, difficulties in obtaining business services, and a shortage of capital sources. However, Campbell questions the incubator participation levels of minorities as both enterprise owners and employees.

## THE NATURAL BUSINESS INCUBATOR

The literature on business incubators has overlooked the fact that throughout history people who were interested in starting enterprises have developed methods to provide for the capitalization and to encourage the success of enterprises. These methods, or what we call here, natural incubators, have been the subject of systematic research by scholars in fields such as anthropology and sociology.

In the United States, scholars of ethnic business enterprise have been developing a literature that looks at the economic behavior of immigrant groups. There are three related research frameworks that guide this work: middleman minority theory, enclave theory, and collective theory. Although there are overlaps among these theories, they have each produced a separate body of literature. More important, these theories each concentrate on the development of new ventures within minority communities.

Middleman theory draws its name from the fact that some minority groups have developed enterprises that are located within the "middle" of the economic system. This theory is organized around three primary elements. First, the minority group (often described as sojourners, although this element is used less often in contemporary research) faces discrimination from the majority group, especially with regard to economic opportunities in the primary sector of the labor market. Second, the members of the minority group tend to develop enterprises located in specific industrial sectors. Playing the middleman position means that they negotiate products between producer and consumer, owner and renter, elite and masses, and employer and employees (Bonacich, 1973). Therefore, they are likely to be found in enterprises such as labor contractor, rent collector, money lender, small retail trade, and broker. Most often these enterprises fall into the category of small business. And third, the group exhibits strong elements of solidarity among its members.

While the classic theoretical grounding for this type of study is based on Max Weber's *The Protestant Ethic and the Spirit of Capitalism* (1904) and Werner Sombart's reply (1914), *The Jews and Modern Capitalism*, the term middleman is generally attributed to Hubert Blalock's work *Toward a Theory of Minority Group Relations* (1967). Bonacich and Modell employ this theory in their *The Economic Basis of Ethnic Solidarity* (1980), a study of Japanese-Americans, primarily located in the California area. This work spans three generations to study economic behavior through the creation of organizations. This work joins Bonacich's other work in setting middleman minority theory into the contemporary labor market.

Many other studies have examined the development of new ventures using the middleman minority theory, both historically and in more contemporary settings. Walter Zenner looked at Christians and Jews in Late Ottoman Syria (1987). Min (1988) studied Korean entrepreneurs in Atlanta, and Light (1980) examined the rapid increase in the number of Korean enterprises in California. Butler (1991) has utilized the framework to examine the increase in black firms both before and after the Civil War in the United States. Each of these works analyzes a certain minority population with regard to the group's entrepreneurial behavior.

Enclave theory is similar to middleman theory in that it looks at the rapid increase in the number of business enterprises. But in this case the enterprises are located in a geographically bounded community, thus the term *enclave*. Portes and Bach (1985) utilized this theory to examine the development of enterprises among Cubans in Miami. The number of enterprises grew so rapidly in this city that Gilder (1984) called the phenomenon "The Cuban Miracle."

Finally, collective theory stems largely from the work of Lovell-Troy (1980) and is seen as a response to "rugged individualism."

> The collectivist approach, with an emphasis on self-help institutions, stresses the cultural side in explaining the economic stability of ethnic groups and also brings to bear the idea that these institutions have more of an influence on the development of economic stability through business activity than through the process of assimilation. Unlike middleman theory, where hostility plays a major role in the interpretation of business success, collectivism concentrates on the "cultural baggage" of a group as the major explanatory variable. (Butler, 1991, p. 23)

Although the literature regarding ethnic entrepreneurship is strong on examining the increase in business enterprise, it rarely gives a distinct and systematic consideration to the mechanisms that create, nurture, and sustain enterprises. In addition, Aldrich and Waldinger (1990) stress the critical lack of comparative studies between ethnic and nonethnic enterprises, suggesting that viable enterprises look much the same regardless of the ethnicity of the owner. Indeed, these authors also suggest that researchers focusing on collective approaches to ethnic entrepreneurship may have overemphasized the contribution of ethnicity with regard to resource mobilization.

The study of networks is one avenue of research often used to approach the topic of resource mobilization among small business owners (Aldrich and Dubini, 1991; Aldrich and Zimmer, 1986; Johannisson and Nowicki, 1992; Birley, 1985). Birley (1985) found in her study of small business owners in Indiana that more owners used their informal networks (family, friends, and business contacts) for aid in the establishment of their enterprise, rather than a reliance on formal networks (banks, lawyers, the Small Business Administration, etc.). One possible explanation for the strength of many ethnic entrepreneurial groups studied is the establishment of a quasiformal network. This network is more structured and procedurally oriented than a strictly informal network of family and friends.

Examples of these quasiformal networks can be seen in the study of capitalization techniques. In a major research effort, Geertz (1962) surveyed and analyzed these creative methods of business capitalization, which represent the first stage of what we call the natural business incubator. Although these natural incubators vary in their methods, many share a common ground when it comes to the method of capital generation. This common ground is the building up on a joint capital pool, shared through some method of rotation. Because of this commonality, Geertz put them under the common term *rotating credit system*.

In addition to the importance of fund raising, research in this area has also included the importance of increasing confidence in the building of business institutions. In this way, the natural incubator has been a tremendous asset. Gunner Myrdal (1956) noted the following:

> The building up of a variety of institutions, serving the purpose of promoting individual savings, and organizing them and making them fruitful to the saver and to the community, should be given a high priority in every development plan. To be effective, the institutions have to be adapted to different individual needs and possibilities and must fit into the community patterns; they must aim at encouraging planned and "goal-directed" savings. Even if, at least in the beginning, the financial results would not constitute more than a trickle of new capital disposal, the effects in rationalizing attitudes and mobilizing ambitions might be crucially important. (Myrdal, 1956)

Joel Kotkin's book *Tribes* (1993) places the economic contribution of certain ethnic groups into clearer perspective. Kotkin's theme is the importance of ethnicity in the evolution of the global marketplace. He describes the entrepreneurial behavior of five "tribes": the Jews, the British, the Japanese, the Chinese, and the Indians. The Pakistanis are discussed as part of the Indian diaspora. The success of the collectivist approach to initiating and growing enterprises is emphasized. Kotkin quotes Rakesh Kaul, former senior executive with Beatrice Foods and Shaklee Corporation, as to the importance of the collective over the individualistic approach:

> In the West we have been living under the technocratic imperative. We have believed in the supremacy of the individual ego. We forget that there are things bigger than the individual—such as the family, the tribe, the company—and relationships which extend beyond the contractual to the charismatic. The Japanese, other Asians are not taking the Western contractual form of doing business. They have rejected it—and are changing it into something different. (Kotkin, 1993, p. 123)

It is Kaul's premise that Asian tribal values are rapidly overtaking those of the "formerly triumphant" West.

Kotkin (1993) specifically describes the strength of the Pakistani presence in the North American marketplace, particularly the ownership of hotels and motels. The Pakistani community in this study is part of such an ethnic network. This community falls under the jurisdiction of a Pakistani community in a larger neighboring city. In 1992, there were approximately 31,000 Parkistani immigrants in the United States. Given the determined approach to business ownership, the potential for value creation and enterprise growth is very large.

However, while Kotkin's discussion of the Indian diaspora is informative, it masks important within-group differences that could extend our understanding of the business creation process. Participation in trade and the importance of family are shown as being of critical importance to the members of the Indian diaspora in general. However, in this study we extend that analysis to consider how a collectivist approach based on institutional beliefs and values adds to the analysis of a group's economic behavior.

The idea of looking to social institutions for an increased understanding of economic behavior is anchored in institutional theory (Scott, 1987). The individual is seen as an integral part of a group (collective) acting under a shared system of beliefs and values. The actions of individuals make sense when placed into the context of the group (Dugger, 1990). Therefore, middleman minority theory informs us as to looking at the group, whereas institutional theory reinforces the need to examine the beliefs and values of the culture.

## SAMPLE AND METHOD

The development of middleman minority theory was originally prompted by an interest in groups bonded by religion. More contemporary studies using this framework focus on race and ethnicity. While the community in this study is generally recognized by its ethnic identity, Pakistani, it is the community members' shared religion that actually defines the nature of the collectivity. The members of this community are Ismaili, a branch of the Shiite Muslims.

Islamic societies are based upon religion, both individual and collective (Akbar, 1990). Therefore all economic, political, and social activities within that society are based on Islamic norms. Max Weber's critique of Islam concluded that Islam was not a path to rational capitalism; however, his conclusions have been criticized and questioned (Turner, 1974). Indeed, Akbar suggests that because Weber's analysis is predicated on a link between rationality and capitalism, the fact that the word "rational" appears in the Koran 50 times itself should raise questions (Akbar, 1990, p. 11).

The Ismailis are defined by their belief in the unbroken chain of leadership from the Prophet Mohammed to the present leader, the forty-sixth Aga Khan. The belief that the Aga Khan holds a position of both secular and spiritual authority sets the Ismailis apart from other Muslims, in many cases making them a "minority within a minority" (Thompson, 1975, p. 30). Historically, the Aga Khan has been instrumental in decreeing the importance of self-help social and economic community activities within Ismaili society. Thompson's description of both the history of the Ismailis and their community self-help activities while living in Uganda illustrates the emphasis placed for many generations upon providing economic and educational opportunities and assistance to members of the community (Thompson, 1975).

The Ismaili Pakistani community in this southwestern city began to develop in the late 1970s from a group of 45 to 50 university students. This community now consists of 368 individuals, making up 82 families who own as individuals a total of 97 businesses. Many of these businesses are small scale, such as convenience stores. However, what makes this particular community interesting and unique is the inclusion of several light manufacturing firms and a continued and explicit emphasis on innovation.

Although the consideration of economic behavior determined by religious beliefs is interesting in its own right, it also raises questions directly related to advancing our understanding of the business creation process. For instance, how does the collectivist process of creating businesses differ from the individualistic approach generally assumed in the United States? What consequences do these different types of approaches have for both the businesses and the founders? For our purposes these questions will be approached through the comparison of the formal business incubator and the minority community business activities that we will refer to as the natural business incubator.

This analysis is based on data gathered from a series of five semistructured interviews of the community business leader, a visit to an Ismaili-owned business, and archival research of newspaper articles featuring Ismaili community members. The interviews were approximately one hour in length and were loosely based on two previously administered surveys—one a survey of Korean entrepreneurs in Atlanta (Min, 1988) and the other, the annual survey of business incubators conducted by the National Business Incubator Association (NBIA, 1990).

## RESULTS

The business leader of this community business, whom we shall refer to as Mr. Hall, is the owner of a chain of seven photo labs, along with a firm which manufactures printed mylar balloons. He received the city 1990-1991 Chamber of Commerce Entrepreneur of the Year award and has been written up in the *Wall Street Journal*. Mr. Hall's philosophy is strongly based on his Ismaili Islamic religion, and his entrepreneurial behavior stems largely from his belief that if a person does not manage his own destiny, someone else will manage it for him. The concept of business failure is simply not accepted.

Mr. Hall emigrated to the United States in 1978 from his native Pakistan. He bought his first business, a photoduplication store, shortly after his arrival and has founded and acquired several businesses since that time. Mr. Hall is a sophisticated businessman who explicitly states a strategy of niche development through specialization. His photographic development enterprises were the first in the country to offer an electronic design center and to use digital photography, an adoption prompted by environmental concerns.

In 1988, Mr. Hall reported that he decided to also adopt a strategy of increased diversification. It was at that time that he decided to develop a mylar balloon manufacturing company. Mr. Hall negotiated for a site in the local Enterprise Zone and obtained a $250,000 government loan with no interest for 15 years. He then added $3.5 million of his own capital. Three years later this balloon company reports annual sales of $7 million.

Mr. Hall attributes his success to incorporating his religious ethics into his business practices. He also follows the motto of "innovate or evaporate." When asked why the immigrant group to which he belonged saw opportunity where so many Americans saw obstacles, Mr. Hall referred to the conditions in his homeland of Pakistan. He told of a friend who recently wanted to begin a business in Pakistan. Many months and millions of rupees later the friend had only managed to obtain the first required permit from the government.

Figure 6-1 illustrates the process of enterprise implementation within the context of a natural business incubator. The left side of the figure represents the deep integration of the community. The Ismaili Pakistani community studied uses an explicit collectivist approach to not only economic activity, but also many other aspects of their lives. The community maintains committees designed to handle health, education, social events, youth and sports, and religious education. Members of the community meet once a month to discuss business ethics; they also publish a magazine dedicated to the discussion of ethics.

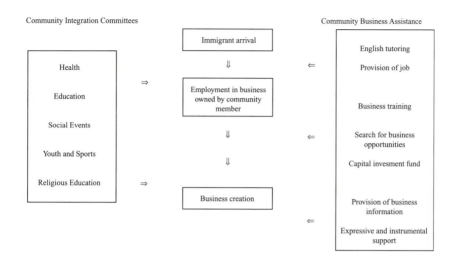

**Figure 6-1** The natural business incubator.

Group decisions are made on topics which impinge on the welfare of the community. For example, the community worked together to identify the best school district in the area. They next developed a plan to move community families into that area so that their children could receive the best education possible. The education committee developed a plan which specifically set an objective of moving 95 percent of their families into the designated school district by the 1993-94 school year. This percentage is exclusive of the children who are already in private schools. During 1992, 17 families moved to that district.

The integration of the community provides the background for our discussion of the pathway this community has developed to encourage the initiation of enterprises. When a new immigrant arrives from Pakistan or certain areas of India, that immigrant already knows the name of the person referred to as the coordinator. Once the immigrant contacts the coordinator of the community, the first step is for community members to tutor the new arrival in English. This tutoring continues throughout the creation process until the recent immigrant is able to conduct business in English. For the next step, the coordinator matches the recent immigrant to an economically stable member of the community. This sponsor provides the recent immigrant with a job, often in a convenience store owned by a community member, and the new arrival is expected to work and save for two years. The new worker's time in the convenience store is an apprenticeship. During this time, his language training continues and is supplemented with exposure to and training in business practices.

Toward the end of the apprenticeship, certain members of the community begin helping the immigrant to look for business opportunities. Sites are scouted and ideas are evaluated. The potential business owner is advised as to relevant aspects of the purchase decision by experienced business owners in the community. Once an opportunity is identified as feasible, capital additional to the immigrant's savings is made available. This Pakistani community controls an internally raised capital investment fund of $1.2 million.

Community help is available on an ongoing basis for business plans, support, and management consulting regarding such business considerations as inventory control, expansion, and security. Other types of specialized consulting are also available by drawing from the collective knowledge and experience of community members. This assistance from the natural business incubator is given in both expressive and instrumental forms. For instance, community business leaders advised convenience store owners of the necessity of increasing security after a rash of convenience store robberies in a neighboring city. Members of the community joined together to purchase video security cameras, and then traveled from convenience store to convenience store to install the surveillance equipment. The installation crew included other business owners, bankers, and community members of all types of occupations.

## CONCLUSION

Our theoretical comparison shows that the minority business community is performing the same nurturing function in the process of business formation as the formal business incubator and using many of the same tools. Table 6-2 provides a summary of characteristics of the incubator types. Both incubators can be seen as institutions with a common desired outcome, the creation of new businesses. The major differences in service offerings are the lack of a dedicated physical plant and administrative support services in the natural incubator. The businesses initiated by the natural business incubator are not based in a common facility and, in fact, are not necessarily located in a geographic area defined by minority group membership, but instead location of the businesses is based on market considerations. However, the Ismaili community meeting site is used for business meetings and counseling.

The types of management and technical consulting services vary in the formal incubator according to the individual facility; the consulting services in the natural incubator are more generally available as needed by the business owner. Financing sources are also different in that the

**TABLE 6-2   Comparison of Incubator Types**

| Formal Business Incubator | Shared Characteristics | Natural Business Incubator |
|---|---|---|
| | Desired outcome: creation of new business | |
| Physical plant | | Community meeting site |
| Motivation varies by sponsorship type | | Motivated by institutional beliefs |
| | Importance of manager/ coordinator | |
| Services vary by type of incubator | | Services vary by need of business owner |
| | Access to consulting | |
| External funding sources | | Internal funding sources |
| Services limited to business arena | | Services provided for all life arenas |
| Finite sponsorship | | Indefinite sponsorship |

formal business incubator is more involved in locating external funds, whereas the natural business incubator has a significant fund of internal capital available for the creation of businesses.

There are, however, three primary differences that relate to the institutional nature of these incubators. First, the motivation driving the activities of a formal business incubator varies by sponsorship, but overall the concern is with the work arena. Businesses are initiated and grown and jobs are created, but despite the legendary long hours required in the business creation process, the beliefs, values, and activities of the individuals involved are concentrated on economic behavior. At a point in time determined by business activity, the relationship between the incubator and the tenant businesses will come to an end.

In comparison, the motivation behind the natural business incubator comes from the underlying religious beliefs institutionalized in their community. The positive relationship between creating businesses and community welfare is a part of Ismaili life that goes beyond the economic to include the social life as well. Assisting a new arrival to the community in starting a business is contributing to the overall good of the community. Therefore, both the intensity and the duration of the business assistance goes beyond that feasible for providers in a formal business incubator.

This study uses a background of existing theory, middleman minority theory in particular, to show the relevance of examining the relationship between minority group membership and economic behavior. This type of research reinforces the importance of examining what the individual brings to the creation process—in this case, a group membership with an institutionalized drive for business creation. This collective approach does make the ethnic business process look different from that of the majority population.

While we illustrate differences in process, we also recognize a need for continued research in the differences in outcome, both for the business created and the individuals involved. A continued interest in the institutional elements of this process leads to questions concerning the replication and survival rates of organizational types. A question also exists concerning the relationship between business succession issues, community survival, and the assimilation of the next generation of Ismailis into Western society. In addition, the empirical question remains of the value of the economic contribution of this type of community. These types of questions have important implications for both research and application.

As the study of entrepreurship advances, it is important to build theory on data that reflect all forms of business startup processes. The study of alternative forms of the beginning of the business process adds to our understanding of the entire entrepreneurial process. And finally, it broadens the base of our knowledge about the relationship between the business founder, business enterprises, incubators, and business success in society.

## REFERENCES

Abkar, M.A.(1990). *Entrepreneurship and Indian Muslims* Manak Publications Pvt. Ltd., Delhi.

Aldrich, Howard E., and Dubini, Paola. (1991). Personal and extended networks are central to the entrepreneurial process. *Journal of Business Venturing, 6* (September), 305–314.

Aldrich, Howard E., & Catherine Zimmer. (1986). Entrepreneurship through social networks. In Donald Sexton & Raymond W. Smilor (eds.), *The art and science of entrepreneurship.* Cambridge, MA: Ballinger Publishing Company, 3–23.

Allen, David N., & R. McCluskey. (1990). Structure, policy, services, and performance in the business incubator industry. *Entrepreneurship Theory and Practice, 14* (Winter), 61–77.

Birley, Sue. (1985). The role of networks in the entrepreneurial process. *Journal of Business Venturing, 1* (Winter), 107–117.

Blalock, Hubert. (1973). *Toward a theory of minority group relations.* Hauppauge, NY: John Wiley and Sons.

Bonacich, Edna. (1980). A theory of middleman minorities. *American Sociological Review, 38* (October), 583–594.

Bonacich, Edna, and Modell, John. (1980). *The economic basis of ethnic solidarity: Small business in the Japanese-American community.* Berkeley: University of California Press.

Butler, John Sibley. (1991). *Entrepreneurship and self-help among black Americans.* Albany: State University of New York Press.

Campbell, Candace. (1989). Changing agents in the new economy: Business incubators and economic development. *Economic Development Review, 7* (Spring), 56–59.

Dugger, William. (1990). The new institutionalism: New but not institutionalist. *Journal of Economic Issues, 24* (June), 423–431.

Gartner, William. (1989). "Who is an entreprenuer?" is the wrong question. *Entrepreneurial Theory and Practice, 13* (Summer), 47–68.

Gatewood, Elizabeth, Lee Ogden, & Frank Hoy. (1986). Incubator centers evolution—The next five to ten years. *Frontiers of Entrepreneurship Research.* Wellesley, MA: Babson College, 526–544.

Geertz, Clifford. (1962). The rotating credit association: A "middle rung" in development. *Economic Development and Change, 10* (April), 241–263.

Gilder, George. (1984). *The spirit of enterprise.* New York: Simon & Schuster.

Johannisson, Bengt, & Krzysztof Nowicki. (1992). Using networks to organize support for entrepreneurs. Paper presented at the Babson College Entrepreneurship Conference, INSEAD, Fontainebleau, France.

Kotkin, Joel. (1993). *Tribes* .NewYork: Random House.

Light, Ivan. (1980). Asian enterprise in America: Chinese, Japanese, and Koreans in small business. In Scott Cummings (ed.), *Self-help in urban America: Patterns of minority economic development..* Port Washington, NY: Kennikat Press, 33–57.

Lovell-Troy, L. A. (1980). Clan structure and economic activity: The case of Greeks in small business entreprise. In Scott Cummings (ed.), *Self-help in urban America: Patterns of minority economic development..* Port Washington, NY: Kennikat Press, 58–85.

Merrifield, D. B. (1987). New business incubators. *Journal of Business Venturing, 2* (October), 277–284.

Min, Pyong Gap. (1980). *Ethnic business enterprise: Korean small business in Atlant.a.* New York: Center for Migration Studies.

Myrdal, Gunnar. (1956). *An international economy.* New York: Harper.

National Business Incubator Association. (1990). *State of the business incubator industry.* Athens, OH.

Portes, Alejandro, & Robert L. Bach. (1985). *Latin journey.* Los Angeles: University of California Press.

Rice, Markm, & Pier Abetti. (1992). Intervention mechanisms utilized by business incubators to influence the critical success factors of new ventures: An exploratory study. Paper presented at Babson College Entrepreneurship Conference, INSEAD, Fontainebleau, France.

Scott, W. Richard. (1987). The adolescence of industrial theory. *Administrative Science Quarterly, 32* (September), 493–511.

Small Business Administration. (1985). Small business incubator perspectives. *Incubator Times.* Office of Private Sector Initiatives. May.

Smilor, Raymond W. (1987). Managing the incubator system: Critical success factors to accelerate new company sevelopment. *IEEE Transactions on Engineering Management, 34* (August), 146–155.

Smilor, Raymond W., & M. D. Gill, Jr. (1986). *The new business incubator: Linking talent technology, capital, and know-how.* Lexington, MA: Lexington.

Sombart, Werner. *The Jews and modern capitalism,* trans. M. Epstein (1914). New York: E. P. Dutton.

Spitzer, Jr., D. M.,& R. H. Ford. (1989). Business incubators: Do we really understand them? (1989). *Frontiers of entrepreneurship research.* Wellesley, MA: Babson College, 436–446.

Thompson, Gardner. (1975). The Ismailis in Uganda. In Michael Twaddle (ed.), *Expulsion of a minority: Essays on Ugandan Asians*. London: Athlone Press, 30–52.

Turner, Bryan S. (1974).*Weber and Islam: A critical study*. London: Routledge and Kegan Paul.

Weber, Max. (1989). *The Protestant ethic and the spirit of capitalism*. London: Unwin [1904].

Zenner, Walter. (1987). Middleman minorities in the Syrian mosaic. *Sociological Perspectives, 30* (October), 400–421.

# 7

# Women Entrepreneurs: An Explanatory Framework of Capital Types

*Patricia Gene Greene and Candida Greer Brush*

## INTRODUCTION

Women entrepreneurs are increasingly in the public eye over the last few years as the target and subject of numerous books, magazines, surveys, assistance programs, and media attention. In this chapter we address that surge of interest by organizing the discussion of women-owned businesses according to various types of capital. First, we summarize the current economic impact of women-owned businesses, including the number of businesses, the distribution among industrial sectors, and the size of business receipts. Second, we present results of a current literature review that shows the gap in existing empirical research. Third, from an analysis of the contextual factors—work, family, and organized social life—we show why the process of women's venture creation may differ. From this we propose a framework of capital types that allows us to articulate potential gender differences. Our discussion concludes with a discussion of implications for both academics and practitioners.

Analyses of entrepreneurial phenomena are complicated by an array of definitions of the "entrepreneur" and "entrepreneurship" (Venkataraman, 1997; Bull & Willard, 1993; Lumpkin & Dess, 1996; Gartner, 1985). Furthermore, operationalizations vary widely from small businesses, to new ventures, to self-employed, with each not necessarily being the same thing (Balkin, 1989). Though a narrow definition is theoretically preferred, the quantity of empirical literature on women's entrepreneurship is comparatively small, representing only about 7 percent of all studies in the field (Baker, Aldrich, & Liou, 1997). Hence limiting the definition to only aspects of self-employment, new ventures, or small firms would overly restrict the scope of our discussion. We choose to follow Boyd (1991), who in his study of black self-employment uses the terms self-employment and entrepreneurship interchangeably, justifying this practice by saying:

> Self-employment is considered to be entrepreneurial activity because, whether it is motivated by exclusion or opportunity, self-employment involves management, risk assumption, and ownership (or control) of an enterprise, all of which are central to the most widely accepted definition of the concept. (p. 425)

We adopt Boyd's precedent by discussing female entrepreneurship as a phenomenon encompassing all women who start their own business, or in other words, women who push or are pulled into the creation of their own employment opportunities, as opposed to women who work for someone else.

Recognizing the overall contribution of small business to the U.S. economy further helps us to understand the context of the economic impact of women entrepreneurs. Small business itself is categorized by various definitions—some based on the size of sales tied to a particular industry, and more frequently, others based on the number of employees. The broadest definition used by the U.S. government is that a small business is one with fewer than 500 employees. In 1994, 22 million businesses filed a business tax return, of which only 14,000 (less than 1 percent) of the filing businesses could be classified as large when using the more than 500 employees definition (SBA, 1994a, 1998). However, of those filing, approximately 16 million businesses (72 percent) were full- or part-time self-employed individuals with no employees. A significantly smaller number, 6 million, were businesses that employed at least 1 but fewer than 500 employees (SBA, 1998). In addition, data from the Economic Survey conducted by the Department of Commerce documents the further contributions of the small business sector, showing us that 54 percent of the labor force is working in small businesses and that this sector of the U.S. economy is generating 52 percent of U.S. sales dollars (SBA, 1994a).

## THE ECONOMIC IMPACT OF WOMEN ENTREPRENEURS

Women have long been active participants in the small business economic arena. While the phenomena of women's entrepreneurship often are approached as new and important phenomena for study, the history of women entrepreneurs in America is actually lengthy and diverse. Prior to the early 1900s women were legally restricted in most states from holding their own property, much less owning their own businesses. That legality did not stop many women with an entrepreneurial bent. Although unrecorded as to numbers and economic impact, women have historically contributed to the household economy, often through petty businesses run from their own home (Wertheimer, 1977; Kessler-Harris, 1982; Bergmann, 1986; Ferree, 1987). Early examples include descriptions of Native American women as "proprietors" of fields and white immigrant women in the 1600s who were active in selling or bartering extra goods created within the household (Werthei-mer, 1977).

The contemporary numbers are striking. Women's share of small businesses increased rapidly from 1.5 million in 1976 to more than 5.8 million by 1992, representing a 32.1 percent share of all small firms. The share of women-owned businesses became more difficult to calculate due to changes in the definitions used by the Small Business Administration. Results of the 1997 economic census indicate that women currently own 5.4 million businesses, with an additional 2 million jointly owned (husband and wife). These numbers represent an increase of 16 percent from the 1992 records.

The gains in receipts generated by women business owners also show substantial increases. Between 1982 and 1987, the number of women-owned businesses increased 57.4 percent; however, the amount of receipts increased 182.97 percent. Between 1982 and 1992 the increase in women-owned businesses was 125.4 percent, with 1992 total receipts of women-owned firms reaching $1.5 trillion. The current number is again difficult to extrapolate from the new reporting standards of the Small Business Administration. The report no longer includes publicly traded companies. This eliminates only a small number of businesses, but a large proportion of revenues; 1997 total receipts totaled $818.7 billion (U.S. Census Bureau, 1997).

The industrial sector location of these businesses also helps us better understand their impact. In 1987, 1992, and 1997 the three most common types of businesses owned by women were consistently found in the Services (55 percent, 54 percent, 55 percent), Retail Trade (19 percent, 19 percent, 17 percent), and F.I.R.E., a category including combined fire, insurance, and real estate business ownership activities (11 percent, 10 percent, 9 percent). Whereas these industrial categories represent the distribution of the overall economy, they are not the fastest growing categories for women business owners. Figure 7-1 illustrates the sectors with the largest increases in numbers of businesses. Construction, Agriculture, and Transportation (which category also includes Communications and Public Utilities) register increases of 67 percent, 55 percent, and 62 percent respectively. Those industries not classified exhibit the largest increase of 123 percent. The Mining sector actually exhibits a decline of 24 percent (Survey of Women-Owned Business Enterprises, 1987, 1992, 1997).

The patterns are similar in the analysis of sources of dollar receipts. In 1987 the sectors that generated the highest receipts were Retail ($85.4 million), Wholesale Trade ($42.8 million), and Services ($61.1 million). These positions remained the same in 1997 ($152.0 million, $188.5 million, and $186.2 million, respectively). However, with the exception of Wholesale Trade, once again they are not the sectors showing the greatest amount of growth. Figure 7-2 illustrates that the three industrial sectors that registered the greatest increases in level of receipts, were Manufacturing (268 percent), Wholesale Trade (340 percent), and Mining (272 percent) (Survey of Women-Owned Business Enterprises, 1987, 1997).

The increase in the level of receipts is attributable to greater numbers of women in business, but also to the increased size and sophistication

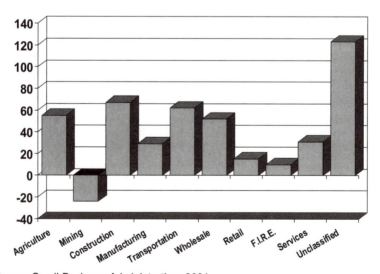

Source: Small Business Administration, 2001.

**Figure 7-1**  Women-owned businesses, industrial sector growth: 1987–1997.

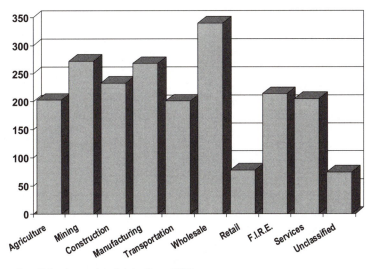

Source: Small Business Administration, 2001.

**Figure 7-2**  Women-owned businesses, growth in receipts: 1987–1997.

of the individual businesses. This can be illustrated by calculating the average receipts per sector for the industrial sectors with the largest growth rates. In 1987 the average receipt per business in the Manufacturing sector was $329,013. In 1997 the average receipt increased to $939,016, showing an increase of approximately 185 percent. The overall growth for the average receipts in Wholesale Trade between the years 1987 and 1997 was 189 percent, an increase from $518,761 to $1,500,168; and the average receipts in the mining sector grew 390 percent, from $73,195 to $358,767 (Survey of Women-Owned Business Enterprises, 1987,1997).

Businesses are growing in terms of both revenues and number of employees. Employment by women-owned businesses rose 28 percent between 1992 and 1997 compared to an 8 percent increase for all firms—more than three times the rate for all U.S. firms of similar size (NFWBO, 2001). Earlier statistics show that women-owned businesses employ more than 18.5 million people, one of every six workers (NFWBO, 1998).

Although these statistics remain problematic due to the use of different units of analysis, the overall direction of these trends is unambiguous. Women are owning an increasing number of businesses, participating more broadly across industrial sectors, generating higher receipts, and providing increasing numbers of jobs through their entrepreneurial activities.

## BACKGROUND

In contrast to the presence and growth of women as entrepreneurs, empirical research is comparatively sparse. Surveys of scholarly journals show that approximately 10 percent of all articles published in the entrepreneurship area between 1988 and 1993 focuses on or includes women entrepreneurs (Brush, 1997). Another survey of academic journals found that the number of articles about women in general over the years 1980–1995 showed a decline from 44 percent in 1980 to 14 percent in 1995, with studies of women owners being about 7 percent (Baker et al., 1997).

Several reasons are offered for the disparity between the practice and research. One argument is that academic reward systems and incentives favor the study of large, publicly traded firms rather than subsets of entrepreneurial populations. Another possibility is that the study of women's entrepreneurship may be perceived as less "legitimate" or important than others such as high tech or venture capital (Churchill, 1992). Alternatively, it might be hypothesized that there are no gender differences, or that if there are, they do not matter.

Research findings on differences between women and men entrepreneurs are equivocal; demographic characteristics, experience, education, and some motives differ, but other aspects such as risk and reasons for becoming an entrepreneur are similar (see Brush, 1992, 1997 for literature reviews). Business characteristics differ in terms of size, age, goals, and performance, but many of the problems faced are similar for both men and women owners (Brush, 1997). When viewed with the growth of women entrepreneurs, it might be argued that obstacles are fewer and differences do not matter.

Yet this conclusion is based on an extremely small number of studies. Baker and his colleagues (1997), in a survey of four management and entrepreneurship journals published between 1982 and 1995, noted that there were only 22 studies (of 3,206) that featured women as business owners or entrepreneurs; Brush (1995), in a review focused on entrepreneurship journals, noted only 79 (of 552) published between 1988 and 1993. A large majority of these studies are descriptive, are exploratory, and rely on convenience samples. Moreover, more than 50 percent of these focus on individual characteristics rather than the organization, the process, or environmental factors. Not surprisingly, the majority of theories upon which studies are based derive from psychology, with more current work utilizing sociological and feminist theories. Because of this small number of studies, the ability to generalize findings is limited concerning similarities or differences between men and women and their businesses.

There is also significant concern with the heterogenous nature of women entrepreneurs. Though there is some recognition of this in the academic, the vast majority of academic articles and trade magazine journals are skewed to women business owners with some tangible measure of success. There are at least two potential reasons for this bias, one methodological and one ideological. The methodological issue is bias due to the sample selection process. It is extremely difficult and expensive to collect individualized data on a large sample of self-employed women. It is far easier to survey members of an organization than to locate individual respondents. However, membership in a business organization carries with it problems of self-selection. These members may be the most aggressive, outgoing, growth-oriented business owners. Also, membership in an organization requires some degree of resources—for example, time to go to the meetings and money to pay for the dues. Therefore, survey studies including only those women who belong to business network organizations potentially skews our perception of these women.

In regards to the ideological bias, this applies more to the women we see represented in the trade journals. Ideologically, the presentation of successful women business owners serves to provide role models for the readers of the magazines, to show that it can be done. It also makes for sexier reading and sells more magazines. Overall, it reinforces the belief that this is the image of a woman business owner.

This limited research provides a starting point; however, future studies can benefit from a stronger theoretical foundation. First, it is important to understand why we might expect differences in the behaviors and activities of women-owned firms. One approach is through a review of the contextual factors influencing women's entrepreneurship. In this case, context can be approached through the social structures (work, family, and organized social life) that influence women's access to entrepreneurial opportunities (Aldrich, 1989; Lerner, Brush, & Hisrich, 1997; Brush, 1997). An examination of these influences provides the basis for discussing a framework for future research in women's entrepreneurship.

## CONTEXTUAL FACTORS INFLUENCING WOMEN'S ENTREPRENEURSHIP

Entrepreneurs are faced with a variety of changing circumstances during their transition from employee to business owner. One of the most pressing involves decisions about resources—where to obtain them, which to acquire, how to use them (Hart, 1995). Resources are fundamental to all organizations because without resources an organization cannot produce products/services, develop unique advantages, or design and implement strategies (Penrose, 1959; Wernerfelt, 1984). Over time, complex combinations of resources create the potential for achieving competitive advantages, which are valuable, inimitable, rare, and organizationally specific (Penrose, 1959; Barnard, 1938; Yuchtman & Seashore, 1967; Andrews, 1971; Rumelt, 1984; Wernerfelt, 1984; Connor, 1991; Peteraf, 1993; Barney, 1986, 1991). In other words, businesses are created from the resources that the entrepreneur can initially acquire or control (Brush, Greene, Hart, & Edelman, 1997). These resources represent various types of capital, and are essentially the building blocks of business. There are various types of capital and each contributes to the creation and operation of a business, regardless of characteristics of the business (industrial sector, size, age, etc.) or characteristics of the owner (gender, age, etc.) (Greene, Brush, & Brown, 1997). Types of capital include human, social, financial, physical, and organizational (Greene & Brown, 1997; Greene, Brush, & Brown, 1997).

Whether creating a new venture, succeeding to a family business, or acquiring an existing business, each entrepreneur begins with a unique set of endowments, or building blocks, that form the initial resource base of the organization (Penrose, 1959). For the entrepreneur at the point of business start-up, succession, or acquisition, the initial resource endowments provide the basis from which they might acquire other resources. At a basic level, the entrepreneur begins with her set of human and social capital. Human capital consists of achieved attributes of the entrepreneur, including education, experience, and reputation (Becker, 1964; Cooper, 1981), but may also be extended to terms of judgment, insight, creativity, vision, and intelligence (Dollinger, 1999). Social capital is comprised of relationships, networks, family, race, ethnicity and political connections of the entrepreneur (Bourdieu, 1983; Glade, 1967). These two sets of endowments provide the basis from which an entrepreneur will acquire physical resources (i.e., assets, facilities) or financial resources, as well as create the organizational resources of the business (Brush et al., 1997).

For women entrepreneurs, initial endowments of human and social capital can be substantially different than for men due to differences in contextual factors. Three contextual factors influence women's endowments of human and social capital: work, family, and organized social life (Aldrich, 1989).

## Work

Occupational segregation and underrepresentation of women at upper management levels continue to persist. Although women have made progress in entering nontraditional areas, still fewer than 16 percent of all undergraduates in engineering are female. Women are highly concentrated in clerical, sales, and administrative positions, with fewer employed in transportation, manufacturing, or agriculture (The World's Women, 1991). Further, salary differentials range from $12,000 to $30,000 depending on the sector (Good for Business, 1995).

Participation of women in executive, administrative, and managerial occupations averages 36 percent of the total, but the range goes from 15 percent in construction to a high of 66 percent in social and health services. Utilities, manufacturing, and public administration are also male dominated in executive and managerial positions. In addition, women's employment is frequently interrupted, as they leave the workforce to have children and care for dependents more often than men do (Powell, 1993).

At the upper executive level, the numbers of women continue to be small. Fewer than 5 percent of all corporate board members of Fortune 1000 companies are women, and less than 5 percent of vice presidents and executives of corporations are female (*Wall Street Journal*, 2/29/94). Franchising and biotechnology are sectors showing extremely low numbers, with women presidents comprising only 7 percent in each area (Dant, Brush, & Iniesta, 1996).

These facts suggest that women have less opportunity to gain experience that will enhance their endowments of human capital for business ownership. A lack of opportunity to gain experience at the chief executive level decreases the leadership decision-making experience that women need to start or acquire companies. In addition, occupational segregation may qualify women for service and retailing entrepreneurial endeavors, but prevent them from gaining experience in nontraditional areas.

On the other hand, the predominant experiential history of women in services and middle-level administrative jobs may affect their abilities to deal with customers and manage people. Whereas networks are a universal tool for all entrepreneurs, female entrepreneurs may draw from other life roles to inform their work role, resulting in a balance of care and calculation, and the ability to listen to others. The caring capacity of women becomes an element in taking the initiative to make network contacts (Johannisson, 1996). Thus, enhanced social skills, mutual relationships, and an ability to gain trust and commitment may be assets for women entrepreneurs (Johannisson, 1996), and indeed may be identified as a relational competence (Liou & Aldrich, 1995).

## Family

Women also face differential influences in family life. Expectations about family roles restrict women in terms of time and acceptance as business owners. Though U.S. women have made significant progress, most women are expected to manage the household and assume a primary care role for their family (Aldrich, 1989; Powell, 1993). A United Nations report emphatically states that "women everywhere retain the primary responsibility for unpaid housework" (The World's Women, 1991, p. 83). Although prevailing family values encouraging women to marry, have children, and stay at home have changed since World War II, it is still estimated that women spend at least 12 more hours per week in unpaid housework than their male counterparts (29.2 to 17.4 hours) (The World's Women, 1991).

These expectations for women's role in the family may mean that women have less opportunity to devote to full-time work endeavors. The expectation that women should be the primary caretakers for children and elder relatives may mean that they spend extra in these endeavors. This may decrease a women's ability to develop and nurture social networks that can be leveraged to obtain other essential business resources. Alternatively, a view that women's primary responsibility is at home may lead to lowered expectations about financing needs, growth goals, and the seriousness of the business in the eyes of others. On the other hand, women may develop better abilities to manage multiple roles, deal with time fragmentation, and be more flexible in the business management process (Brush, 1997).

### Organized Social Life

Organized social life continues to be different for women than men. Although networking behavior and this process does not vary by gender (Aldrich, Reese, & Dubini, 1989), the composition of networks for women and men differ. Women have a higher proportion of females in their networks. Further, social institutions (service organizations, eating clubs, and country clubs) still exist where business networking among high-level executives takes place and women are excluded. Increasingly women are forming their own vehicles for networking—for instance, the National Association of Women Business Owners and the National Association of Female Executives, as well as local organizations such as South Shore Women in Business (Massachusetts) and the Missouri Women's Council. In the volunteer area, women tend to participate more in school, church, and volunteer fundraising activities (Driscoll & Goldberg, 1993), which certainly have a social network component.

These circumstances suggest that women may be left out of critical information networks. Some women believe they are left out of venture capital networks, which, on the surface, appears to be true. Less than 0.1 percent of the $3 billion institutional venture capital was awarded to women-owned businesses in 1993 (*Wall Street Journal*, 1994). However, on the other hand, research shows that women may be just as successful at gaining other types of resources (information, accounting, or legal assistance) through the use of their networks (Aldrich et al., 1989).

In sum, an assessment of contextual factors (work, family, and organized social life) suggests that women come to entrepreneurship with different endowments of human and social capital. This conclusion leads to an expanded discussion of a capital framework for women-owned businesses.

## A CAPITAL FRAMEWORK FOR WOMEN-OWNED BUSINESSES

The purpose of the capital framework is to organize the discussion of women business owners in order to recognize the variety inherent in the group, as well as between the genders. The framework explains both initial and emerging types of capitals. Table 7-1 provides a guide to the theoretical grounding for each of the capital categories.

### Human Capital

The concept of human capital consists of achieved attributes, which are linked to increased levels of productivity (Becker, 1964). Education and work experience are the components of human capital most often

**TABLE 7-1  Literature Support for Capital Categories**

| Resource Type | Definition | Associated Authors |
|---|---|---|
| Human | achieved attributes | Becker, 1964 |
| | education and experience | Cooper, 1981 |
| Social | relationships and networks | Bourdieu, 1983 |
| | family | Liebenstein, 1968 |
| | race and ethnicity | Glade, 1967 |
| | religion | Weber, 1904; Sombart, 1914; Biggart, 1989 |
| Physical | tangible assets necessary for business operations | Hofer & Schendel, 1978 |
| | facilities and equipment | Hofer & Schendel, 1978 |
| | technology | Dollinger, 1995 |
| Organizational | organizational relationships, structures, routines, culture, knowledge | Tomer, 1987 Hofer & Schendel, 1978 Dollinger, 1995 |
| Financial | funds used to start and grow the business | Bygrave, 1992 |

*Source:* Derived from Greene, Brush, & Brown, 1997.

considered in the analysis of labor force participation. In the area of entrepreneurship, human capital approaches are used to discuss differential rates of returns (Bates, 1985; Sullivan & McCracken, 1988; Evans & Leighton, 1989). Indeed, education and experience are included as part of most any analysis of the entrepreneur or entrepreneurial performance (Cooper & Gimeno-Gascon, 1992) with findings on the positive relationship between education and engaging in entrepreneurship being highly robust. Brush and Hisrich (1991), Hisrich and Brush (1983, 1987), Brush (1992), Hisrich and O'Brien (1981, 1982), and Neider (1987) all describe the woman entrepreneur as either being college educated or having more education than her wage and salary counterpart. Gender comparisons also have been made regarding levels of education, finding similar levels for both male and female entrepreneurs (Birley, Moss, & Saunders, 1987). However, differences have been found regarding the content of the education. Women entrepreneurs are more likely to have had a liberal arts education instead of a background in business or engineering (Brush, 1992; The World's Women, 1991; Hisrich & Brush, 1983; Honig-Haftel & Martin, 1986; Carter, Williams, & Reynolds, 1997). Whereas the immediate assumption is a positive relationship between a business education and entrepreneurial behavior, that assumption may not be appropriate. A female entrepreneur interviewed in a regional newspaper credited her liberal arts education with the ability to teach herself (Wilen & Wilen, 1998).

The question of types of education becomes even broader as programs of entrepreneurial education become more available. Kourilsky and Walstad (1998) found that young women are more aware of gaps in their entrepreneurial knowledge than are young men; however, respondents of both genders rated entrepreneurial education as important or very important. School-based and freestanding entrepreneurial education and awareness programs are becoming available, some targeted to young women (Godfrey, 1992; Kourilsky, 1994). However, the contribution of these types of programs is as yet unmeasured.

Experience, as human capital, is relevant on three dimensions: management, industry, and start-up. These experiential dimensions tie us to the contextual consideration of what types of work experience women are currently getting in the labor force. Women entrepreneurs are less likely to have had experience in executive management or technical jobs (Watkins & Watkins, 1984; Stevenson, 1986), and more likely to have had experience in teaching, retail sales, or the secretarial area (Hisrich & Brush, 1983; Neider, 1987). Research on both male and female entrepreneurs also shows a very robust finding of a positive relationship between prior work experience in the same business and survival/success rate of the business (Cooper & Bruno, 1977; Van de Ven, Hudson, & Schroeder, 1984; Carter et al., 1997). However, findings show that women business owners possess fewer years of industry experience than their male counterparts (Carter et al., 1997). In addition, women are less likely to have experience in a start-up venture (Carter et al., 1997).

### Social Capital

"Social capital is an outcome of networks and relationships which are usable, by conscious or unconscious design, in an economic sense" (Bourdieu, 1983, p. 249). It is a form of noneconomic knowledge that, although having a separate foundation from formal learning or instruction, directly impacts the economic behaviors of individuals (Kelly, 1994). Social capital emerges from the norms, networks, and relationships of the social structure in which an individual lives, potentially producing useful resources for business through the development of sets of obligations and expectations, information channels, and social norms, which reinforce certain types of behaviors (Coleman, 1988).

In his analysis of the social capital of black business owners, Fratoe (1988) provides a direct example of the contribution of social capital to the operation of a business. Fratoe operationalized social capital as the business owners' role models, training, financial support, attitudes, values, as well as the sources of labor, customers, and business contacts. Significant contributions were attributed to both the amounts and types of social capital (Fratoe, 1988).

The social capital gained from an individual's family of origin is better understood through an examination of the family's group memberships, specifically groups defined by race or ethnicity and religion. The interaction between race, ethnicity, religion, and economic behaviors is another area of renewed research interest. Light and Karageorgis (1994) described the ethnic economy and summarized the classic literature pertaining to the concept. Directly related to this discussion, Portes and Sensenbrenner (1993) expressed social capital as a manifestation of social embeddedness. Kotkin (1993) used the concept of tribes to discuss race, religion, and identity in the global economy. However, although in these discussions gender is not usually a focal point, empirical and anecdotal exceptions are starting to be more frequent and noticeable. One woman interviewed in a southwestern city described a busy day of managing a multi-office family business. On the other side of the country, the *New York Times* reported a story on a garment industry sweatshop owned by a Chinese woman (Lii, 1995). Maggie Zheng took over the business when her brother, the former owner, fled town owing the workers approximately $80,000. Zheng's mother, a restaurant owner, had originally bought the factory for her son, and then subsequently encouraged her daughter to reopen the business. These are entrepreneurial women about whom we know little.

The relationship between religion and economic behavior is also one that needs to be revisited. Much of the classic work on minority entrepreneurs stems from recognition of the different economic behaviors between groups defined by religion (Weber, 1904; Sombart, 1914). In a more contemporary discussion, Biggart (1989) describes the foundation of several direct selling operations as having a spiritual base. Indeed, for many of the women in Biggart's study, a prioritizing of a woman's life into God, family, and the business is an integral part of the determination of their economic behavior. The recent increase in attention paid to conservative Christians, and indeed to conservatism in general, reinforces the need for an increased awareness of the types of social capital being developed and whether that capital does impact entrepreneurial behaviors.

A specific example of the type of attitudes that may be considered social capital is an attitude toward recognizing risk, constraints, and opportunities. Lauren Wood, a New Jersey business owner, comes from a family of entrepreneurs. She states, "Coming from an entrepreneurial family is different—we never saw any limits, there were no limits." Wood also developed a different attitude toward risk. When discussing fear she quoted the old adage, "The difference between $100 and $1 million is really only a couple of zeros" (Wood, 1995).

Networks as social capital may be considered in two ways. The individual networks of the founder or founding team serve as conduits for various types of capital to launch the business. These networks of the business founder(s) often serve as the basis for the development of subsequent organizational networks. The development and maintenance of both types of networks are critical to the creation and growth of most types of small businesses; however, significant gender differences in networking behavior have not been identified (Aldrich et al., 1989; Katz & Williams, 1997). Significant  differences are seen between the genders in the composition of the network. The networks of women entrepreneurs have repeatedly been found to be smaller and more predominantly female (Aldrich et al., 1989; Aldrich, 1989). Differences also have been found between female entrepreneurs and female salaried managers. When measuring weak-tie networking as participation in various types of groups (fraternal organizations, hobby groups, political organizations, etc.), the managers report higher levels of networking.

## Organizational Capital

Organizational capital is "human capital in which the attribute is embodied in either the organizational relationships, particular organization members, the organization's repositories of information, or some combination of the above in order to improve the functioning of the organization" (Tomer, 1987, p. 2).

External organizational relationships have been studied under the concept of networks as a means of obtaining both information and resources (Brush, 1992; Carsrud, Gaglio, & Olm, 1986). These external networks can be explicit providers of both instrumental and expressive support. Ellen Silverman, owner of Ellen Silverman Advertising and president of the Middlesex chapter of the New Jersey Association of Women Business Owners, credits her association with providing almost half her business. She states, "I did business with 40 NJAWBO members last year, either buying from or selling to." Silverman further stipulates that this number does not count referrals from members, but refers only to the direct transactions (Silverman, 1995).

Organizational capital is also concerned with particular organization members and the relationships between those members within the organization. Edith Penrose (1959) provides a strong foundation for the inclusion of people, specifically the entrepreneur, as part of the firm's resource base. Cooper and Gimeno-Gascon (1992) describe the entrepreneur as "the primary resource of a new firm" (p. 306). However, because the capital embodied in the entrepreneur is more specifically considered as human capital, organizational capital captures the attributes of others within the business.

The generally accepted dictum is that small businesses have difficulty in attracting top employees. Several explanations are proffered for this difficulty: inability to pay competitive salaries, unavailability of group benefit packages, and the perceived risk of accepting an unstable job due to the fear of small business failure rates. Gender may even be an exacerbating factor, interacting with other business variables to give female business owners a greater disadvantage in hiring talent. Anecdotal evidence exists, however, that female business owners may lead in recognizing and acquiring organizational capital from an underutilized source—women returning to the labor force after time away due to family responsibilities. These women often bring a variety of useful and productive skills and experiences, acquired in a domestic context but applicable within the business organization as well.

Internal organizational relations are another important element of organization capital, and gender differences have also been reported regarding these relationships as evidenced in management styles. Chaganti (1986) describes women business owners as having a more feminine management style. Neider (1987) suggests that women business owners develop a more participative management style. However, additional research is needed regarding the relationship of these findings to outcomes as well as the robustness of the findings themselves.

### Physical Capital

Physical capital is the equipment and tangible assets used in the creation and operation of a company. The type of business a woman chooses to enter to a great extent dictates the type and amount of physical capital needed. Indeed, it is more likely that the type and amount of physical capital needed has a strong determining role in the types of business a woman starts. Hisrich and O'Brien (1981, 1982) categorize traditional types of women-owned businesses as services, retail trade, and wholesale trade; and services and retail trade are still reported as the sectors with the greatest numbers of women participating in business ownership (SBA, 1994a). The businesses considered nontraditional for women to own include manufacturing, construction, and contracting. Though there are many causal relationships regarding the decision of type of business for a woman to enter, the level of investment needed for physical capital can be a significant factor in that start-up decision. For instance, manufacturing businesses in general require more physical capital than do service industries; therefore an individual entering the manufacturing industry will need more money than one entering most types of service industries. Indeed, one reason given to explain why women enter service industries in such large numbers is the reduced need for financial capital in order to start the business. These businesses instead require greater levels of human capital and social capital than physical capital. The initial basic resource inputs are substantially different.

The types of physical capital available must also be considered. Changes in the computer and telecommunications industries contribute to record numbers of women owning their own businesses. A personal computer can now be bought for less than $1,000, with professional quality peripherals priced accordingly. It is also no longer necessary to buy a building, or even to rent an office. Many women work at home, some for pay from an employer (Presser & Bamberger, 1993), but many more for themselves. In addition, the physical capital used to run the business may be the same as the physical capital used to run the family.

Physical capital also plays a role in the growth of the business. A business dependent on physical capital—for example, machinery—must also deal with the subsequent problems of maintenance and obsolescence. However, on the other hand, the accumulation of physical capital may also be considered as an accumulation of collateral for subsequent loans for increased business growth.

## Financial Capital

Obtaining the necessary financing to start and grow a business is generally considered to be one of the entrepreneur's major problems. Entrepreneurial funds come from many sources, including personal savings, banks, government programs, venture capital funds, and business angels. Each of those sources has different ramifications for the business and business owner.

The vast majority of owners of start-ups use personal savings for their initial stages, combining these savings with funds borrowed from family and friends (Vesper, 1996). For many women this source of capital can be a prime determinant of the type of business selected. Women with greater sources of personal capital, possibly through a working spouse, have more opportunities for choice in regards to the initial resource base. This stands in contrast to women with very low levels of household income or personal savings having fewer resource options.

Various studies approach the question of whether women have a more difficult time obtaining financial capital from banks than do men (Riding & Swift, 1990; Buttner & Rosen, 1988, 1989). However, the results remain somewhat inconclusive. Though there seem to be some differences regarding the likelihood of obtaining bank funds for growth, this difference lessens as a woman business owner's business matures and she develops a business track record (Brush, 1992).

One technique used to improve the possibilities of obtaining a bank loan is to arrange for a loan guarantee through either a direct government program, or one of the various microlender programs administered through either economic development or community-based organizations. Johnson's (1998) discussion of the rapid increase in microlender programs targeted to women business owners informs us as to the scope and agendas of these programs. The intent is not only to improve women business owners' access to capital but also to generate a sense of solidarity among women for both instrumental and affective purposes.

Venture capital is generally reserved for high-flyer, later stage, and often high-tech types of businesses. Only approximately 3 percent of all businesses started obtain venture capital at any time in their existence, and many of these are technology-related businesses. Because these types of businesses are already the exception for a woman business owner to start, it is understandable that women obtain a correspondingly smaller slice of venture capital funds. On the other hand, an increasing number of private investors, or angels, in both the profit and nonprofit sectors are interested in women-owned businesses.

## IMPLICATIONS FOR WOMEN-OWNED FIRMS

An overlay of dimensions of family, work, and organized social life helps to explain stocks of capital, particularly human and social capital. If accepted that these are the foundation resources for the creation of the organization, these contextual dimensions become critical explanatory factors for both the supply of entrepreneurs and the practice of entrepreneurial behaviors. The identification and acquisition of subsequent resources as well as the formation of any organizational capabilities and competencies are dependent upon these initial individual inputs.

### Practitioner and Policy Oriented

The stylized facts are that although women are starting businesses at a faster pace than men, these businesses remain smaller (Hisrich & Brush, 1987), make less money (Loscocco, Robinson, & Hall, 1991), and are generally considered less successful. They are not necessarily more likely to fail (Kalleberg & Leicht, 1991). These findings prompt the reconsideration of our measure of success. However, the fact remains that in order for women-owned businesses to continue to have a significant impact on the economy, there is much that can be done. The proposed approach focuses on the basic resource inputs for the creation of new business.

Human capital is acquired through education and experience. The White House Conference on Small Business Issues Handbook (SBA, 1994a) includes human capital as one of the eleven main issues driving the yearlong discussion on U.S. small businesses. One of the key points under this issue is entrepreneurial education, posing the question, "Should small business and government support entrepreneurial education?" (p. 46). The underlying assumption is that school children could gain an increased awareness of "the world of work," in this case an entrepreneurial world, through programs including mentoring, tutoring, and informal apprenticing. At the time of the conference, entrepreneurial education programs existed within 22 community and technical colleges, 16 high schools, and 90 colleges and universities in the United States and Canada (p. 46). These numbers continue to grow, and various programs also exist at different government levels and through different government agencies to assist individuals. Some of these programs are specifically addressed to women and members of minority groups, encouraging them to engage in entrepreneurial activities. Many types of volunteer organizations, such as the Service Corps of Retired Executives (SCORE), supplement these programs.

The concern is that due to limited access to all types of capital, these programs perpetuate the pattern of women's entrepreneurial activities in "traditional" types of business in which growth and financial success are less likely. One way to prevent this is through an explicit effort to expose women to opportunities in nontraditional, growth-oriented, moneymaking types of businesses. This approach can be organized using a resource framework based on the types of capital needed to start and grow a business. For instance, programs encouraging young women to study in science and technical fields need to be reinforced. Work opportunities in nontraditional, technical positions need to be developed. An early emphasis on the type of human capital acquired by women can have a direct and significant effect on the types of businesses started.

Nontraditional businesses—manufacturing, construction, and the like—generally require more physical capital to operate; therefore there is a need for increased access to financial capital. Women currently borrow very little to start their businesses. A true dedication to encouraging women to break out of industrial segregation into more lucrative sectors would require a commitment to the provision of increased funding for the growth of the business.

Government contracts and certain other types of large contracts operate under a set-aside situation. Currently an explicit percentage of all contracts awarded for a project must be awarded to a woman- or minority-owned business. However, the procurement process for these contracts, including the certification process necessary in order to be eligible to submit a bid, is expensive and cumbersome. A more streamlined, readily understandable process would encourage increased participation from women business owners.

## Implications for Future Research

We suggest three main areas of future research on female entrepreneurs in terms of the development of entrepreneurial practices, the future supply of women business owners, and the impact on society of the increasing numbers of women entrepreneurs. These questions are critical to the understanding of the gendered nature of entrepreneurship, and each can be explored using the contexts of family, work, and organized social life and an organizational framework of the relevant capital types.

First, what is the influence of differential contextual influences on women's entrepreneurial practices? This question relates to differences between the genders but also across groups of women determined by various factors. Some of these factors are associated to types of capital, including age cohort, types of experiences, family status, and so on. Others relate more to environmental characteristics such as geography. Whatever the factor, the concern is how dimensions of family, work, and organized social life differentially impact the manner in which a women starts, manages, or grows her business. One approach may be to examine the integration of roles in a woman's life and the relationship of such to the business outcome. Another is to examine the effect of starting endowments in venture creation.

Second, how do contextual dimensions affect the potential supply of women business owners? This question can be approached through both human and social capital. Changes in the educational and work experiences of women may be analyzed as to the subsequent impact on the rate of women entering entrepreneurship as well as the types of entrepreneurial behaviors observed. Also, mothers need to be added into the study of entrepreneurial backgrounds. Given the rapid increase in the number of entrepreneurial mothers over the last two and a half decades, it seems probable that the instrumental and expressive lessons gained from these mothers can contribute greatly to our increased understanding of the phenomenon, especially in regard to the generation of social capital.

Finally, what is the social and economic impact of the trend of women toward business ownership? To better address this question, researchers need to undertake more longitudinal studies of women owners of both traditional and nontraditional businesses. In addition we must add gender and class to the study of economic behaviors of individuals defined by race or ethnic background. The potential interactions of these characteristics considered from various theoretical perspectives can help us reach a better understanding of the broad range of experiences that comprise women's entrepreneurial behaviors.

## NOTE

An earlier version of this chapter was presented at the 1995 Conference on Immigrant and Minority Entrepreneurship, IC2 Institute, Austin, TX, March. Our sincere thanks go to Margaret Owen for research assistance.

The authors would like to thank John Sibley Butler for comments on this chapter.

## REFERENCES

Aldrich, Howard. (1989). Networking among women entrepreneurs. In Oliver Hagan, Carol Rivchun, & Donald Sexton (eds.), *Women-Owned Businesses*, pp. 103–132.

Aldrich, Howard, Pat Ray Reese, & Paola Dubini. (1989). Women on the verge of a breakthrough: Networking among entrepreneurs in the United States and Italy. *Entrepreneurship & Regional Development, 1*, 339–356.

Andrews, Kenneth R. (1971). *The concept of corporate strategy*. Homewood, IL: Richard D. Irwin.

Baker, Ted, Howard E. Aldrich, & Nina Liou. (1997). Invisible entrepreneurs: The neglect of women business owners by mass media and scholarly journals in the USA. *Entrepreneurship and Regional Development, 9*, 221–238.

Balkin, Steven. (1989). *Self-employment for low-income people.* New York: Praeger.

Barnard, Chester. (1938). *The functions of the executive.* Cambridge, MA: Harvard University Press.

Barney, Jay B. (1986). Types of competition and the theory of strategy. *Academy of Management Review, 11*, 791–800.

Barney, Jay B. (1991). Firm resources and sustained competitive advantage. *Journal of Management, 17*, 99–120.

Bates, Timothy. (1985). Entrepreneur human capital endowments and minority business viability. *The Journal of Human Resources, 20*, 540–554.

Becker, Gary S. (1964). *Human capital.* New York: Columbia University Press.

Bergmann, Barbara R. (1986). *The economic emergence of women.* New York: Basic Books.

Biggart, Nicole W. (1989). *Charismatic capitalism.* Chicago: University of Chicago Press.

Birley, Sue, Caroline Moss, & Peter Saunders. (1987). Do women entrepreneurs require different training? *American Journal of Small Business, 12* (1), 27–35.

*Bourdieu, Pierre. (1983). Forms of capital. (pp. 241–258). In J. Richardson (ed.), Handbook of theory and research for the sociology of education.* New York: Greenwood Press.

Boyd, Timothy. (1991). A contextual analysis of black self-employment in large metropolitan areas, 1970–1980. *Social Forces, 70*, 409–429.

Brush, Candida G. (1992). Research on women business owners: Past trends, a new perspective and future directions. *Entrepreneurship Theory and Practice, 16*, 5–30.

Brush, Candida G. (1995). *Women entrepreneurs: Contributions, concerns and changes needed for the future.* Working Paper. Boston University.

Brush, Candida G. (1997). Women owned businesses: Obstacles and opportunities. *Journal of Developmental Entrepreneurship, 2*, 1–25.

Brush, Candida G., Patricia G. Greene, Myra M. Hart, & Linda F. Edelman. (1997). Resource configurations over the life cycle of ventures. *Frontiers of Entrepreneurship Research.*

Brush, Candida G., & Robert D. Hisrich. (1991). Antecedent influences on women-owned businesses. *Journal of Managerial Psychology, 6*, 9–16.

Bull, Ivan, & Gary E. Willard. (1993). Towards a theory of entrepreneurship. *Journal of Business Venturing, 8*, 183–195.

Buttner, E. Holly, & Benson Rosen. (1988). Bank loan officers' perceptions of the characteristics of men, women, and successful entrepreneurs. *Journal of Business Venturing, 3*, 249–258.

Buttner, E. Holly, & Benson Rosen. (1989). Funding new business ventures: Are decision makers biased against women entrepreneurs? *Journal of Business Venturing, 4*, 249–261.

Carsrud, Alan L., Connie Marie Gaglio, & Kenneth W. Olm. (1986). Entrepreneurs, mentors, networks, and successful new venture development: An exploratory study. In *Frontiers of Entrepreneurship Research* (pp. 229–235). Wellesley, MA: Babson College.

Carter, Nancy M., Mary Williams, & Paul D. Reynolds. (1997). Discontinuance among new firms in retail: The influence of initial resources, strategy, and gender. *Journal of Business Venturing, 12*, 125–145.

Chaganti, Radha. (1986). Management in women-owned enterprises. *Journal of Small Business Management, 24* (October), 18–29.

Churchill, Neil C. (1992). Research issues in entrepreneurship. In Donald L. Sexton and John D. Kasarda (eds.), *The state of the art of entrepreneurship* (pp. 579–596). Boston: PWS-Kent Publishing.

Coleman, James. (1988). Social capital in the creation of human capital. *American Journal of Sociology, 94* (Supplement), S95–S120.

Connor, Kathleen. (1991). A historical comparison of resource-based theory and five schools of thought within industrial organization economics: Do we have a theory of the firm? *Journal of Management, 17,* 121–154.

Cooper, Arnold C. (1981). Strategic management: New ventures and small businesses. *Long Range Planning, 14,* 39–45.

Cooper, Arnold C., & A. V. Bruno. (1977). Success among high-technology firms. *Business Horizons, 20,* 16–22.

Cooper, Arnold C., & F. J. Gimeno-Gascon. (1992). Entrepreneurs, processes of founding and new firm performance. In Donald L. Sexton & John D. Kasarda (eds.), *The State of the Art of Entrepreneurship* (pp. 301–340). Boston: PWS-Kent Publishing.

Dant, Rajiv P., Candida G. Brush, & Francisco P. Iniesta. (1996). Patterns of participation of women in franchising. *Journal of Small Business Management, 36,* 81–89.

Dollinger, Marc J. (1999). *Entrepreneurship: Strategies and resources.* Boston: Irwin.

Driscoll, Dawn-Marie, & Carol R. Goldberg. (1993). *Members of the club; The coming of age of executive women.* New York: Free Press.

Evans, David S., & Linda S. Leighton. (1989). Some empirical aspects of entrepreneurship. *American Economic Review, 79,* 519–535.

Ferree, Myra Marx. (1987). She works hard for a living: Gender and class on the job. In Beth B. Hess & Myra Marx Ferree (eds.), *Analyzing Gender* (pp. 322–347). Newbury Park, CA: Sage Publications.

Fratoe, Frank. (1988). Social capital of black business owners. *Review of Black Political Economy, 16,* no. 4 (Spring), 33–50.

Gartner, William B. (1985). A conceptual framework for describing the phenomenon of new venture creation. *Academy of Management Review, 14,* 696–706.

Glade, William P. (1967). Approaches to a theory of entrepreneurial formation. *Explorations in Entrepreneurial History, 4,* 245–259.

Glass Ceiling Commission. (1995). *Good for business: Making full use of the nation's human capital.* Washington: The Glass Ceiling Commission.

Godfrey, Joline. (1992). *Our wildest dreams: Women making money, having fun, doing good.* Champaign, IL: HarperBusiness.

*Good for business: Making full use of the nation's human capital.* (1995). Washington: The Glass Ceiling Commission.

Greene, Patricia G., Candida G. Brush, & Terrence E. Brown. (1997). Resource configurations in new ventures: Relationships to owner and company characteristics. *Journal of Small Business Strategy, 8,* 25–40.

Hart, Myra M. (1995). *Founding resource choices: Influences and effects.* Doctoral dissertation, Harvard Graduate School of Business.

Hisrich, Robert D., & Candida Brush. (1983). The women entrepreneur: Implications of family, educational and occupational experience. In *Frontiers of Entrepreneurship Research* (pp. 54–77). Wellesley, MA: Babson College.

Hisrich, Robert D., & Candida Brush. (1987). Women entrepreneurs: A longitudinal study. In *Frontiers of Entrepreneurship Research* (pp. 187–199). Wellesley, MA: Babson College.

Hisrich, Robert D., & Marie O'Brien. (1981). The woman entrepreneur from a business and sociological perspective. In *Frontiers in Entrepreneurship Research* (pp. 21–39). Wellesley, MA: Babson College.

Hisrich, Robert D., & Marie O'Brien. (1982). The woman entrepreneur as a reflection of the type of business. In *Frontiers of Entrepreneurship Research* (pp. 54–77). Wellesley, MA: Babson College.

Honig-Haftel, Sandra, & L. Martin. (1986). Is the female entrepreneur at a disadvantage? *Thrust: The Journal for Employment and Training Professionals, 7*, 49–64.

Johannisson, B. (1996). Existential enterprise and economic endeavor—Women's use of personal networks in the entrepreneurial career. In *Aspects of Women's Entrepreneurship* (pp. 115–142), Stockholm, Sweden: NUTEK.

Johnson, Margaret A. (1998). New approaches to understanding the gendered economy. Paper presented at the annual meetings of the American Sociological Association, San Franciso.

Kalleberg, Arne L., & Kevin T. Leicht. (1991). Gender and organizational performance: Determinants of small business survival and success. *Academy of Management Journal, 34* (1), 136–161.

Katz, Jerome A., & P. M. Williams. (1997). Gender, self-employment, and weak tie networking through formal organizations. *Entrepreneurship and Regional Development, 9* (Special Issue), 183–197.

Kelly, M. Patricia Fernandez. (1994). Towanda's triumph: Social and cultural capital in the transition to adulthood in the urban ghetto. *International Journal of Urban and Regional Research, 18* (March), 88–111.

Kessler-Harris, Alice. (1982). *Out to work.* New York: Oxford University Press.

Kotkin, Joel. (1993). *Tribes.* New York: Random House.

Kourilsky, Marilyn L. (1994). *MADE-IT (Mothers and Daughters Entrepreneurs— IN Teams).* Kansas City, MO: Center for Entrepreneurial Leadership, Inc., Ewing Marion Kauffman Foundation.

Kourilsky, Marilyn L., & William B. Walstad. (1998). Entrepreneurship and female youth: Knowledge, attitudes, gender differences, and educational practices. *Journal of Business Venturing, 13* (3), 77–88.

Lerner, Miri, Candida G. Brush, & Robert D. Hisrich. (1997). Israeli women entrepreneurs: An examination of factors affecting performance. *Journal of Business Venturing, 11,* 315–339.

Light, Ivan, & Stavros Karageorgis. (1994). The ethnic economy. In Neil Smelser & Richard Swedberg (eds.), *Handbook of Economic Sociology.* Princeton, NJ: Princeton University Press.

Lii, Jane. (1995, March 12). Week in sweatshop reveals grim conspiracy of the poor. *New York Times.*

Liou, Nina, & Howard E. Aldrich. (1995). *Women entrepreneurs: Is there a gender-based relational competence?* Paper presented at the annual meetings of the American Sociological Association, Washington.

Loscocco, Karyn A., Joyce Robinson, & Richard H. Hall. (1991). Gender and small business success: An inquiry into women's relative disadvantage. *Social Forces, 70,* 65–86.

Lumpkin, G. T., & Gregory C. Dess. (1996). Clarifying the entrepreneurial orientation construct and linking it to performance. *Academy of Management Review, 21,* 135–172

National Foundation for Women Business Owners (NFWBO). (1998). *Research findings.* Silver Springs, MD.

National Foundation for Women Business Owners (NFWBO). (2001, April 23). *Key facts and NFWBO fact of the week.*

Neider, Linda. (1987). A preliminary investigation of female entrepreneurs in Florida. *Journal of Small Business Management, 25,* 22–29.

Penrose, Edith. (1959). *The theory of the growth of the firm.* London: Basil Blackwell.

Peteraf, Margaret. (1993). The cornerstones of competitive advantage: A resource-based view. *Strategic Management Journal, 14,* 179–192.

Portes, Alejandro, & Sensenbrunner, Julia. (1993). Embeddedness and immigration: Notes of the social determinants of economic action. *American Journal of Sociology, 98,* 1320–1350.

Powell, Gary N. (1993). *Women and men in management.* Newbury Park, CA: Sage Publications.

Presser, Harriet B., & Elizabeth Bamberger. (1993). American women who work at home for pay: Distinctions and determinants. *Social Science Quarterly.*

Riding, Allan L., & Catherine S. Swift. (1990). Women business owners and terms of credit: Some empirical findings of the Canadian experience. *Journal of Business Venturing, 5,* 327–340.

Rumelt, Richard P. (1984). Towards a strategic theory of the firm. In R. Lamb (ed.), *Competitive strategic management.* Englewood Cliffs, NJ: Prentice-Hall.

Silverman, Ellen. (1995). Personal conversation.

Sombart, Werner. (1914). *The Jews and modern capitalism.* (M. Epstein, Trans.). New York: E.P. Dutton.

Stevenson, Lois A. (1986). Against all odds: The entrepreneurship of women. *Journal of Small Business Management, 24* (October), 30–36.

Sullivan, Teresa A., & Stephen D. McCracken. (1988). Black entrepreneurs: Patterns and rates of return to self-employment. *National Journal of Sociology, 2,* 168–185.

Tomer, John F. (1987). *Organizational Capital.* New York: Praeger.

U.S. Small Business Administration. Office of Advocacy. (1994a). *Handbook of small business data.* Washington: Government Printing Office.

U.S. Small Business Administration. Office of Advocacy. (1994b). *The White House conference on small business issues handbook.* Washington: Government Printing Office.

U.S. Small Business Administration. (1998). *State of small business.* Washington: Government Publishing Office.

Van de Ven, Andrew, R. Hudson, & D. Schroeder. (1984). Designing new business start-ups among men- and women-owned firms in rural areas. *Rural Sociology, 59,* 289–310.

Venkataraman, S. (1997). The distinctive domain of entrepreneurship research. In Jerome A. Katz & Robert H. Brockhaus (eds.), *Advances in entrepreneurship, firm emergence and growth* (Vol. 3, pp. 119–138). Greenwich, CT: JAI Press, Inc.

Vesper, Karl. (1996). *New venture experience.* Seattle: Vector Books.

*Wall Street Journal.* February 29, 1994.

Watkins, Jean, & David Watkins. (1984). The female entrepreneur: Background and determinants of business choice–some British data. *International Small Business Journal, 2,* 21–31.

Weber, Max. 1989 [1904]. *The Protestant ethic and the spirit of capitalism.* London: Unwin-Hyman.

Wernerfelt, Brigid. (1984). A resource-based view of the firm. *Strategic Management Journal, 5,* 171–180.

Wertheimer, Barbara Mayer. (1977). *We were there: The story of working women in America.* New York: Pantheon Books.

Wilen, Joan, & Lydia Wilen. (1998, August 30). They weren't afraid to take a chance. *Kansas City Star,* pp. 16–17.

Women-Owned Businesses, 1987 Economic Census, *Survey of women-owned business enterprises*, U.S. Census Bureau.

Women-Owned Businesses, 1992 Economic Census, *Survey of women-owned business enterprises*, U. S. Census Bureau.

Women-Owned Businesses, 1997 Economic Census, *Survey of women-owned business enterprises*, U.S. Census Bureau.

Wood, Lauren. February 23, 1995. Personal interview.

The World's Women—1970–1990. (1991). *Trends and statistics*. New York: United Nations.

Yuchtman, Ephraim, & Stanley E. Seashore. (1967). A systems resource approach to organizational effectiveness. *American Sociological Review, 32,* 891–903.

# 8

# New Approaches to Understanding the Gendered Economy: Self-Employed Women, Microcredit, and the Nonprofit Sector

*Margaret A. Johnson*

During the second half of the twentieth century, the United States transitioned from an industrial to a post-industrial economy. This transformation brought significant changes to all aspects of U.S. society, and we examine two of them—the increase in self-employed women in the for-profit sector and the growth of microenterprise programs in the not-for-profit sector to support self-employment. The rapidly growing field of nonprofit micro-enterprise organizations in the United States provides an example of interconnections between the not-for-profit and for-profit sectors in the post-industrial economy. With a focus on self-employed women, it becomes evident that economic changes during the past thirty years affected men and women differently, and for women these trends were reinforced by a nonprofit sector that is "gendered female" (Steinberg & Jacobs, 1994; Odendahl & Youmans, 1994). By considering trends in women's self-employment and the role of nonprofit activities, this chapter exposes a unique case where the gender dynamics of the non-profit and for-profit sectors overlapped to produce mutually beneficial outcomes.

Much researched are economic trends for women as employees, such as the increase in labor force participation rates, especially among mothers with young children (Oppenheimer, 1970; Bianchi & Spain, 1986; Reskin & Padavic, 1994; Spain & Bianchi, 1996), the extent and stability of sex segregation of the labor force (Goldin, 1990; Reskin & Hartmann, 1986; Lloyd, 1975; England & Farkas, 1986), and the earnings gap between women and men (Goldin, 1990; Bianchi & Spain, 1986). Less researched are women as self-employed, although this nascent literature has proceeded at a rapid rate (Brush, 1992; Cromie & Hayes, 1988; Fisher, Reuber, & Dyke, 1993; Hisrich, 1986; Loscocco & Robinson, 1991; Greene & Johnson, 1995). Unlike most previous analysis of self-employed women, this chapter connects the trends of self-employed women to gendered trends in the larger economy. In terms of gender and the nonprofit sector, scholars have advanced the notion that it is gendered female (Steinberg & Jacobs, 1994; Odendahl & Youmans, 1994), but gender issues are much less discussed as compared to literature on the for-profit sector. Although some research contrasts sex differences in earnings and promotions between the nonprofit, for-profit, and government sectors (Steinberg & Jacobs, 1994; Wharton, 1989), little to no attention has been given to how gender plays a role in the interconnections between the for-profit and not-for profit sector. This chapter explicitly considers the links between gendered economic trends in the economy at large and nonprofit sector activities.

To discuss these issues of sector connections and gender effects, we first consider the gendered trends in the economy that led to the rapid rise in self-employment among women, followed by a summary of how the nonprofit sector is "gendered female." These discussions provide a context for examining microenterprise organizations, a type of nonprofit organization that has grown rapidly in the United States. These micro-enterprise organizations support the for-profit activities of "micro" and small business owners. Microenterprise organizations are an example of mediating social structures where nonprofit and for-profit activities are mutually reinforcing. This illustration is particularly useful because it provides a framework to understand trends in self-employment among women as well as the issues and potential for micro-enterprise programs, a rapidly growing tool for welfare reform and community development.

## ECONOMIC CHANGES IN THE U.S. ECONOMY

Since the 1970s, the United States has witnessed a boom in female entrepreneurship. Changes in the economy created a situation favorable to a rapid growth in female entrepreneurship. With this growth, needs for financing increased and policy makers began to view micro-enterprise organizations and self-employment as a new approach to community development. In just a few years, the nonprofit sector produced a rapid increase in microenterprise organizations and other support services for business owners.

Increases in female entrepreneurship and creation of alternative financing schemes, such as microenterprise programs, become explainable and even predictable when we view economic changes through a gendered lens. That is, structural transformations of the economy affected men and women differentially, and gender-specific patterns in economic behavior emerged. Specifically, changes in the economy created space favorable to the development of female entrepreneurship at the same time that women were poised to take advantage of these changes. Moreover, the nonprofit sector of the economy is "gendered female." Thus, as women experienced difficulty in obtaining financing for their businesses through traditional routes, the nonprofit sector developed supporting organizations and programs. The development of such organizations to support women entrepreneurs complemented and reinforced the gendered trend of female entrepreneurship in the broader economy.

The economic changes in the 1970s, 1980s, and 1990s had gendered outcomes—increases in women's small business development and difficulties for women in obtaining business loans.[1] Microenterprise and mutual aid organizations in the nonprofit sector proliferated to overcome the deficiencies in the for-profit sector of the economy. Besides providing funding, these organizations also provided the means and support for fostering solidarity and community building. In what follows we consider the gendered nature of the economy, the particular development of women's small businesses, and the use of alternative financing sources.

## The Permanently New Economy

In the second half of the twentieth century, the United States economy experienced significant and far-reaching changes. These changes are best characterized by two well-known outcomes—rapid movement to a global economy and changes in the United States industrial base from a predominantly goods-producing economy to a non–goods-producing economy (i.e., a service, professional, trading, information-providing economy). This "permanently new economy" (Ritzer, 1989, p. 243) of the United States is characterized by global interconnectedness, a much smaller manufacturing base, and radical changes in the way work organizations and labor are organized.

The permanently new economy is distinguished by movement to a global economy and the eroding economic dominance of the United States. The global economy witnessed the proliferation of transnational corporations, global joint ventures, international contracting, growth of off-shore affiliates, and outsourcing (Ritzer, 1989, p. 248). In the United States, personal, professional, health, and business service industries and finance and real estate industries grew rapidly, whereas manufacturing and trade industries declined (U.S. Bureau of the Census, 1994).

During this time, the power of organized labor decreased significantly. When company profits started to decline in the 1970s, management devised a new strategy to control the cost of labor—threat of capital mobility; that is moving or threatening to move production elsewhere (Bluestone & Harrison, 1982, p. 16–17). New technology in transportation and communication made these threats a real possibility by providing companies the means to move production much more quickly and efficiently than in the past. Unions moved their focus away from wage increases to preserving their jobs and benefits (Ritzer, 1989). Increasingly, union efforts concentrated on resisting management efforts to subcontract work previously done by union firms (Bennet, 1994; Lavin, 1994).

Along with a decline in the power of organized labor, companies increasingly relied on subcontracting work and the use of temporary workers to accommodate market fluctuations and to hold down labor costs (Belous, 1989; Chevan, 1992). In fact, by the 1990s, for many companies temporary workers were integrated to such a degree that temporary services became a line item in company budgets, and some companies even established temporary services departments (Fernberg, 1989, p. 116; McGhee, 1985). The use of the term "Just-in-Time" workers by trade magazines (e.g., Gruer & Moore [1992] in *Industrial Management* and Lincoln [1993] in *Office*) to describe temporary workers underscores the institutionalization of temporary workers as an organizational strategy.

The dramatic increase in temporary services permeated all industries, but was concentrated in office, industrial, medical, and engineering and technical areas (Carey & Hazelbaker, 1986). Companies relied on "Rent-an-Executive" (Gruer & Moore, 1995, p. 31) to rent lawyers, human resource professionals, chief financial officers or other professionals as needed for special projects. This changing organization of work resulted in a temporary services industry with an annual growth rate of 19 percent with billings in the late 1980s of $13.9 billion (Fernberg, 1989). The direct effect on self-employment was twofold: a rapid proliferation of temporary service firms and small firms that serviced larger companies and an increase in self-employment of professionals who worked as independent contractors.

Many of these trends—declining profit margins in the 1970s, faster transition to a global economy, declining power of organized labor, changes in organizational strategies—were the same trends that some researchers cite as leading to the growth of the informal economy (Castells & Portes, 1989). Castells and Portes (1989) discussed how these trends created a situation conducive to the development of businesses among immigrants in the United States because immigrant entrepreneurship in its early stages and sometimes even later stages often occurs in the informal economy. Here, the contention is that these economic changes also had gender-specific outcomes, and these gendered outcomes resulted in a situation conducive to the development of women-owned enterprises.

### Gendered Economic Trends

The trends just described led to a climate favorable for small business development.

> Between 1980 and 1987, *Fortune 500* companies laid off over three million employees while companies with less than 100 employees created 12 million new jobs. These small companies alone were three times more productive than the entire Japanese economy in terms of job creation. (Ritzer, 1989, p. 251)

Conditions were especially favorable for the growth in self-employed women to the point that by 1994, women-owned businesses employed 35 percent more people in the United States than the Fortune 500 companies employed worldwide (NFWBO, 1995). The economic trends previously described impacted the growth of self-employment among women in the following ways.

First, growth in the economy occurred in industries where women were concentrated. Figure 8-1 provides the percentage of women in each industry and the rate of growth from 1983 to 1993. In 1993, women were concentrated in retail trade, finance, insurance, real estate, and services, and these were also among the fastest growing industries. Transportation and public utilities also experienced significant growth, but women were not concentrated in this industry. These changes in industrial distribution occurred along with changes in the organization of the economy and workplace as described previously. Through small business development, women were able to take advantage of the changing opportunity structure in the United States economy.

Second, at the same time that the opportunity structure changed, women had reached a point where they had the skills and experience to take advantages of the opportunities. Large numbers of women had

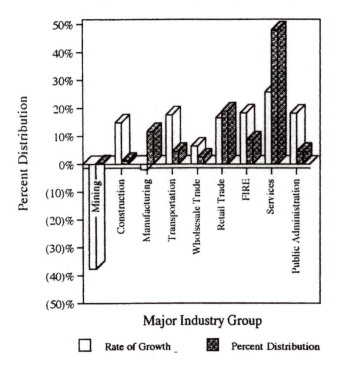

**Figure 8-1** Percentage distribution of all female workers by industry, 1993, and rate of growth from 1983 to 1993 by industry. *Source: Employment and Earnings, 1984 and 1994. Note. FIRE is Finance, Insurance, and Real Estate.*

spent sufficient time in the labor force to accumulate skills and experience. Women's educational attainment was approaching parity with men's. By 1993, women were just as likely as men to have obtained some college education, although graduation rates for all men age 18 and over were still higher than for women (U.S. Department of Education 1994, p. 18). Moreover, many women had experienced firsthand the "glass ceiling effect," the limits to advancement in corporate America (Freeman, 1990). Many more women lived the typical female job—dead-end and low paying (Reskin & Padavic, 1994). The United States also participated in the maturing of the women's movement along with an increasing recognition that women can be and are successful in business. The end result of these trends was that a large number of women possessed the skills, experience, and motivation necessary to be successful in small business development. Thus, a comparison of the growth rate of women's small business development by industry to the overall growth rate of industry reveals that women's rate of self-employment was greater than that of industry growth (U.S. Department of Commerce, 1990).

In fact, since the 1970s, women's self-employment rose significantly faster than male self-employment. The U.S. Bureau of the Census 1992 economic census reported a 43 percent growth in the number of women-owned firms between 1987 and 1992—considerably greater than the 26 percent growth for all U.S. businesses during that time (U.S. Department of Commerce, 1990, 1996). In addition, by 1992, the growth in sales and receipts was 131.3 percent, and women owned 34.1 percent of all nonfarm sole proprietorships, partnerships, and subchapter S corporations for a total of 5.89 million firms (U.S. Bureau of the Census, 1994).

In addition, women entrepreneurs, like men, possessed a variety of motivations for starting a business, yet overall some of their motivations could be differentiated from men's (Cromie & Hayes, 1988). Although profit was usually important (for exceptions, see a discussion by Goffee and Scase [1983]), many women entrepreneurs stressed other factors as at least equally important. For example, a flexible lifestyle was paramount, and for many women entrepreneurs their work and family life overlapped (Brush, 1992). Brush (1992) suggested that "many women business owners conceive of their businesses as a cooperative network of relationships rather than primarily as a separate profit-making entity" (p. 17). Also, creating a certain kind of work environment was important (Fried, 1989). "Many experts believe that women business owners often seem to emphasize employee training, teamwork, reduced hierarchy, and quality far more than their male counterparts" (Zellner, King, Byrd, DeGeorge, & Birnbaum, 1994, p. 105). Scholars reported that women entrepreneurs measured success differently (Neider, 1987). Profits were important, but success depended more on developing employees, meeting customer expectations, and achieving a balance between work and family (Brush, 1992). In short, for female entrepreneurs, small businesses were an arena where they could shape a personal vision of how work should be organized. Some women pursued entrepreneurship as a way to gain control over work processes and advance a particular vision.

No consensus exists in research studies on whether or not women have more difficulty in obtaining loans than men. Experimental studies and surveys of hypothetical situations (Buttner & Rosen, 1988, 1989; Fay & Williams, 1993) found few to some gender differences in banker decisions about granting loans, although one survey found that bank loan officers "rated women as significantly less likely successful entrepreneurs compared to men" (Buttner & Rosen, 1988, p. 249). Studies of actual experiences found some gender bias in loan requirements even for similar male- and female-owned firms (Riding & Swift 1990). These conflicting findings might be due to the fact that banks are unlikely to make small business loans to women *or* men who need less than $50,000. Bankers prefer to make start-up loans for at least $50,000, whereas the start-up costs of the typical small business is only $4,000 to $5,000. However, because female businesses tend to be smaller than male businesses, their loan needs are smaller. Thus, women encounter significant barriers in financing their small businesses through traditional financial institutions such as banks (Loscocco & Robinson, 1991). The National Women's Business Council (NWBC) identified "the lack of access to capital as the most serious problem facing women entrepreneurs today" (Fraser, 1993, p. 60). The 1992 National Foundation of Women Business Owners (NFWBO) survey of their members found that women business owners cited availability of capital as one of the most significant barriers to business growth (NFWBO, 1993). In general, reasons for difficulty include that most lending officers did not have experience with giving loans to women and thus were hesitant to loan to women; women were more likely to start companies, such as service companies, that had low to no capital that could be used as collateral; limited track records; and that microlending was not profitable for banks (Cocheo, 1986; Fraser, 1993; NFWBO, 1993; Touby, 1992). "A surprising 20% of women business owners reported that their loan officer insisted upon their spouse's signature in order to obtain a loan," and 14 percent believed that being a woman-owned business was detrimental for their attempts to obtain financing (NFWBO, 1993). Women reported using several tactics to overcome these difficulties. To finance or start their businesses, many women turned to personal sources of financing—credit cards, home-equity loans, second mortgages, or 401 (k) retirement accounts (Klein, 1993; NFWBO, 1993). Women wryly referred to the interest from a credit card as the "business woman's tax" (Klein, 1993).

To overcome financing difficulties, women have sought solutions in another gendered area of the economy—the nonprofit sector. Through nonprofit organizations, women have created alternative financing sources in the form of nonprofit microlending organizations. Once again, an examination of the economy with a gendered lens helps explain why we have seen this rapid growth in microlending mutual aid associations.

### Trends in the Nonprofit Sector

The previous section discussed how changes in the economy created opportunities for women at the same time that women were poised to take advantage of the changing economy. We now examine a part of the economy that has been called "gendered female" (Steinberg & Jacobs, 1994; Odendahl & Youmans, 1994)—the nonprofit arena. From 1977 to 1990, the nonprofit sector experienced a 63 percent growth in revenue and a 57 percent increase in employment (Hodgkinson, Weitzman, Toppe, & Noga, 1992). In addition, this sector consists of industries in which women are concentrated—education, health, and social welfare (Preston, 1994). In fact, by various estimates, women were two thirds to three fourths of the 7.8 million workers in nonprofits (O'Neill, 1994). In addition, more than half of the 90 million volunteers were women, and women have been in the majority in the nonprofit sector throughout American history (O'Neill, 1994).

The gender composition in the nonprofit sector is dramatically different than in business or government. For example, "65 percent of nonprofit employees are women, as opposed to 44 percent in business and 53 percent in government" (O'Neill, 1994, p. 5). Moreover, the nonprofit wage distribution reveals greater gender equality than anywhere else in the economy, although some economists elaborate that this is not an indication of gender equality given that the wages in the nonprofit sector overall are lower relative to the for-profit sector (Steinberg & Jacobs, 1994, p. 87). On average, women's wages are 92 percent of men's wages in the nonprofit sector, but the wages of managerial women are more than 20 percent below wages of men in the same occupations (Preston, 1994). Moreover, from 1973 to 1991 the wages of women in the nonprofit sector increased relative to those of women in governmental employment to the point that by 1991, the typical female nonprofit employee earned a higher hourly wage than her government counterpart (Preston, 1994). Also, women are much more likely to be in professional and managerial positions in nonprofit organizations than in business or government, and they are much more likely to head the largest nonprofit organizations. "[F]or instance, in 1992, sixteen of the nation's one hundred largest nonprofits had chief executive officers who were women, whereas only one Fortune 500 corporation was headed by a woman" (O'Neill, 1994, p. 6).

During the 1980s women were faced with increasing employment options, and more and more were turning to nonprofit employment (Preston, 1994). At this time, the government sector was downsizing and reducing employment opportunities, whereas the nonprofit sector greatly increased management opportunities for women (Preston, 1994). In addition, this sector offered flexibility in employment. It had the highest percentage of part-time workers, and part-time female workers earned higher wages in the nonprofit sector than in the for-profit sector (Preston, 1994).

Despite what on the surface might seem a rosy situation for women in the nonprofit sector, two distinctive views have emerged among scholars regarding women's position. Some researchers take the view that the nonprofit sector is "gendered female" and that this situation has negative consequences for women (Steinberg & Jacobs, 1994; Odendahl & Youmans, 1994). These scholars describe the usual situation in the nonprofit sector as a large female workforce under the direction of an elite male power structure that sets the agenda, while occupations are distributed according to gender (Steinberg & Jacobs, 1994, p. 94). Proportionately fewer women advance to positions of organizational governance (Shaiko, 1996). The scholars state that "the images, stereotypes, ideologies and metaphors used to describe the work" are gendered female, while the "missions of nonprofit organizations are 'soft'—encompassing the provisions of services, a preoccupation with moral and ethical concerns, producing beauty, helping people" (Steinberg & Jacobs 1994, pp. 99–100). This gendering of the nonprofit sector leads to the devaluation of women's work and subordination of women by men. In short, these scholars argue that the same gender dynamics that occur in the governmental and private sector occur to an even greater extent in the nonprofit sector.

However, another view stresses an opposite perspective. This view says that because of the preponderance of women in this sector and the dominance of industries that are "characteristically female," the nonprofit arena provides fertile ground for women's leadership. It historically has been an arena where women are able "to wield power in societies intent upon rendering them powerless" (McCarthy, 1990, p. 1). In addition, significant trends in wages and employment opportunities support women's greater development and expression through leadership roles in the nonprofit arena and the for-profit arena. Rose (1994) documents the growth of Women's Funds that are feminist, philanthropic funds run by women to support programs that empower women and girls. Thus, the nonprofit sector provides a niche for women to reach their fullest potential and to support goals that they think are important.

One way to reconcile these divergent pictures of the nonprofit sector is to consider distinctions among occupational levels. The studies cited here show that at the higher occupational levels, women have had greater opportunities for advancement and leadership than in for-profit sector companies. However, like the for-profit sector, most women in the not-for-profit sector are in low-wage, low-prestige occupations. This fact aligns with the negative assessment of Steinberg and Jacobs (1994).

Similarities between the gendered-female nonprofit sector and the growth in female small businesses are evident. Both the nonprofit sector and women's small businesses are concentrated in industries that are predominantly female. They both provide leadership roles for women and arenas where women can take an activist role in shaping their personal vision. Each offers a more flexible work environment where women can adapt their work situation to family needs. And they both offer an arena where women can rise to self-sufficiency through carving out a space in the economy suitable to their visions and lives.

To summarize, changes in the economy opened up opportunities for women in the area of small business development. Women through their labor market experience, skills, and motivations took advantage of these emerging opportunities. These motivations included desire for a more flexible work schedule, control over the work processes and work time, ability to advance and to shape personal visions of how work should be ordered (e.g., sensitivity to employee needs, emphasis on quality products and service). But in their quests, women encountered barriers in financing. The growth of micro-enterprise organizations in the nonprofit sector occurred, in part, to help overcome these hurdles.

Here, economic trends and motivations merged in a specific type of intermediary organizations—nonprofit organizations that support women's small businesses through training, technical assistance, and financing. The gendered-female nonprofit sector is increasingly complementing and reinforcing the gendered trends in the broader economy. Women's small business growth has collided with the nonprofit sector to form mediating institutions that support community building through the development of female entrepreneurship. The type of organization of particular interest is nonprofit micro-enterprise organizations.

## MICRO-ENTERPRISE ORGANIZATIONS

A micro-enterprise has been defined as a very small business with less than five employees that does not have access to the commercial banking sector because initial loan needs are usually less than $15,000 (Clark, Huston, & Meister, 1994). The most common case is for the business to be run by only one person. However, micro-enterprises are far from being insignificant. Two-thirds of businesses in the United States start with less than $10,000, and women start most of them (NWBC, 1994, p. 22).

Micro-enterprise nonprofit organizations assist in "job creation, business and community development, poverty alleviation, and economic self-sufficiency" (CEI, 1994). In the United States (see Figure 8-2), when these programs first started, most nonprofit micro-enterprise organizations usually made "micro" business loans to women and low-income and minority entrepreneurs who have had difficulty obtaining credit through conventional sources. Increasingly, programs are broader and target anyone needing a business loan of less than $25,000; many programs loan much more. Microlending organizations receive their funds from a variety of sources, including foundations, private donations, program revenues, banks, corporations, state and federal funding (especially SBA dollars), and funding from Native American tribes (Clark et al., 1994).[2]

During the 1990s, it was difficult to assess the size and scope of the rapidly growing field of micro-enterprise organizations. The Self-Employment Learning Project (SELP) of the Aspen Institute provided the most comprehensive information. They compiled a mailing list of "over 4,000 individuals and organizations involved or interested in micro-enterprise development" (Severens & Kays, 1997). They used this list to conduct a mail survey from August 1996 to February 1997 that resulted in a directory of 328 micro-enterprise development programs. Their earlier 1994 directory provided information on the year each program was established. This data from survey respondents illustrated the dramatic growth of these nonprofit organizations.

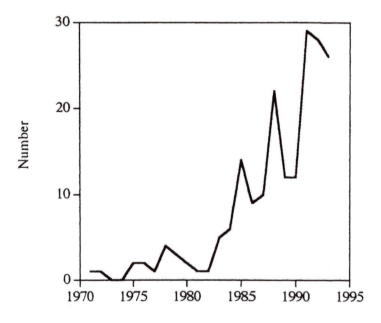

**Figure 8-2** Number of microenterprise programs by year. *Source: Compiled from the 1994 Directory of U.S. Microenterprise Programs.*

Micro-enterprise programs provide a combination of technical assistance and lending (individual and/or group lending) either as practitioner programs or support programs (Clark et al., 1994). Practitioner programs offer services and loans directly to the entrepreneur, whereas support programs provide assistance to the practitioner programs. Many micro-enterprise programs receive some or all of their funding from governmental funds. For example, funds from the Office of Refugee Resettlement support a few microlenders that assist refugee populations. Nonprofit organizations administered the SBA pilot microloan program whose purpose was "To provide capital to women, low-income and minority entrepreneurs and small businesses unable to obtain credit through conventional sources" (Coastal Enterprises Inc., n.d.). It offered loans from less than $5,000 to $25,000 with an average loan of $10,000. As of 1994, more than 43 percent of SBA microloans had been made to women (NWBC, 1994).

According to the SELP project, of those programs responding to their survey, micro-enterprise programs had loaned $126 million and in 1995 assisted 36,211 business (Severens & Kays, 1997). Fifty-six percent of the programs featured in the directory provided support for AFDC clients, and 55 percent worked with low-income clients (Severens & Kays, 1997).

In less developed countries, micro-enterprise programs have usually targeted women, and most of the participants have been women. In the United States, micro-enterprise programs have had a more diverse client base. Nonetheless, a portion of micro-enterprise organizations can be identified as targeting women and designed specifically to empower women. Examples have included the Women's Business Development Center established in 1993 "[t]o support women and their families in their quest for economic self-sufficiency through entrepreneurship" (Clark et al., 1994, p. 268). This program has provided business training courses, business planning, individual business counseling, peer support, and mentoring. They also have made individual microloans of up to $5,000 and larger loans ranging from $20,000 to $100,000 to businesses that have been operating for more than one year. WBDC has targeted AFDC recipients (40 percent), low- (20 percent) and moderate- (35 percent) income women, and 5 percent "other." Similar programs have included the Women's Business Development Corporation, established in 1988 in Bangor, Maine; the Women's Business Initiative Corporation of Milwaukee, Wisconsin, established in May 1989; and the Women's Economic Self-Sufficiency Team established in 1988 in Albuquerque, New Mexico. The American Woman's Economic Development Corporation, established in 1977 (AWED) has been a national nonprofit organization that offered business, training, counseling, conferences, and seminars to over 35,000 women from all

50 states and Canada (Nelton, 1987). Another example has been WomanVenture in St. Paul, Minnesota, an organization that made loans from $50 to $25,000, primarily to startups.

Using information provided in the *1994 Directory of U.S. Micro-enterprise Programs*, the following characteristics were identified. Of the 195 practitioner and support organizations identified by the SELP project in 1994, 122 or 63 percent had a female contact person. Forty-six percent (89) specified that their organization targeted women. The remaining provided services to women, but did not specify women as a target group. Twenty-five (12.8 percent) organizations targeted women only, and of the 38 organizations that offered group lending, 17 or 44.7 percent specifically targeted women. This situation could be changing rapidly, as the 1996 directory listed only 12 programs (5 percent) that served women exclusively and 75 percent of programs with a client base that was 50 percent or more female (Severens & Kays, 1997, p. xvii).[3]

Some micro-enterprise programs have made loans directly to individuals, and others have used a group model. The Women's Self-Employment Project (WSEP) in Chicago has been "the largest nonprofit entrepreneurial-services program targeting low-income and moderate-income women in the city" (Welles, 1994, p. 92). WSEP has concentrated on providing support for women in the start-up stage. Women interested in borrowing must join a "lending circle" consisting of five women (Welles, 1994, p. 94). The lending circle was based on the "Grameen model" whereby borrowing occurs in succession with the next group member borrowing only after the previous borrower has repaid her loan or established a history of repayment (Welles, 1994). Using a lending group has helped to foster peer pressure for repayment and provided social support. In Less Developed Countries the model has been associated with a high rate of loan repayment.

Connie Evans, the president of WSEP, "believes that having the circle composed of just women imparts solidarity and a sense of security that might not result if a man were allowed into the circle and sought to dominate it" (Welles, 1994, p. 94). Since 1986, WSEP has been serving low-income and moderate-income, mostly minority (90 percent) women. Altogether, "WSEP had lent out nearly $650,000, with the average first loan being $1,500." The lending circles have boasted a repayment rate of 100 percent (Welles, 1994, p. 94).

> Evans believes that the jump in interest reflects a changing economy. In the inner city, people are losing jobs, and those jobs are disappearing for good. Second, she says, the rising interest reflects a desire by many inner-city women to escape the debilitating clutches of welfare. It's a way for people to dig themselves out of isolating experience of poverty and to develop a sense of self by connecting with other people whose experiences

they share. It's as much a community development project as it is a program to foster entrepreneurship. "People in poverty live such isolated lives," says Evans. "We want to reduce that isolation and free people up to address other issues in their lives." (Welles, 1994, p. 94)

Servon (1996) echoed these sentiments in her case study of the Women's Initiative for Self Employment (WISE), a micro-enterprise program for women with a client base of 44 percent very low income, 23 percent moderate income, 20 percent high income, and no information available for 13 percent (Servon, 1996, p. 40). One of her key findings was that women needed access to more than just credit and training. WISE has used a holistic approach to address a complex set of needs faced by low-income women. In fact, less than 10 percent of participants eventually received a loan through the program (Servon, 1996, p. 44). In a survey, participants indicated other benefits including increases in self-esteem, career options, work skills, the potential for success, and independence (Servon, 1996, p. 45). This holistic, social welfare approach has stressed personal development as necessary for economic empowerment.

Micro-enterprise organizations emphasize communal effort, support, and a desire for economic self-sufficient. The goal is to dig oneself out of poverty by connecting with others. The results have been increased solidarity among women, successful small businesses, and a remarkably high loan-repayment rate. Here we see a merging of the goals of the "gendered female" nonprofit sector—community and support—combined with a goal of the for-profit sector—economic growth.

Micro-enterprise organizations have served as mediating institutions where the gender trend of increases in women small businesses and the nonprofit sector have met. Through these nonprofit organizations, women entrepreneurs have engaged in community building and the development of solidarity among participants. Of course, not all women entrepreneurs have relied on nonprofits, and micro-enterprise programs cannot meet the needs of all women entrepreneurs, especially those who require larger amounts of financing. The point is that this phenomenon has occurred—rapid increase in female entrepreneurs and rapid rise in nonprofit micro-enterprise organizations. How can we understand these trends? By using gendered lenses to view the changes in the economy and by understanding the gendered nature of the nonprofit sector, these trends become understandable. The particular shape of female entrepreneurship—small business, low capital, and concentrated in a few industries—becomes reinforced and complemented with nonprofit organizations. By examining how the trends are connected, we become aware of the interrelationships of the sectors, of how flexible we are in creating structures that do not fit rigid definitions of for profit and not for profit.


## DISCUSSION

This analysis highlighted the connections between the not-for-profit and for-profit sectors, the importance of gender for understanding these connections, and the cooperative activities between the sectors. By examining self-employment among women and supporting micro-enterprise programs, we see connections between the sectors. By definition, making a profit is not the goal of not-for-profits, but helping others better their lives, restoring communities, and building social networks are common aims of nonprofit activities. When the means to these goals are economic empowerment through small business development, we see that activities in the nonprofit and for-profit can become complementary.

Gender informed our understanding of these connections between the not-for-profit and for-profit sectors. Understanding gendered economic trends was the bridge to seeing the link between economic trends and nonprofit sector activities. By paying attention to increases in women's self-employment as a result of changes in the economy, the connections between for-profit sector activity of increases in female self-employment and nonprofit sector activities of micro-enterprise nonprofit organizations become apparent. But gender was important for more than just understanding these connections. For micro-enterprise programs, a common gender of participants served as a source of empowerment and solidarity. This idea of empowerment crossed over into for-profit activities as self-employment itself has been an arena where women can be economically empowered and empowered to enact a personal vision. For women, a common gender can provide a source of empowerment and solidarity. These common goals help link the sectors' activities. Thus, for some women, self-employment became the answer to their lack of advancement in the broader economy. The micro-enterprise programs provided a way to empower them, to build the skills necessary to succeed, and to give access to financial resources that make self-employment possible.

However, to more fully understand the gendered outcomes related to self-employment in the post-industrial economy, it is necessary to consider the occupational level of women entrepreneurs. Like the dichotomy in the not-for-profit sector of enhanced leadership opportunities and low-wage, dead-end jobs, self-employment experiences for women differ significantly. Although highly skilled, entrepreneurial women might be able to achieve greater successes once they are no longer under the corporate glass ceiling, low-skilled, self-employed women often find themselves in even less favorable conditions than their counterpart in wage labor. The average salary for self-employed women is lower than the average salary of women employees. Moreover, self-employed women of microbusinesses are less likely to have health insurance and other benefits. The higher level of sex segregation among the self-employed means that women business owners are more likely to be in female-dominated industries with their lower wages and prestige. In fact, some researchers reject micro-enterprise programs on the grounds that they encourage women to start businesses in marginalized sectors of the economy (Ehlers & Main, 1998). Thus, although self-employment offers greater leadership opportunities and potential for capital growth as compared to wage and salary employment, for women with microbusinesses, self-employment also can mean lower incomes and less job stability.

Micro-enterprise organizations can be thought of as mediating structures between not-for-profit and profit-making activities. They serve as a meeting place for women to come together, to learn about themselves, to acquire training and job skills, and decide if self-employment is appropriate for them. If they choose self-employment, the micro-enterprise organization provides a foundation on which to build a support network, establish a credit history, and receive ongoing technical support, all activities promoting business success. These mediating structures that are conducive to personal and economic empowerment become launching pads into for-profit activities.

As the field of micro-enterprise programs matures in the United States, we see organizations evolving away from target populations to serving anyone in need of a microloan. Individual borrowing is becoming the norm, and group lending is becoming the exception. Though we do not know how representative the Aspen Institute directory is of U.S. micro-enterprise programs, there were fewer programs in the 1996 directory as compared to the 1994 directory that were targeted exclusively toward women. These trends raise an interesting question: As micro-enterprise programs evolve, are they becoming more like for-profit lending programs?[4] That is, are micro-enterprise programs moving away from focusing on personal development and empowerment through group lending, training, and using alternative collateral requirements to becoming more like bank lending programs with strict collateral and credit history requirements and individual lending? For many micro-enterprise programs, training has become the most important activity, and credit has become less important. What role is gender playing? How do organizations make the decision to focus on a specific group versus making their services available to all? As micro-enterprise programs evolve, will they still serve as mediating organizations or will they look more like for-profit entities? Will these changes occur because of increasing pressures on micro-enterprise programs to become economically self-sustaining? The evolution of micro-enterprise provides a fertile ground for future research on the links between the for-profit and not-for-profit sectors and the gender dynamics of these interactions.

## NOTES

1. The economy has had many other gendered effects such as declining wages for men and continued sex segregation. However, these effects are not the focus of this chapter.

2. For a comprehensive discussion of the different types of micro-enterprise programs, see Johnson 1998b.

3. It should be noted that these directories do not represent a random sampling of microcredit programs (none exists), but the information does reveal the significant role of women in these programs. It is not necessary that *all* programs be geared toward women and run by women to say that gender plays a significant role in the formation and practices of some microcredit programs.

4. For a discussion of issues facing micro-enterprise programs, see Johnson 1998a.

## REFERENCES

Belous, R. S. (1989). How human resource systems adjust to the shift toward contingent workers. *Monthly Labor Review, 112* (3), 7–12.

Bennet, J. (1994, August 26). Strike at G.M. parts plant ends after idling 46,000. *New York Times,* A14.

Bianchi, S. M., & D. Spain. (1986). *American women in transition.* New York: Russell Sage Foundation.

Bluestone, B., & B. Harrison (1982). *The deindustrialization of America: Plant closings, community abandonment, and the dismantling of basic industry.* New York: Basic Books.

Brush, C. G. (1992). Research on women business owners: Past trends, a new perspective and future directions. *Entrepreneurship Theory & Practice, 16* (4), 5–30.

Buttner, E. H., & B. Rosen. (1988). Bank loan officers' perceptions of the characteristics of men, women, and successful entrepreneurs. *Journal of Business Venturing, 3* (3), 249–258.

Buttner, E. H., & B. Rosen. (1989). Funding new business ventures: Are decision makers biased against women entrepreneurs? *Journal of Business Venturing, 4* (4), 249–261.

Carey, M. L., & K. C. Hazelbaker. (1986). Employment growth in the temporary help industry. *Monthly Labor Review, 109* (4), 37–44.

Castells, M., & A. Portes. (1989). World underneath: The origins, dynamics, and effects of the informal economy. In A. Portes, M. Castells, & L. A. Benton (Eds.), *The informal economy: Studies in advanced and less developed countries.* Baltimore: Johns Hopkins University Press.

Chevan, H. (1992). Temporary workers help businesses manage peaks and valleys. *Office Systems, 9* (4), 25–28.

Clark, M., T. Huston, & B. Meister. (1994). *1994 directory of U.S. micro-enterprise programs.* Washington: Aspen Institute.
Coastal Enterprises Inc. (n.d.). *SBA microloan program.* Wiscasset, ME: CEI.
Coastal Enterprises Inc. (1994). *Creating opportunities for Maine people: 1994 annual report.* Wiscasset, ME: CEI.
Cocheo, S. (1986). Trading ideas with small business. *ABA Banking Journal, 78* (3), 48–50.
Cromie, S., & J. Hayes. (1988). Towards a typology of female entrepreneurs. *Sociological Review, 36* (1) 87–113.
Ehlers, T. B., & K. Main. (1998). Women and the false promise of micro-enterprise. *Gender and Society, 12* (4), 424–440.
England, P., & G. Farkas. (1986). *Households, employment, and gender: A social, economic and demographic view.* Hawthorne, NY: Aldine Publishing Company.
Fay, M., & L. Williams (1993). Gender bias and the availability of business loans. *Journal of Business Venturing, 8* (4), 363–376.
Fernberg, P. (1989). Enjoying impressive growth and diversity. *Modern Office Technology, 34* (1), 116.
Fischer, E. M., A. R. Reuber, & L. S. Dyke. (1993). A theoretical overview and extension of research on sex, gender, and entrepreneurship. *Journal of Business Venturing, 8* (2), 151–168.
Fraser, J. A. (1993). Desperately seeking capital. *Working Women, 18* (7), 59–79.
Freeman, S. J. M. (1990). *Managing lives: Corporate women and social change.* Amherst: University of Massachusetts Press.
Fried, L. I. (1989). A new breed of entrepreneur—women. *Management Review, 78* (12), 18–25.
Goffee, R., & R. Scase. (1983). Business ownership and women's subordination: A preliminary study of female proprietors. *Sociological Review, 31* (4), 625–47.
Goldin, C. (1990). *Understanding the gender gap: An economic history of American women.* New York: Oxford University Press.
Greene, P. G., & M. A. Johnson. (1995). Social learning and middleman minority theory: Explanations for self-employed women. *National Journal of Sociology, 9* (1), 59–84.
Gruer, W. E., & H. L. Moore. (1992). Staffing a company with the just-in-time employee. *Industrial Management, 34* (1), 31–32.
Hisrich, R. D. (1986). The woman entrepreneur: Characteristics, skills, problems, and prescriptions for success. In D. L. Sexton & R. W. Smilor (Eds.), *The art and science of entrepreneurship.* Cambridge, MA: Ballinger Publishing Company.
Hodgkinson, V. A., M. S. Weitzman, C. M. Toppe, & S. M. Noga. (1992). *Nonprofit almanac 1992–1993: Dimensions of the independent sector.* San Francisco: Jossey-Bass.
Johnson, M. A. (1998a). Basic issues facing micro-enterprise organizations in the United States. *Journal of Developmental Entrepreneurship, 3* (1), 1–19.
Johnson, M. A. (1998b). Developing a typology of nonprofit micro-enterprise programs in the United States. *Journal of Developmental Entrepreneurship, 3* (2), 165–184.
Klein, E. (1993). Getting credit when credit is due. *D&B Reports, 42* (2), 28–31, 55.
Lavin, D. (1994, March 15). Two GM facilities are struck by UAW over 'outsourcing.' *Wall Street Journal,* A4.
Lincoln, C. (1993). Temporary services and the global economy. *Office, 117,* 48.
Lloyd, C. B. (Ed.). (1975). *Sex discrimination and the division of labor.* New York: Columbia University Press.

Loscocco, K. A., & J. Robinson. (1991). Barriers to women's small business success in the United States. *Gender and Society, 5* (4), 511–532.

McCarthy, K. D. (Ed.). (1990). *Lady bountiful revisited: Women, philanthropy and power.* New Brunswick, NJ: Rutgers University Press.

McGhee, N. (1985). Temporary workers help insurers to avoid long-term staffing woes. *National Underwriter, 89,* 4 and 68.

National Foundation for Women Business Owners. (1993). *Financing the business: A report on financial issues from the 1992 biennial membership survey of women business owners.* Washington: NFWBO.

National Foundation for Women Business Owners. (1995). *Women-owned businesses: Breaking the boundaries.* Washington: NFWBO.

National Women's Business Council. (1994). *1994 annual report to the President of the United States and the Congress of the United States.* Washington: NWBC.

Neider, L. (1987). A preliminary investigation of female entrepreneurs in Florida. *Journal of Small Business Management, 25* (3), 22–29.

Nelton, S. (1987). Polishing women entrepreneurs. *Nation's Business, 75* (7), 61–63.

Odendahl, T., & S. Youmans. (1994). Women on nonprofit boards. In T. Odendahl & M. O'Neill (Eds.), *Women & power in the nonprofit sector.* San Francisco: Jossey-Bass Publishers.

O'Neill, M. (1994). The paradox of women and power in the nonprofit sector. In T. Odendahl & M. O'Neill (Eds.), *Women & power in the nonprofit sector.* San Francisco: Jossey-Bass Publishers.

Oppenheimer, K. M. (1970). *The female labor force in the United States: Demographic and economic factors governing its growth and changing composition.* Berkeley: University of California Press.

Preston, A. E. (1994). Women in the nonprofit labor market. In T. Odendahl & M. O'Neill (Eds.), *Women & power in the nonprofit sector.* San Francisco: Jossey-Bass Publishers.

Reskin, B., & H. I. Hartmann (Eds.). (1985). *Women's work, men's work: Sex segregation on the job.* Washington: National Academy Press.

Reskin, B., & I. Padavic. (1994). *Women and men at work.* Thousand Oaks, CA: Pine Forge Press.

Riding, A. L., & C. S. Swift. (1990). Women business owners and terms of credit: Some empirical findings of the Canadian experience. *Journal of Business Venturing, 5* (5), 327–340.

Ritzer, G. (1989). The permanently new economy: The case for reviving economic sociology. *Work and Occupations, 16* (3), 243–272.

Rose, M. S. (1994). Philanthropy in a different voice: The Women's Funds. *Nonprofit and Voluntary Sector Quarterly, 23,* 227–242.

Servon, L. J. (1996). Micro-enterprise programs and women: Entrepreneurship as individual empowerment. *Journal of Developmental Entrepreneurship, 1* (1), 31–55.

Severens, C. A., & A. J. Kays. (1997). *1996 directory of U.S. micro-enterprise programs.* Washington: Aspen Institute.

Shaiko, R. G. (1996). Female participation in public interest nonprofit governance: Yet another glass ceiling? *Nonprofit and Voluntary Sector Quarterly, 25* (3), 302–320.

Spain, D., & S. M. Bianchi. (1996). *Balancing act.* New York: Russell Sage Foundation.

Steinberg, R. J., & J. A. Jacobs. (1994). Pay equity in nonprofit organizations: Making women's work visible. In T. Odendahl & M. O'Neill (Eds.) *Women & power in the nonprofit sector.* San Francisco: Jossey-Bass Publishers.

Touby, L. (1992). The new bankrolls behind women's business. *Business Week,* September 21, 70–71.

U.S. Bureau of the Census. (1994). *Statistical abstract of the United States: 1994.* 114th edition. Washington: U.S. Government Printing Office.

U.S. Department of Commerce, Bureau of the Census. (1990). *1987 economic census: Women-owned businesses.* Washington: Government Printing Office.

U.S. Department of Commerce, Bureau of the Census. (1996). *1992 economic census: Women-owned businesses.* Washington: Government Printing Office.

U.S. Department of Education. (1994). *Digest of education statistics.* Washington: National Center for Education Statistics.

Welles, E. O. (1994). It's not the same America. *Inc., 16* (5), 82–98.

Wharton, A. (1989). Gender segregation in private-sector, public sector, and self-employed occupations, 1950–1981. *Social Science Quarterly, 70* (4), 923–940.

Zellner, W., R. W. King, V. N. Byrd, G. DeGeorge, & J. Birnbaum. (1994). Women entrepreneurs. *Business Week,* April 18, 110.

# 9

# Korean Rotating Credit Associations in Los Angeles

*Ivan Light, Im Jung Kwuon, and Zhong Deng*

Also sometimes called rotating credit and savings associations, rotating credit associations (RCAs) are informal social groups whose participants agree to make periodic financial contributions to a fund which is "given in whole or in part to each contributor in rotation."[1] Familiar in many developing countries, and a frequent subject of anthropological inquiry,[2] RCAs have also attracted sociological attention for two reasons. First, RCAs facilitate the entrepreneurship of immigrant and ethnic minorities in developed market economies, thus becoming a factor in ethnic minorities' income attainment.[3] Second, depending on naked social trust, RCAs are theoretically interesting organizations.

The provision of investment capital is the more studied issue. Obtaining loan capital poses an obstacle for all small business ventures, but the problem is especially severe for immigrant or ethnic minority entrepreneurs, who lack credit ratings, collateral, or are the victims of ethnoracial discrimination. RCAs reduce the severity of this financial obstacle. First, RCAs encourage saving. Second, RCAs make the whole group's savings available to member households for consumption or investment. Those to whom the RCAs extend credit are typically im-

migrants or disadvantaged minorities whose financial needs mainstream institutions cannot or will not service because the borrowers
lack credit ratings and/or collateral. Third, like numbers gambling
syndicates, RCAs circumvent the slow, unfriendly, and bureaucratic
channels of banks and insurance companies, the mainstream financial
institutions of market societies.[4] Finally, RCAs are educational institutions in which the more skilled teach money-handling to less-skilled
coethnics.[5] For these reasons, RCAs represent cultural resources that
support the consumption, home purchase, and commercial enterprise
of groups endowed with the tradition.[6]

RCAs have a special importance in the literature of Asian entrepreneurship, underscoring the claim that Asian cultural traditions influence and influenced Asian entrepreneurship in North America. Rooted
ultimately in Weber's Protestant ethnic thesis, cultural theory stresses
the contribution of ethno-cultural heritages to entrepreneurship independent of class resources or of market conditions. When specifically
applied to the entrepreneurship of immigrant or of ethnic minorities, a
special case of the general theory, cultural theory attributes differential
entrepreneurial performance to differential endowment with appropriate cultural resources, net, of course, of class resources and market
conditions.[7] To the extent that RCAs provide an informal vehicle for
saving and lending, groups that possess the institution (like Chinese,
Japanese, and Koreans) are in a position to solve the credit problems
that inhibit the entrepreneurship of groups (like American blacks) that
lack this informal institution.[8]

## FUNCTIONALIST ANALYSIS OF THE RCA

Although entrepreneurship research has been the most active source
of interest in RCAs, and the sole source of evidence, the RCAs are also of
theoretical importance outside entrepreneurship studies because of the
organization's dependence upon naked social trust. Three positions
characterize that related theoretical literature: Parsonian functionalism,
transaction cost analysis, and embeddedness theory. Parsonian and
neo-Parsonian functionalists claim that modernization promotes the
autonomy of economic behavior from social roles and social networks
by its universalism, specialization, and bureaucratization.[9] In a seminal
functionalist work that still represents the orthodox view of rotating
credit associations, Geertz defines modernization as a "process of social
structural differentiation and reintegration" in the course of which actors learn to distinguish social contexts in which economic calculation is
legitimate from those in which it is illegitimate.[10] Because RCAs are tied
to social networks, particularistic, and non-bureaucratic, Geertz pre-

dicts their disappearance in the course of modernization. According to Geertz, RCAs are "self-liquidating, being replaced ultimately by banks, cooperatives, and other economically more rational types of credit institutions."[11] In the functionalist view, it is irrational to utilize RCAs when depository institutions are alternatively available, and, when finally given a choice, people will cease to use RCAs for this reason.

Like other functionalist theorists,[12] Geertz does not explain how differentiation proceeds, but he intimates that economic competition causes more differentiated financial institutions to survive less differentiated ones. This formula leaves unanswered the role of conflict, of elites, and of law in effecting the change as well as the evenness of differentiation among economic sectors. Also, when specifying that differentiation will ultimately prevail, Geertz provides no time frame. Nonetheless, functionalists could hardly derive satisfaction from the longevity of RCAs, especially in developed market economies.

Because so little is known about RCA operation, functionalism's success turns on several still unanswered questions of fact. First, functionalists claim that RCAs cannot compete effectively with financial bureaucracies because RCAs offer inadequate financial services. For example, Reitz maintains that RCAs cannot assemble sums of money sufficiently large to permit the capitalization of viable firms in an advanced market economy.[13] Second, Graves and Graves treat RCAs as an "adaptation to poverty" rather than a means of escape from it.[14] This interpretation identifies RCAs as benighted products of economic backwardness, and condemns them to extinction as advancing economies liquidate pockets of residual poverty. Finally, it might be alleged that RCAs are only useful among marginal social groups locked out of bureaucratic credit institutions by temporary barriers (such as racial discrimination, ignorance, foreign origin) that must in time disappear.

## TRANSACTION COST ANALYSIS OF RCAs

Transaction cost analysis adopts a viewpoint partially compatible with that of sociological functionalism.[15] From a transactional perspective, RCAs are of interest because of their reliance on naked social trust. Long acknowledged a critical condition of business or financial transactions,[16] social trust does not go naked in advanced market economies. Instead, it depends upon law, contracts, collateral, credit agencies, banks, and escrow and insurance companies. These formal organizations permit creditors and debtors to trust strangers in complex and long-term financial transactions.[17] When debtors prove untrustworthy, lenders recover by foreclosure, lawsuits, or insurance. With this security available, lenders can provide funds to strangers, and credit exists in financial markets.

Because the problem of social trust is so serious and intractable, Western market economies have abandoned market-coordinated provision of business, consumer, and real property credit to giant financial bureaucracies, tacitly accepting the overhead costs they impose. In Williamson's terms, giant financial bureaucracies absorb the "opportunism" otherwise present in market-coordinated financial transactions. Therefore, bureaucracies exist.[18] Although an economist, Williamson dismisses economistic apriorism which assumes that actors are omniscient and self-interested. Instead, he substitutes "bounded rationality" for omniscience, and "opportunism" for self-interest.[19]

Deeming these assumptions realistic characterizations of "human nature as we know it," Williamson nonetheless excludes from analysis "the social context in which transactions are embedded" even while acknowledging that "customs, mores, habits, and so on" do "have a bearing" upon transaction cost economizing.[20] Of course, the more important their bearing, the less satisfactory a theory that excludes social factors from analysis. Nonetheless, Williamson's premises are compatible with sociological functionalism's exclusion of social factors from economic behavior in differentiated societies.[21]

## EMBEDDEDNESS THEORY

Derived from social anthropology, embeddedness theory claims that "structures of social relations" always influence economic behavior to the extent that overlooking their influence is a grave error even when treating differentiated institutions in advanced societies.[22] On this point, embeddedness theory departs from transaction cost analysis, which ignores any influence of purely social relationships upon economic behavior. Embeddedness theory departs from sociological functionalism in its stress upon the continuing influence of social relationships upon economic action even in fully modern societies. This last point of difference is, however, relative, not absolute. Embeddedness theory concedes that the fusion of business and social roles recedes with modernization. However, embeddedness theorists deny that the historical disjuncture is so sharp as functionalists believe. Whereas functionalists (and most American Marxists) accept the economists' utilitarian vision of economic action in advanced market economies, rejecting only their account of economic action in premodern societies, embeddedness theory rejects the economists' asocial version of economic behavior in modern, modernizing, and premodern societies.[23] Embeddedness concedes that social influences recede in modernization, but it claims that they never disappear or become so faint in their effects that analysts can ignore them.

RCAs utilize social trust to solve the problem of business trust. In Williamson's terms, RCAs reduce the "transaction costs" of non-bureaucratic credit by limiting access to participants whose probity and responsibility is informally assured on the basis of family and social networks.[24] In current Korean practice, participants need not know one another personally.[25] It suffices that the organizer vouch for each. RCAs represent decentralized, non-bureaucratic solutions to credit problems that Western market economies require gigantic bureaucracies to resolve. Minimizing transaction costs, RCAs also avoid the overhead costs that result from bureaucratic internalization of market transactions.[26] This reduction renders RCAs effective credit agencies that compete with banks and insurance companies, the modern and bureacratized solution to the problem of social trust in credit.[27]

## COMPARATIVE RESEARCH ON RCAs

RCAs pose no theoretical anomaly in backward economies so long as they exist without competition from bureaucratic institutions of credit. But in differentiated economies, the spectacle of a premodern RCA's surviving competition with huge banks and insurance companies poses a theoretical anomaly. At this point, entrepreneurship research becomes of more general theoretical relevance because, as a matter of empirical fact, Afro-Asian immigrants in the United States have long utilized rotating credit associations to support their independent business and they continue to do so. According to Moon, RCAs also contribute to the entrepreneurship of Korean immigrants in the United States between 1903 and 1918.[28] In Britain and France, historical studies are missing, but current research demonstrates that Afro-Asian immigrants currently utilize rotating credit associations for business capitalization.[29] However, it has proven difficult to document just how big a role RCAs play and have played in immigrant entrepreneurship whether in Europe or North America. Granted, RCAs exist, but how important is the credit they provide to the communities that use them?

On this issue, the entrepreneurship literature raises two key questions: what proportion of entrepreneurs used rotating credit associations, and how much of their start-up capital did RCAs provide? If RCAs were of negligible importance, then one can dismiss their influence on entrepreneurship because, whatever inter-group differences in entrepreneurship exist, RCAs did not cause them if the possessor groups do not utilize RCAs for entrepreneurial purposes. The same two questions have a different salience in the theoretical literature. If the RCA plays a negligible role in the immigrant entrepreneurs' capitalization, then evidence supports the arguments of those who expect RCAs to fail when confronting competition with rationalized, bureaucratic institutions of saving and credit. To the extent that immigrant RCAs play an important role in capitalization in the United States, transaction cost theory is confounded, embeddedness theory strengthened, and functionalist theory is handed back the still unsolved problem of how differentiation actually proceeds.

## KYE: A KOREAN RCA

The rotating credit association has a centuries-long history in Korea. Its first known usage is described in a census volume of 1663. Koreans call their RCA *kye* (pronounced keh). The word means "contract" or "bond," but it is often translated as voluntary association.[30] The earliest kyes were non-monetary associations for mutual aid among subsistence-farming peasants. Mutual aid kyes continue to exist, and Chun identifies funerals, weddings, ceremonial foods, and seasonal ceremonies as occasions for the formation of mutual aid kyes. As modernization theory predicts, money kyes became more important with the commercialization of Korean agriculture and society. According to Chun, money kyes are more common in "urban commercial settings" than in the countryside.[31] Moreover, rural money kyes are commonly interest-free whereas urban money kyes have evolved complex methods for the payment of interest to the fund. Janelli and Janelli declare money kyes "an extremely popular form of savings and investment in South Korean cities."[32]

Kennedy declares that money kyes became more popular in urban areas after the Korean War. He also maintains that the money kyes "successfully competed with other sectors of the money market," a claim he confirmed by Bank of Korea publications dated 1969.[33] Because kyes diverted funds from the banking system, Korean banks regard and regarded them as economic competitors, and studied their practices and extent in hope of emulating their market appeal. Nonetheless, more recent survey evidence suggest that kyes probably peaked in popularity around 1969. In that year's survey of South Korea, the Bank of Korea found that 72 percent of adult respondents were kye members. Another survey found that member households invested about 26 percent of their monthly income in kyes.[34] Subsequent bank surveys of urban Korean households recorded declines in kye participation. In 1976, the Bank of Korea found that 42.5 percent of urban households were kye members, and in 1986 only 34.1 percent were still kye members.[35]

Because of their convenience and high interest payments, kyes encouraged popular thrift. Yi declares kye "the only way the poor have" of acquiring lump sums of money as well as "the most frequent and profitable investment activity of the poor."[36] In the mid-1970s, "middle and upper income savers" were especially attracted to kyes, utilizing their cash withdrawals for "such costs as childrens' educational expenses."[37] Contrary to what one would expect on a functionalist view, Korea's peasantry included fewer money kye participants than did Korea's intelligentsia. If money kyes were simply disappearing, one would expect rural and backward population segments to retain the practice longer than progressive urban segments as, for example, peasants retain folk music and costume longer than do urban non-manual workers.

Nearly all Korean kye participants were and are women.[38] This fact has encouraged the functionalist claim that kye participants are economically irrational, as women are supposed to know less about money than men. However, in their study of women kye participants in Seoul, Janelli and Janelli demonstrate that kye bidders structured their offers in full knowledge of the interest rate advantage of different turns. Financial analysis reveals that the first and last turns in kye are always the most advantageous, and the middle turn is least advantageous. True, the Seoul women did not use mathematical interest formulas to make these calculations. Instead they used "common sense" and "crude mathematical intuition" to reach a judgment that was roughly correct. When the women adjusted their interest bids to accommodate social relationships, as they frequently did, they knew what the accommodation cost them.[39]

Another common fallacy maintains that kyes involve only "pin money," and that the kyes' functions were and are social, not economic. Compatible with a functionalist view of kyes, this fallacy rests upon unexamined Western assumptions about family roles. Although Korea is a patriarchal society, women customarily manage family finances and investments in Korea whereas, in the West, husbands perform this role.[40] Because women manage household finances, they have the whole earned income of their household to invest in kyes, not just domestic allowances. Korean women utilize RCAs to save and to invest whatever income their households save or invest, routinely a great deal, as South Korea's saving rate was second only to Japan's in East Asia.[41] Naturally, most of the money returned to households from kyes is utilized for consumption. But, especially in South Korea, where a third of workers are self-employed, the line between household income and enterprise income is faint. Therefore, some portion of money invested in Korean kyes ultimately finances family firms.

## KYEs IN THE UNITED STATES

Koreans were among the most entrepreneurial of America's immigrants in the 1970s and the 1980s. In view of the ubiquity and importance of kyes in South Korea, the hypothesis naturally arises that

Korean entrepreneurs in the United States utilized kyes to support their numerous firms, a position enthusiastically endorsed in the popular media.[42] If so, kye presumably represented a cultural resource that partially accounts for the entrepreneurial record of the Korean immigrants. Reviewing the research on Korean RCAs in Los Angeles and elsewhere in the United States, Light and Bonacich reported unambiguous evidence that such was, indeed, the case. Their evidence showed that kye was a frequent practice among Korean Americans, that kyes raised substantial sums of money, and that this money often supported the capitalization, expansion, or cash flow of Korean-owned business firms.[43] Indeed, the use of kye is so widespread in the Los Angeles Korean-American community that the Hanmi Bank, a Korean-American organization, developed kye-like savings plans in order to compete with the kyes.[44]

At the same time, a number of puzzling methodological issues surfaced. Contrasting the results of three ethnographic and four survey research studies of Korean kyes, Light and Bonacich found systematic discrepancies in the extent of kye participation reported. Although both methods yielded evidence of kye participation, ethnographic research yielded much larger estimates of the probable extent of kye participation than did survey research. For example, in the most generous survey result, Kim and Hurh interviewed 94 Korean business owners on Chicago's South Side. Thirty-four percent of respondents indicated that they had "accumulated some of their own capital through the rotating credit system."[45] However, using ethnographic methods, Kunae Kim found 82 percent participation in kye among 77 Los Angeles Koreans she studied.[46]

To explain this discrepancy, one might suppose that more Korean-Americans used the kye for consumption, housing, or business than used it for business alone. Although this conclusion is probably fair, it does not resolve the methodological puzzle. Ethnographic researchers also reported problems of respondent rapport and candor which have implications for the survey results too. In evaluating the discrepancy between ethnographic and survey results, one must pay some attention to methodological issues.[47]

According to the ethnographers, Korean-American respondents were reluctant to discuss kye participation at all. In fact, finding respondent suspicion and hostility unbearable, one Korean-American ethnographer prematurely terminated his research rather than face it.[48] Assessing the problem of respondent candor, Kunae Kim concluded that survey research "could not elicit intimate and honest response regarding the kye from respondents."[49] On these grounds, Kim dismissed results obtained from survey research.

Why should Korean-Americans be so reluctant to discuss kyes? Light and Bonacich proposed a number of explanations.[50] First, many Korean-American respondents erroneously believed that kyes are illegal in the United States, a belief supported by poorly researched articles in the American press. However, although not unlawful in themselves, kyes were routinely utilized in unlawful ways.[51] Few kye participants report interest income to the U.S. tax authorities any more than they had reported it to Korean tax authorities.[52] Therefore, kye interest income unlawfully escapes taxation in both countries. Additionally, intrest rates prevailing in kyes typically exceed statutory maxima both in the United States and in Korea. Interest rates earned by kye members in the United States generally exceed 30 percent a year, an amount in excess of what the federal usury statute permits.[53] As recipients of usurious income, kye users did "not wish to identify themselves" to policemen or tax authorities in Korea, and one supposes that immigrant kye users have the same reluctance in the United States.[54]

These legal issues probably affected Korean respondents' willingness to participate in research about kyes. Many Korean-American respondents fear that social science researchers will report their findings to the tax collector. In view of this mistrust, researchers require respondent confidence before they can obtain candid answers. Unfortunately, even if respondents expect personal anonymity, they may deem it unwise to permit too much to be learned about the usurious and tax-evading kyes in which they participate. Here we confront a little studied methodological issue: conflict of interest between respondents who benefit from public ignorance of their activities and sociologists who live by enlightening the world.

Question wording has posed another methodological problem. Survey questionnaires have asked respondents whether they ever participated in a kye. In most cases, respondents were men but their wife, sister, mother or other female relative was the kye participant. In such cases, a male respondent properly answers "No" to this question. He never participated; his wife did. However, a "No" answer causes underestimation of the true household participation rate in kyes.

Finally, surveys did not distinguish between an RCA's savings function and its credit function.[55] Therefore, when kye participants invested in a business funds they had saved in a completed kye, they might subsequently identify the money's source as "own savings," thus obscuring kye's role in assembling those savings.

Unaware of how serious is the problem of respondent candor, surveys of kyes have had difficulty in obtaining respondent agreement to participate at all. Woodrum, Rhodes, and Feagin conducted the most successful survey study of participation in rotating credit associations. Thanks to the Japanese American Research Project, a research effort paid for and promoted by Japanese community organizations, the authors had a list of every surviving Issei who had migrated to the United States before 1924. From this list of 18,000 Issei, the authors took a systematic sample of 1,024, with a 99 percent response rate. Among their aged respondents, 38.1 percent reported participation in *ko*, the Japanese rotating credit association.[56] Participation rates were higher among urban self-employed than among farmers, and higher among self-employed than among wage earners. This patterning suggests that business owners used rotating credit association more than workers, and that the most modern (urbanized) segment of the business owners used it more than the less progressive rural segment.

These Japanese-American results provide a basis for comparing contemporary Korean-American results. Because the Japanese-Americans surveyed were of the prewar immigrant generation, they are comparable in respect to foreign-born status to contemporary Korean-American adults, few of whom are native born. In the absence of the massive, twenty-year effort undertaken by the Japanese American Research Project, available Korean-American results derive exclusively from low-budget efforts that suffered serious problems of sample randomness and respondent candor. H. C. Kim obtained a non-exhaustive list of Korean-American business firms in 4 cities from which he sampled 300. However, only 52 firms responded to his mailed questionnaire survey, a response rate of 17 percent. Of those who did respond, only 2 percent had obtained all their capital from kye, but Kim's question left undisclosed the proportion who had used kye to obtain any of their business capital.[57]

Young interviewed 40 Korean-American owners of produce stores in New York City, approximately 5 percent of all Korean-American produce merchants in the city.[58] These stores he had obtained from a comprehensive list of all produce stores in New York City. However, Young selected respondents on the basis of location in four clusters rather than randomly. Although Young declared that his respondents were "cooperative," he did not indicate what refusal rate his research encountered. Among his 40 respondents, only one acknowledged that kye had provided "most of his start-up capital," but 21 knew of other Koreans who had participated. When respondents attribute familiarity to others like themselves, but disavow personal involvement, analysts must suspect that respondents did not provide candid answers.

Light and Bonacich completed a telephone survey of Korean entrepreneurs listed in the Korean yellow pages directory of Los Angeles.[59] This telephone directory was not a comprehensive list of Korean-owned business firms. Of more than 1,000 listees, only 325 valid telephone contacts were obtained, a result attributed to inaccuracies and outdated information in the telephone directory. Although the survey was conducted in the Korean language, of 325 listees validly contacted, only 63 percent agreed to participate in the survey. Of 213 entrepreneur respondents, only 1 percent acknowledged making any use of kye in financing their business firms.

In a study of Korean merchants in black neighborhoods, Kim and Hurh obtained a list of Korean merchants on Chicago's South Side from the Korean Chamber of Commerce of Chicago. This list did not include all Korean merchants on the South Side, and it excluded all Korean merchants outside the South Side black community, the majority of Chicago-area Korean merchants. Kim and Hurh were able to interview only 75 percent of the original list. Others refused or could not be located. However, they found several unlisted Korean stores in the neighborhood, bringing to 94 the number of entrepreneurs they finally interviewed. Their survey disclosed that 34 percent of store owners acknowledged accumulating "some of their capital" through kye. Of those who did thus utilize kye, most indicated they had utilized kye capital for their first business. Only six had used kye as a method of capital accumulation in their current business.[60]

Clearly these survey research efforts suffer from imperfect sampling frames, high refusal rates, and lack of respondent candor. Still, flawed as they are, these results represent the existing knowledge about Korean RCAs in the United States. With the exception of Kim and Hurh, the survey results uniformly portray negligible kye use among Korean entrepreneurs. True, Kim and Hurh's results show levels of kye utilization higher than those reported in the other survey literature and comparable with levels reported among aged Japanese-Americans. However, none of the survey studies reported levels of kye utilization consistent with those suggested in the ethnographic literature.

## METHODS OF RESEARCH

Although ethnographers dismiss all survey research because of the candor issue, such dismissal excludes any hope of exact measurement of kye use. If possible at all, it would certainly be desirable to obtain the exact results that only survey research can yield. To this end, when an opportunity presented itself, we designed a survey of kye utilization intended to minimize the objections to previous survey research while retaining the advantages of the survey method.

Rather than sampling the Korean community or some business neighborhood, as others have done already, we located an important Korean trade association in a manufacturing industry. This trade association forms our sampling universe. In June 1987 the Korean American Garment Industry Association had 368 entrepreneur members in Los Angeles. Each entrepreneur owned and operated one or more garment manufacturing factories. Entrepreneur members represented about 50 percent of the Korean entrepreneurs in the Los Angeles garment industry, and approximately 11 percent of the entire garment entrepreneur population of Southern California.[61] The median entrepreneur member employed 40 workers in her or his factories.

The research team explained our scientific purpose to the Director of the KAGIA, and, thanks to a family friendship connection, elicited his cooperation in a study of kye utilization among the KAGIA membership. Declining to release his Association's membership list for sampling, the Director agreed to mail our questionnaire to the entire KAGIA membership along with the Association's monthly newsletter.

We developed a short, self-administered questionnaire of 10 items along with an explanatory letter of introduction. Bailey recommends the mailed survey when respondents must be assured anonymity because a topic is sensitive.[62] Our letter explained the scientific importance of our research, indicating also that RCAs were not, in fact, illegal. Questionnaire and letter were translated into Korean, pretested, revised, and mailed to the entire KAGIA membership along with the Association's April 1987 newsletter. At our request, the Association's director included a communication in Korean, vouching for the bona fides of the research and urging all members to complete and return the survey questionnaire in the postage-paid envelope provided. We hoped this endorsement would increase the respondents' willingness to participate.[63]

By June 1, 1987, we had received only 74 completed questionnaires. Therefore, we included a follow-up questionnaire in the June 1987 KAGIA newsletter. By September 1, 1987, we had received 110 replies in all, a response rate of 29.9 percent of the total KAGIA membership. Although this response rate is low, there are four mitigating circumstances.[64] First, we did not have and could not obtain access to a master list of KAGIA members, and could not identify non-respondents for additional follow-ups. Second, our research addressed a sensitive subject of which respondents were already known to resist discussion. Third, our results are based on 29.9 percent of the sampling *universe*, not 29.9 percent of a sample thereof.

## RESULTS OF THE SELF-ADMINISTERED SURVEY

Twenty-two of our respondents were female, and 88 were male. The KAGIA director reported that only eight of the Association's members were female. However, the director also indicated that in some cases, women operate factories whose nominal owner is their husband or son.

In other cases, wives have secretarial and accounting responsibilities that apparently included filling out our questionnaire. In any event, we found no statistically significant differences between male and female respondents in respect to factory size or household participation in kye, whether in the United States or in Korea.

Asked whether, when still living in Korea, any member of their household had participated in a kye, 54.5 percent responded "Yes," and 43.6 percent "No." Other responses were uninterpretable. Asked whether, since moving to the United States, any member of their household had participated in a kye, 77.3 percent answered "Yes," and 20.9 percent "No." Of 60 entrepreneurs whose households had not utilized kye in Korea, 44 had used it in the United States. Conversely, of 47 whose households had utilized kye in Korea, only 7 became non-users in the United States. We found no statistically significant difference in mean employment size of factory between entrepreneurs who had and who had not used kye in the United States.

Our respondents used kye more in the United States than they had used it in Korea. The change resulted from two causes. First, entrepreneurs use kye more frequently than non-entrepreneurs. Therefore, an increase in entrepreneurship pursuant to immigration would increase kye usage among immigrants. Only one-fifth of Korean American entrepreneurs had been self-employed in Korea prior to emigration.[65] Assuming that the same increase in self-employment occurred among the garment owners we surveyed, their increased kye use in this country probably reflected their choice of self-employment in this country.

Second, Korean garment entrepreneurs utilized kye because they encountered gaps in the American financial system. Small business owners typically fall outside the service market of mainstream financial institutions. However, when kyes fill gaps in financial service they compete effectively with mainstream financial institutions that cannot serve adequately and often *cannot offer service at all* to certain communities. Additionally, the immigrant entrepreneurs' increased utilization of the Korean RCA in the United States is mute evidence that the kyes facilitated their social mobility rather than their accommodation to inferior status.

Asked whether, when they started their garment factory, any of the funds invested as start-up equity capital had originated in a kye, 36.3 percent answered "Yes," and 58.2 percent answered "No." Other responses were uninterpretable. Even if we assume that those 40 respondents who indicated kye use were, as a result of self-selection, the only Korean entrepreneurs who had used the institution at all, all of the 258 non-respondents being non-users, we still confront an 11 percent rate of kye utilization among the garment entrepreneurs. As that 11 percent must represent the lowest possible estimate of kye use in the KAGIA, we are on safe ground in concluding that between 11 and 36 percent of the Korean manufacturers utilized kye funds for business capitalization.

Money derived from concluded kyes represents personal saving; money derived from a continuing kye (against the future necessity to repay) represents credit. Of those who had obtained investment capital from kye participation, 55 percent indicated that they had invested money saved from an already concluded kye in their business; 40 percent indicated that money borrowed from a continuing kye, an unpaid loan, was invested as start-up equity; and 5 percent indicated that they had utilized both completed and continuing kyes. This result may explain why other survey studies reported much lower levels of kye utilization among Korean entrepreneurs. Those studies did not distinguish kye's savings function from its credit function. They asked only about kye's credit use. When credit use is distinguished from savings use, it becomes apparent that the credit use was less important than the previously ignored savings use.

Entrepreneurs were more reluctant to indicate what percentage of their start-up equity had actually been generated by kyes, whether as savings or as loans. Of those 39 who had already indicated that their own firm had utilized equity capital originating in a kye, only 26 specified the exact percentage of start-up capital they had obtained in this manner. However, among those 26 kye users who did respond, kye's mean contribution to total equity was 62.1 percent. Concluded kyes and continuing kyes made unequal contributions to this total. Among those who used kyes for business investment and indicated its percentage contribution to their initial capitalization, concluded kyes generated 40.6 percent of start-up capital and continuing kyes generated another 21.5 percent. As the concluded kyes represented a form of personal saving, the results indicate that the frequently encountered category "own savings" probably glosses over the utilization of rotating credit associations as a method of saving, thus underestimating the financial importance of the rotating credit association in entrepreneurship.

We asked kye users which persons in their household were or had been the actual participants in a U.S. kye. Among male entrepreneurs, two-thirds reported that their wife had been the kye participant. As kye participants in Korea are almost exclusively women, a male participation rate of one-third represents masculinization of the institution in the United States. The increased proportion of male users in the United States is hard to reconcile with the hypothesis that kyes became less important in Los Angeles than they had been in Korea. If the "pin money" theory has any truth, then masculinization of American kyes presumably indicates an increased importance of kyes in this country, a conclusion incompatible with the functionalist view of this institution. If the pin money argument is unsound, as urged above, then masculinization of American kyes would have no importance for the financial importance of kyes, even though it might suggest Americanization of family roles among the immigrants.

Among all respondents, male and female, 57 percent indicated that another household member had participated in the kye, utilizing household funds. If a survey asked respondents only whether they had participated in a kye, 43 percent of those from kye-using household would truthfully have answered "No" to this question. As other surveys have asked exactly that question, their results underestimated kye use.

Of those entrepreneurs who had personally participated in a kye, 59.6 percent owned bigger than average garment factories. Of those whose household had been represented by another member, usually a wife, only 38.1 percent owned bigger than average factories. This difference was statistically significant at the .05 level. The result implies that owners of bigger factories more frequently assumed personal responsibility for overseeing their household's kye participation than did owners of smaller factories, who delegated this function to their wives. Therefore, masculinization of kyes in the United States is compatible with the claim that kye use generally increased in this country in response to increased entrepreneurship among the Korean immigrants.

## DISCUSSION

Obtaining information about kye participation is difficult because respondents had a motive to conceal it. Nonetheless, we have shown that future research on entrepreneurial utilization of RCAs must consider their thrift as well as their credit role as well as the participation of women, especially of wives. If these distinctions are not made, estimates of RCA use will be too small. Additionally, researchers should distinguish household participation in RCAs and investment of RCA proceeds in a business. If this distinction is ignored, estimates of entrepreneurial use of RCAs will be too large.

Between two-thirds and nine-tenths of Korean entrepreneurs made no business use of kye, whether for credit or savings, but kye's role in the Korean garment industry was nonetheless significant. Among kye users and non-users combined, but excluding inconclusive responses, mean utilization of kye for start-up capital amounted to 18.1 percent of total capitalization. Among the kye-using one-fifth, kyes produced almost two-thirds of total start-up capital. As the sums involved were not small, we can reject the claim that RCAs cannot raise capital sums sufficiently large to organize viable firms in advanced market economies. As the kye users were Algeresque garment entrepreneurs, we can also reject the claim that RCAs organize adaptation to poverty rather than an escape route from it.

Running on naked social trust, kyes filled some of the financial needs of these Korean entrepreneurs in Los Angeles and, in so doing, permitted more Koreans to finance business firms than would have been able to achieve this goal without recourse to kyes, thus increasing the size of the Korean business population. To this extent, the Korean kyes underscore the continuing and supportive influence of RCAs upon entrepreneurship, now as in the past. Admittedly, only a minority of manufacturing entrepreneurs in Los Angeles opted for kyes. The majority stayed away. This split is what one would expect from a functionalist view, although small business owners rarely borrow from banks either.[66]

Since the Korean entrepreneurs used kyes more in the United States than in Korea, we can rule out ignorance of financial alternatives as the cause of their enhanced utilization of RCAs in this country. Clearly, the Korean immigrant community institutionalized social trust to an extent that kyes continued to offer some Korean entrepreneurs a useful tool for saving and borrowing. Conceivably, acculturation of Korean immigrants will erode their community solidarity, thus depriving their descendants of access to the traditional kye. If so, kye's obsolescence would occur because acculturation destroyed the social solidarity that the institution required—thus eliminating kye's transaction cost advantage. Although compatible with the functionalist prognosis, such an ending would not signal the expected outperformance of kye in a straight economic competition.

On the other side, so long as social trust persists, kye enjoys a transaction cost advantage relative to bureaucratic financial institutions.[67] In turn, this transaction cost advantage supports the premodern social trust that makes kyes possible. Like ethnic business generally, kyes encourage the ethnic solidarity they require.[68] In short, social trust reciprocally shapes credit institutions and is shaped by them, being helped to persist where credit institutions require a high level of social solidarity in the user population and destroyed where general social (not economic) life undermines the requisite solidarity. This result supports the claim that bureaucratized financial institutions accelerated the atomization of the population rather than having, as previously thought, served the otherwise intractable needs of already atomized people.[69]

Korean RCAs are impossible to accommodate to Williamson's transaction cost analysis since the trusting relations of the participants depend on social mores that Williamson excludes from analysis. Worse, the transaction cost approach cannot explain the evolution of financial institutions in Korea since kyes were and are critical parts of that evolution. Therefore, transaction cost must prove of limited value in explaining the evolution of financial institutions anywhere since relations of social trust are so basic to this whole subject.

Finally, the kye evidence suggests some modifications to Parsonian functionalism. First, kye use in Korea did not decline linearly. Although kye use was increasing when he wrote, a fact evidently unknown to him, Geertz correctly predicted the post-1970 shift from mutual aid to money kyes in Korea as well as the post-1970 decline in kye participation there.[70] In this sense, events in Korea since 1970 have tended to vindicate Geertz's functionalist predictions, even though events before 1970 did not. Moreover, the survival of kyes is the product of three structural features that Geertz overlooked. First, the kyes operate in hard-to-reach populations (such as immigrant communities) that bureaucratic institutions of finance serve with difficulty or not at all. This situation arises because of uneven capitalist development, a universal of capitalist development. Even if kyes ultimately disappear, as functionalism predicts, they may linger longer than functionalists once expected because some financial markets are hard for banks to penetrate. Indeed, since there is no guarantee that banks will ever penetrate all the recalcitrant financial markets, kyes could in principle survive forever.

Second, in Korea and in Los Angeles, kyes benefitted from the rich possibilities for tax evasion and usurious interest-taking that they afforded. Ironically, modernization bequeathed these legal advantages to kyes, thus encouraging their persistence. Mainstream financial institutions cannot violate usury or tax statutes so easily as can kyes. Until and unless modernization strips kyes of their unlawful advantages, kyes shall enjoy an economic advantage in free competition with bureaucratic institutions. There is no guarantee that modernization will ever strip kyes of this advantage. Indeed, the modernization of societies renders ascribed trust of unique value in all illegal business transactions, a condition that could exist forever.[71]

Third, kyes survive because Korean women have feminine networks, motives, values, and attitudes. So long as Korean women control saving, but remain feminine in their financial outlook, Korean households will manage money in RCAs. If the attitudinal and behavioral homogenization of Korean women and Korean men is a necessary prerequisite to the end of kyes, we shall have to wait until women become men before kyes disappear. In that sense, the ultimate financial differentiation of Korea as well, one supposes, of Korean America waits upon a homogenization of gender roles and achievement roles, a realignment that is still very far in the future for Koreans as, indeed, for everyone else.

## NOTES

The authors acknowledge with thanks small research grants from the Asian American Studies Center and the Student Research Program at UCLA. However, only the authors are responsible for errors of fact or opinion found in this article.

1. Shirley Ardener, "The Comparative Study of Rotating Credit Associations." *Journal of the Royal Anthropological Institute* 94, pt. 2, p. 213; David Y. H. Wu, "To Kill Three Birds with One Stone: the Rotating Credit Associations of the Papua New Guinea Chinese," *American Ethnologist* 1 (1974), pp. 565–584. See also: Thierry Pairault, *L'Integration Silencieuse: La Petite Entreprise Chinoise en France*, (Paris: Editions L'Harmattan, 1995), pp. 138–182.

2. Carlos G. Velez I, *Bonds of Mutual Trust: The Cultural Systems of Rotating Credit Associations among Mexicans and Chicanos* (New Brunswick: Rutgers University, 1981); Dan Soen and Patrice de Comarond, "Savings Associations among the Bamileke: Traditional and Modern Cooperation in Southwest Cameroon," *American Anthropologist* 74 (1972), 1170–1179; Clifford Geertz, "The Rotating Credit Association: A 'Middle Rung' in Development," *Economic Development and Cultural Change* 10 (1962), 241–263; Marvin P. Miracle, Diane S. Miracle and Laurie Cohen, "Informal Savings Mobilization in Africa," *Economic Development and Cultural Change* 28 (1980), 701–724.

3. Ivan H. Light, *Ethnic Enterprise in America* (Berkeley and Los Angeles: University of California, 1972); Eric Woodrum, Colbert Rhodes, and Joe R. Feagin, "Japanese American Economic Behavior," *Social Forces* 58 (1980), 1235-1254; Janet Chan and Yuet-Wah Cheung, "Ethnic Resources and Business Enterprise: A Study of Chinese Businesses in Toronto," *Human Organization* 44 (1985), 149; Roger D. Waldinger, *Through the Eye of the Needle* (New York and London: New York University, 1986), 5–6.

4. Ivan H. Light. "Numbers Gambling among Blacks: A Financial Institution," *American Sociological Review* 42 (1977), 892–904.

5. Soen and de Comarond, p. 1178; Geertz, p. 260; Maurice Friedman. "The Handling of Money: A Note on the Background to the Economic Sophistication of Overseas Chinese," *Man* 59 (1959), 64–65.

6. Coleman writes that RCAs cannot operate in disorganized groups that lack mutual trust. He evidently supposes that RCAs can operate wherever the requisite trust is present. Admittedly, mutual trust is a necessary condition of RCA operation. However, trust is not also a sufficient condition of RCA use. RCAs embody what Swidler calls a "culturally-shaped skill." Cultural skills do not easily cross cultural boundaries. For example, black Americans have never utilized RCAs even though RCAs are a West African cultural tradition still utilized by black West Indians in the United States. See: James S. Coleman, "Social Capital in the Creation of Human Capital," *American Journal of Sociology* 94, Supplement S95-S120; Ann Swidler, "Culture in Action: Symbols and Strategies," *American Sociological Review* 51 (1986), 275. See also: Aubrey W. Bonnett, "Structured Adaptation of Black Migrants from the Caribbean: an Examination of an Indigenous Banking System in Brooklyn," *Phylon* 42 (1981), 346–355; Light, *Ethnic Enterprise*, ch. 2.

7. Ivan Light, "Immigrant and Ethnic Enterprise in North America," *Ethnic and Racial Studies* (1984), pp. 195-199; Frank Fratoe, "A Sociological Analysis of Minority Business," *Review of Black Political Economy* 15 (1986), 5–29.

8. Light, *Ethnic Enterprise*, chs. 2, 3.

9. Jeffrey C. Alexander, *Action and Its Environments* (New York: Columbia University, 1989), ch. 2; Neil Smelser, *Social Change in the Industrial Revolution* (Chicago: University of Chicago, 1959), pp. 2–3; Marion J. Levy, *Modernization and the Structure of Societies*, vol. 1 (Princeton, NJ: Princeton University, 1966), 38–46, 60–66, 71–74.

10. Geertz, 241–263.

11. *Ibid.*, p. 263; see also John Derby, "The Role of Tanomoshi in Hawaiian Banking," *Social Process in Hawaii* 30 (1983), pp. 66–84.

12. Alexander, ch.2.

13. Jeffrey G. Reitz, *The Survival of Ethnic Groups* (Toronto: McGraw Hill, 1980), 242; see also: Hyung-Chan Kim, "Ethnic Enterprises among Koreans in America," in Hyung-Chan Kim ed., *The Korean Diaspora* (Santa Barbara, CA: ABC-Clio, 1977), 104–105.

14. Nancy B. Graves and Theodore D. Graves, "Adaptive Strategies in Urban Migration," *Annual Review of Anthropology* 3 (1974), 134.

15. Mayer N. Zald, "Review Essay: the New Institutional Economics," *American Journal of Sociology* 93 (1987), 701–708.

16. Stewart Macaulay, "Non-Contractual Relations in Business: A Preliminary Study," *American Sociological Review* 28 (1963), pp. 55–69; Light, *Ethnic Enterprise*, chs. 2,3.

17. Lynne G. Zucker, "Production of Trust: Institutional Sources of Economic Structure, 1840-1920," *Research in Organizational Behavior* 8 (1986), 83; Bernard Barber, *The Logic and Limits of Trust* (New Brunswick: Rutgers University, 1983); Michael Hechter, *Principles of Group Solidarity* (Berkeley and Los Angeles: University of California, 1987), 107–111.

18. Oliver Williamson, *Markets and Hierarchies* (New York: Free Press, 1975), 26-30; Oliver Williamson, "Transaction Cost Economics: The Governance of Contractual Relations," *Journal of Law and Economics* 22 (1979), 233–261; Oliver Williamson, *The Economic Institutions of Capitalism* (New York: Free Press, 1985).

19. Williamson, *Economic Institutions*, 51.

20. Williamson, *Economic Institutions*, 22, 44; Williamson, *Markets and Hierarchies*, 107–109.

21. In contrast, sociological approaches invoke "moral communities" within which trustworthiness is a reasonable assumption. Trustworthiness shifts the transaction cost advantage to the RCA. See: Abner Cohen, "Cultural Strategies in the Organization of Trading Diasporas," in Claude Meillassoux, ed., *The Development of Indigenous Trade and Markets in West Africa* (London: Oxford University Press, 1971), 267.

22. Mark Granovetter, "Economic Action, Social Structure, and Embeddedness," *American Journal of Sociology* 91 (1985), 482, 503; Karl Polanyi, *The Livelihood of Man* (New York: Academic Press, 1977), ch. 4.

23. The theoretical case centers on the cheapness of ascription; the empirical documentation centers on the utility of ethnicity in business. On the cheapness of ascription see: Leon Mayhew, "Ascription in Modern Societies," *Sociological Inquiry* 38 (1968), 105–120; Harold L. Wilensky and Anne T. Lawrence, "Job Assignment in Modern Societies: A Reexamination of the Ascription-Achievement Hypothesis," in Amos H. Hawley, ed., *Societal Growth* (New York: Free Press, 1979), 202–248. On the continuing utility of ethnicity in business and commerce, a vast literature now exists. For a review, see: Edna Bonacich and John Modell, *The Economic Basis of Ethnic Solidarity* (Berkeley: University of California, 1980), chs. 1, 2.

24. Williamson, *Markets and Hierarchies*, 8–10.

25. Gerard F. Kennedy, "The Korean *Kye*: Maintaining Human Scale in a Modernizing Society," *Korean Studies* 1 (1977), 210–211.

26. Light, *Ethnic Enterprise*, ch. 3.

27. As recent events in the savings and loan industry underscore, embezzlement is frequent even in mainstream financial associations. "What has caused the $50 billion or more in savings and loan losses is incompetent, if not criminal, management. Fraud is a major culprit. So are insider borrowing, self-dealing, and loan policies that encourage larceny." See: James Ring Adams, "Post Election Bailout: Congress and the Thrift Industry Must Bear the Blame," *Barron's* 68 (Nov. 7, 1988), p. 9 ff.

28. Nguyen Van Vinh, "Savings and Mutual Lending Societies (Ho)," unpublished paper, Yale University Library, New Haven, Conn.; see also: Light, *Ethnic Enterprise*, ch. 2; Woodrum, Rhoades, and Feagin, 1235-1254; Bonnett, 346-355; Michel S. Laguerre, *American Odyssey: Haitians in New York City* (Ithaca: Cornell University, 1984); Ivan Light and Edna Bonacich, *Immigrant Entrepreneurs: Koreans in Los Angeles, 1965-1982* (Berkeley and Los Angeles: University of California, 1988); James Leung, "Asian Immigrants Tapping Underground Banks for Cash," *San Francisco Chronicle*, May 2, 1988: I, 1; Christine Gorman, "Do-It-Yourself Financing," *Time*, July 25, 62.

29. Hassan Boukbakri, "La Restauration Tunisienne a Paris," in Gildas Simon, ed., *Marchands Ambulants et Commercants Etrangers* (Poitiers, Centre Universitaire d'Etudes Mediterraneennes de l'Universite de Poitiers, 1984), 90; Michelle Guillon and Isabelle Taboada-Leonetti, *Le Triangle de Choisy: Un Quartier Chinois a Paris* (Paris, Editions L'Harmattan, 1986), 114; Pnina Werbner, "Enclave Economies and Family Firms: Pakistani Traders in a British City," in Jeremy Eades, ed., *Migrants, Workers and the Social Order* (London, Tavistock Publications, 1987), 226.

30. Kennedy, "The Korean Kye," 198.

31. Kyung-Soo Chun, *Reciprocity and Korean Society: An Ethnography of Hasami* (Seoul, National University Press, 1984), 139.

32. Roger L. Janelli and Dawnhee Yim Janelli, "Interest Rates and Rationality: Rotating Credit Associations among Seoul Women," *Journal of Korean Studies* 6 (1988), forthcoming.

33. Kennedy, "The Korean Kye," 206.

34. Nina Vreeland, *Area Handbook for South Korea*, 2d ed. (Washington: U.S. Government Printing Office, 1975), 241; Kennedy, "The Korean Kye," 206.

35. Janelli and Janelli, fn 2.

36. Kyn-Tae Yi, *Modern Transformation of Korea*, translated by Sung Tong-Mahn (Seoul: Sejong Publishing Co., 1970), 70.

37. Vreeland, 240.

38. Nathan Benn, "The South Koreans," *National Geographic* 174 (1988), 245; Susan Chira, "It's Clubby, It's Thrifty, and It Can Cover the Bills," *New York Times* Nov. 19, 1987, sect. I, 4.

39. Janelli and Janelli,

40. Gerard F. Kennedy, "The Korean Fiscal Kye (Rotating Credit Association)," Ph.D. Diss. (University of Hawaii, 1973), 155; Benn, 245; Nancy Rivera Brooks, "Women Business Owners Thriving in the Southland," *Los Angeles Times*, Oct. 24, 1988, section 4, 1.

41. Vreeland, 240.

42. Marlys Harris, "How the Koreans Won the Greengrocer Wars," *Money* 12 (March, 1983), 190-198; Merrill Goozner, "Age-Old Tradition Bankrolls Koreans," *Chicago Tribune*, July 19, 1987, Sect. 7, 1; Gorman, 62; Douglas Frantz, "Hanmi Bank Uses Ancient Asian Lending Practice to Help Koreans," *Los Angeles Times*, Oct. 5,

1988, Section 4, 1; Mark Arax, "Pooled Cash of Loan Clubs Key to Asian Immigrant Entrepreneurs," *Los Angeles Times*, Oct. 30, 1988, Sect. 2, 1.

43. Light and Bonacich, ch. 10.

44. Frantz, Section 4, 1.

45. Light and Bonacich, 57; Kwang Chung Kim and Won Moo Hurh, "Ethnic Resources Utilization of Korean Immigrant Entrepreneurs in the Chicago Minority Area," *International Migration Review* 19 (1985), 82–111.

46. Kunae Kim, "Rotating Credit Associations among the Korean Immigrants in Los Angeles," M. A. thesis, Department of Anthropology, University of California at Los Angeles, 1982. These are our calculations from Kim's discussion.

47. Ethnographic research on kyes in Korea encountered the same reticence. "Like people everywhere, Koreans do not like to have their personal affairs, especially their fiscal affairs, the subject of direct investigation." Kennedy, "The Korean Kye," 207. Therefore, Kennedy advised kye researchers to abandon the "ideal" of randomly sampling kye users.

48. Edward Chang, "Korean Rotating Credit Associations in Los Angeles" (1983). Unpublished paper in Library of the Asian American Studies Center, University of California at Los Angeles.

49. Kunae Kim, 13.

50. Light and Bonacich, ch. 10.

51. Although rotating credit associations are legal in the United States, the legal obligations of the organizer remain undefined in American law. Suing on behalf of 23 plaintiffs who alleged fraudulent mismanagement against a defaulting kye organizer, attorney Stanley Cook ("Plaintiffs' Trial Brief," Case No. 3-87-01598T-LK, United States Bankruptcy Court, Northern District of California, in re: Soon Duk Cabling and Rodolfo Cabling, dba Allenbe, Filed May 13, 1988) declared the "case before the court" one of "first impression, and there are no directly applicable authorities." In this case, the defaulting organizer owed the 23 plaintiffs $400,000. The case turned on an issue of law: Can defaulting kye organizers escape liability through a chapter 11 bankruptcy proceeding even when they embezzled or mismanaged the funds entrusted to them? In the first ruling on this point, Judge Thomas Carlson ("Findings of Fact and Conclusions of Law," Adv. No. 3-87-0408-TC, In re: Soon Duk Cabling and Rodolfo Cabling vs. Yung Hwan Chang, *et al.*, United States Bankruptcy Court for the Northern District of California, Oct. 5, 1988) ruled for with the plaintiffs, denying the kye organizer discharge on account of her mismanagement. However, Carlson disallowed the plaintiffs' demands for interest above the statutory usury ceiling, discharging the defendant of this portion of her indebtedness. 52. Kennedy, "The Korean Kye," 206-207; Frantz, Section 4, 1.

53. Carlson, 10; see also Colin D. Campbell, and Chang Shick Ahn, "Kyes and Mujins—Financial Intermediaries in South Korea," *Economic Development and Cultural Change* 11 (1962), 62.

54. Vreeland, 239.

55. See: Janet Chan and Yuet-Wah Cheung, "Chinese Businesses in Toronto," *Human Organization* 44 (1985), 149.

56. Woodrum, Rhodes, and Feagin, 71. This statistic recalculated from their Table 8, 1245.

57. H. C. Kim, "Ethnic Enterprises," 97, 104, 107.

58. Philip K. Y. Young, "Family Labor, Sacrifice and Competition: Korean Greengrocers in New York City," *Amerasia Journal* 10 (1983), 53–71.

59. Light and Bonacich, 441.

60. Kim and Hurh, 92-93

61. Light and Bonacich, 309.

62. Kenneth Bailey, *Methods of Social Research*, 2d edition (New York Free Press, 1982), 156.

63. Thomas A. Heberlein and Robert Baumgartner, "Factors Affecting Response Rates to Mailed Questionnaires," *American Sociological Review* 43 (1978), 449.

64. Bailey, 177-78.

65. Light and Bonacich, 286–289.

66. Light, *Ethnic Enterprise*, ch. 2.

67. Thomas Cope and Donald V. Kurtz, "Default and the Tanda: a Model Regarding Recruitment for Rotating Credit Associations," *Ethnology* 19 (1978), 215.

68. Edna Bonacich and John Modell, *The Economic Basis of Ethnic Solidarity*, (Berkeley and Los Angeles: University of California, 1980), 33-36.

69. Light, *Ethnic Enterprise*, ch. 8; Viviana A. Rotman Zelizer, *Morals and Markets* (New York and London: Columbia University Press, 1979), chapter 8; William G. Ouchi, "Markets, Bureaucracies, and Clans," *Administrative Science Quarterly* 25 (1980), 139–140.

70. Geertz, 241–263.

71. The Mafia is an example. The Mafia is a family business that modernization has not eliminated and may even have encouraged. Yet, the Mafia is resolutely ascriptive and particularistic in its operations. See: Francis A. J. Ianni, *A Family Business* (New York: Russell Sage Foundation, 1972).

# Index

# About the Editors and Contributors

JOHN SIBLEY BUTLER is professor of management and sociology at the University of Texas at Austin and holdst the Gale Chair in Entrepreneurship and Small Business in the graduate achool of business (Department of Management) and the Herb Kelleher Chair in Entrepreneurship. He is the director of the Herb Kelleher Center for Entrepreneurship and the director of the Institute for Innovation, Creativity, and Capital ($IC^2$). He has published extensively in the areas of organizational science (Sociology of the Military) and entrepreneurship. His books include *Entrepreneurship and Self-Help among Black Americans: A Reconsideration of Race and Economics* and *All That We Can Be: Black Leadership and Racial Integration the Army Way* (with Charles C. Moskos).

GEORGE KOZMETSKY (1917–2003) was dean of the McCombs School of Business at the University of Texas at Austin and founder of the Institute for Innovation, Creativity, and Capital ($IC^2$). He was cofounder and executive vice president of Teledyne, Inc. and assisted in developing over 100 technology-based companies, and served on numerous boards. He was an acknowledged expert in high technology and venture capital. His works include *Creating the Technopolis* (co-editor) (1988), *Pacific Cooperation and Development* (co-editor) (Praeger Publishers, 1988), *Modern American Capitalism* (co-author) (Quorum Books, 1990), and *Global Economic Competition* (co-author) (1997).

STEPHEN J. APPOLD lectures in the Department of Sociology at the National University of Singapore. Recent publications include "Patron-Client Relationships in a Restructuring Economy: An Exploration of Inter-Organizational Linkages in Vietnam," (with Dinh the Phong) in *Economic Development and Cultural Change*; "The Control of High-skill Labor and Entrepreneurship in the Early U.S. Semiconductor Industry," in *Environment and Planning*; and "The Employment of Women Managers and Professionals in an Emerging Economy: Gender Inequality as an Organizational Practice" (with Sununta Siengthai and John D. Kasarda) in *Administrative Science Quarterly*. He is developing a Web-based text for the study of work and organizations that incorporates research performed by undergraduates.

CANDIDA GREER BRUSH is an associate professor of strategy and policy director of the Council for Women's Entrepreneurship and Leadership (CWEL), and research director for the Entrepreneurial Management Institute at Boston University. She was a research affiliate to Jonkoping International Business School in Sweden. She is the author of *International Entrepreneurship: The Effect of Age on Motives for Internationalization* and *The Woman Entrepreneur: Starting, Financing and Managing a Successful New Business*, as well as book chapters and articles in scholarly journals such as Journal of Business Venturing, Stategic Mnagement Journal, Journal of Business Research, and others.

ZHONG DENG is a graduate student in sociology at UCLA.

SAMIA EL-BADRY is director of operations at TERA and has a unique business background in marketing, an academic background in demography and economics, and an applied expertise in product shifts and usage. She is vice president and director of operations of Teknecon. Prior to joining Teknecon in 1993, she was a senior research fellow at the $IC^2$ Institute of the University of Texas at Austin. As research director for the Japan Industry program, she directed research on international technology transfer and commercialization. Compiled research topics include legal and regulatory issues; business development; industrial development; and cultural literacy. In addition, she has developed and delivered curricula for a variety of executive seminars; edited several books for the government and corporate sectors; acquired international liaisons for student corporate intern-ships; and given formal presentations to the professional community.

PATRICIA GENE GREENE holds the Ewing Marion Kauffman/Mis-souri Chair in Entrepreneurial Leadership at the University of Mis-souri—Kansas City. She currently serves as the director of the Entrepreneurial Growth Resource Center at UMKC and a scholar in residence at the Ewing Marion Kauffman Foundation. She previously held the New Jersey Chair of Small Business and Entrepreneurship at Rutgers University where she was a founding member of the Rutgers Center for Entrepreneurial Management and the coordinator of the entrepreneurship curriculum. Her work has been published in various journals including *Journal of Business Venturing; Entrepreneurship Theory and Practice; Journal of Business Research; Small Business Economics; Fron-tiers of Entrepreneurship Research; Journal of Small Business Management* and *National Journal of Sociology.*

HAYWARD DERRICK HORTON is Associate Professor of Sociology at the State University of New York at Albany. He specializes in demogra-phy, race and ethnicity, and rural sociology. He has published over 20 articles on topics such as: the demography of rural black families; differences in black-white levels of homeownership; population change and the employment status of college-educated blacks; race, ethnicity and levels of employment; the demography of black entrepreneurship; and the feminization of poverty. He is currently co-authoring a book on the model entitled, *Rebuilding Black Communities: Black Community Devel-opment in Contemporary America.*

MARGARET A. JOHNSON is CEO of Transfirex Translation Services, Inc. This firm specializes in language translation, desktop publishing, and multimedia development for higher education and government agencies. Dr. Johnson brings to the firm more than 10 years of experi-ence as a social scientist, researcher, public speaker, and organizational consultant. During her faculty career in higher education, she pub-lished extensively on entrepreneurship and nonprofit organizations and earned numerous awards for her research and writing.

JOHN D. KASARDA is director of the Frank Hawkins Kenan Institute of Private Enterprise and is the Kenan Distinguished Professor of Man-agement at the University of North Carolina, Chapel Hill. His research areas include demography, logistics, aviation industry, and urban econ-omies. He has published extensively in professional journals.

IM JUNG KWUON is an undergraduate student at UCLA.

MARGARET LEVENSTEIN is visiting associate professor of business economics at the University of Michigan business school and associate professor of economics at the University of Massachusetts at Amherst. She is also a faculty research fellow of the Development of the American Economy Program of the National Bureau of Economic Research in Cambridge, Massachusetts. Her works include *Accounting for Growth: Information Systems and the Creation of the Large Corporation.* Professor Levenstein has also published extensively on a variety of subjects in the history of business and economics, including the evolution of information systems; the relationship between information systems and firm organization; historical changes in the nature of competition; cartels in the chemical industry; and the history of African American entrepreneurship.

MIN ZHOU is Professor of Sociology and Asian American studies at the University of California, Los Angles. Her main research interests are immigration, race, and ethnicity, Asian American studies, and the community and urban sociology. Her works include *Chinatown: The Socioeconomic Potential of an Urban Enclave* and *Growing Up American: How Vietnamese Children Adapt to Life in the United States.*

IVAN LIGHT is Professor of Sociology at the University of California, Los Angeles. He has published extensively in the area of immigrant entrepreneurship. His works include *Ethnic Enterprise in America; Cities in World Perspective; Immigrant Entrepreneurs: Koreans in Los Angeles* (with Edna Bonacich); and *Immigration and Entrepreneurship* (Transactions Publishers, 1993; in collaboration with Parminder Bhachu). His latest book is *Ethnic Economies* (with Steven Gold).